Dan Plesch is the Director of the Centre for International Studies and Diplomacy at the School of Oriental and African Studies, University of London. His previous books include *The Beauty Queen's Guide to World Peace*.

'In this book, Dan Plesch opens a long-locked door and shines a piercing searchlight on a past which has great impact on the present – the virtually unknown origins of the UN in the dark days of World War II. A genuine revelation which he puts into its challenging and troubled modern context.'
— **Jonathan Dimbleby**

'The story of the United Nations between its creation as a war-fighting alliance by Roosevelt and Churchill in January 1942 and its establishment as a global peace-keeping organization at San Francisco three years later has never been fully told; but without it we cannot fully understand either the conduct of the war in its latter stages nor the nature of the imperfect peace that followed. Dan Plesch has now pulled it all together in a lively and provocative study that not only fills this gap but will make us re-examine many currently-held assumptions about the making of the post-war world.'
— **Sir Michael Howard, founder of War Studies at King's College, London**

'There are certainly many lessons in this book that statesmen and leaders in defence, security and international economics would do well to take on board today.'
— **Admiral Lord Boyce, Chief of UK Defence Staff 2001–2003**

'Television histories of World War II have been made obsolete by Dan Plesch's book.'
— **Jerry Kuehl, Associate Producer, 'The World at War'**

'This book should be required reading for the Obama administration and the leaders of other countries as well. It is an historical treasure trove of documents and anecdotes about the origins of the United Nations as a project to win the war and secure the peace.'
— **Thomas G. Weiss, Presidential Professor of Political Science, The City University of New York**

'The United Nations was not created out of nothing. Before it became an organization, it was the name of the wartime alliance against Nazism and fascism. Dan Plesch performs a great service in reminding us of this early history, and of a time when public opinion in the world's great democracies understood the need for binding global arrangements to "save succeeding generations from the scourge of war".'
— **Edward Mortimer, formerly Director of Communications in the Executive Office of the United Nations Secretary-General**

'This book is the most original and groundbreaking reappraisal of the conduct of World War II in 65 years. His thesis that the 'United Nations' (which included Soviet Russia) won the war against Nazi Germany and that subsequent Cold War politics obscured this truth, is meticulously documented and supported. This is a "must read" for every student of modern and contemporary history, international politics and international relations, and modern international policy makers.'

— Chris Bellamy, Director of the Greenwich Maritime Institute
and author of *Absolute War: Soviet Russia in the Second World War*

'A fascinating book full of nice tidbits one doesn't want to skip.'

— Sir Richard Jolly, formerly Assistant Secretary General
of the United Nations holding senior positions in UNICEF and UNDP

'Magnificent. *America, Hitler and the UN* for the first time shows the present United Nations in the full context of its wartime parentage. In doing so, it provides an important new dimension both for the world organization's current and ever-growing responsibilities, and for those who are responsible for charting and developing its future.'

— Sir Brian Urquhart, former Undersecretary-General
of the United Nations

AMERICA, HITLER AND THE UN

HOW THE ALLIES WON WORLD WAR II AND FORGED A PEACE

Dan Plesch

Foreword by Sir Brian Urquhart

I.B. TAURIS

LONDON · NEW YORK

Published in 2011 by I.B.Tauris & Co Ltd
6 Salem Road, London W2 4BU
175 Fifth Avenue, New York NY 10010
www.ibtauris.com

Distributed in the United States and Canada Exclusively by Palgrave Macmillan
175 Fifth Avenue, New York NY 10010

ISBN: 978 1 84885 308 9

A full CIP record for this book is available from the British Library
A full CIP record is available from the Library of Congress

Library of Congress Catalog Card Number: available

Typeset in Palatino by MPS Limited, a Macmillan Company
Printed and bound in Great Britain by CPI Antony Rowe, Chippenham

For Linds, Susie and Robster

Contents

List of Photographs and Illustrations

List of Tables

List of Maps

Map X, the advance across Germany, is from Canadian official history. The cartographers of the other maps were Vaughan Gray, Emil Herlin and Lucas Manditch whose work was published in the 1944 edition of the New York Times's *The War in Maps*.

Foreword

For most people, the United Nations, now with 192 member countries, is a large, untidy organization which often disappoints and is rarely heard of when it succeeds. Only a few now remember that 'The United Nations' came into being in 1942 just after Pearl Harbor. It was the brainchild of President Franklin D. Roosevelt and Winston S. Churchill and described the alliance that was then fighting for its life against Hitler and his Axis allies.

The basis of the United Nations was the fight against Nazism and Fascism based on Roosevelt's 'Four Freedoms'. Roosevelt used the phrase with consummate skill to bring into that fight a steadily increasing number of governments that believed in the cause while not necessarily taking part in military operations. The alliance took the name 'United Nations' in all its main announcements on the progress of World War II. At the end, both Germany and Japan surrendered to all the United Nations.

Thus, in 1945, the victorious alliance had a universal concept on which to build a peacetime organization also called the United Nations, whose Charter was already in an advanced stage of preparation. Its origin as a successful, largely military organization undoubtedly gave the new world organization a united and authoritative appearance which was soon belied by the peacetime differences of its members, in particular the 40-year East–West Cold War. But it also allowed the United Nations to hit the ground running in facing the immense problems of the post-war world.

Dan Plesch's book performs the vital task of, for the first time, showing the present United Nations in the full context of its wartime parentage. In doing so, it provides an important new dimension both for the world organization's current and ever-growing responsibilities, and for those who are responsible for charting and developing its future.

Sir Brian Urquhart

Preface

In my family, the idea that the United Nations was important because it was part of what the war was fought for was obvious. But this idea faded from cultural memory and from my own understanding. In 2004, while writing about the importance of the values of the Atlantic Charter in contrast to those of the War on Terror, I came across references to the United Nations prior to the UN Charter of 1945 and began the research that has produced this book.

The tragedy of our time would be that the USA and other powers stumble into further economic and military crises, ignorant of the techniques of war prevention and economic and social development learnt at such great cost in World Wars I and II.

I have many people to thank for helping me on the way to completing this book. The staff of the British Library and the UK National Archives were unfailingly helpful. I am grateful to Jerry Kuehl for applying to my text the forensic skills he honed as a producer of the TV series *The World at War*, to Poul-Erik Christiansen for his precision and patience with notes and bibliography, Matt Craven for legal advice and Stephanie Blankenburg for aid on economics. Dr Lindsay Forbes provided excellent tuition in sentence surgery. Iradj Bagherzade and his team at I.B.Tauris, particularly Liz Friend-Smith and Joanna Godfrey, were unstinting in their assistance. I am also thankful to Bill Barnard, Chris Bellamy, Nick Branson, John Burton, Stephen Chan, Walter Christman, Matt Craven, Alex Danchev, Kevin Duffy, Richard Falk, Jonah Foran, James Gow, Jill Kastner, Sarah Hibbin, Christopher Hill, Michael Ferber, Jo Husband, Maya Irvine, Sir Richard Jolly, Martin Jones, Alex Lazarowicz, Gail Lelyfeld, Deborah Parfitt, John Pike, Sir Adam Roberts, Inger Sira, Charles Townshend, Sir Brian Urquhart, John Vogler, Tom Weiss and Gordon Wyn Jones for their interest, advice and encouragement. Academics, staff, students and members of the public at both the British International and the Transatlantic Studies Associations, Cambridge, Keele and Kent Universities, Chatham House, Portsmouth Grammar School and the US Navy Postgraduate School all kindly invited me to road-test my ideas. I alone am responsible for the text.

There are many maps and illustrations from the war years that are evocative of the time in a way their modern equivalents have difficulty in achieving. Every effort has been made to trace and contact copyright holders prior to publication. If notified, all reasonable efforts will be made to rectify any errors or omissions in subsequent printings. *The New York Times* atlas of the war, the advertising of Simpson's club in Piccadilly, the cartoons of Dr Seuss and the orders of religious service all have both an immediacy and a poignancy that is hard to capture with modern creations.

Introduction

O n the morning of 29 December 1941, Winston Churchill was in the bathroom of his room at the White House when he heard Franklin Roosevelt calling him. He emerged, a naked pink cherub, drying himself with a towel and without a stitch on, to find the President waiting in a chair. The President pointed at Churchill and exploded, 'United Nations!' 'Good!' affirmed Churchill. And so the United Nations was born. This was already the third year of Churchill's war, but it was barely four weeks after the Japanese attack on Pearl Harbor and Hitler's subsequent declaration of war against the United States.

Churchill, Roosevelt and their advisors were at the White House trying to work out the most effective way to win the war. The previous day, they had been preparing an international political declaration that would unite them with the Soviet Union, China and as many other nations as possible against the Axis powers led by Germany, Italy and Japan. The two politicians had wrestled with the need for a catchy brand name for the proposed alliance, 'Associated Nations' being a term offered by the US State Department but discarded as too boring. Overnight, Roosevelt hit on 'United Nations', perhaps informed by Churchill's rendition of a line from Byron's poem, *Childe Harold's Pilgrimage*.[1]

> 'Their children's lips shall echo them, and say –
> "Here where the sword united nations drew,
> Our countrymen were warring on that day!"'

That morning, as soon as he had finished breakfast, not waiting for a formal meeting, Roosevelt had a servant propel him in his wheelchair down the corridor to Churchill's room. His excitement at his idea was born of a sense of urgency to hit upon a name that would catch the public mood at a time of great uncertainty.

The name and the ideas did catch on. Between the announcement of the Declaration by United Nations on New Year's Day 1942 and the creation of the UN we know today at San Francisco in 1945, 'The United Nations' was mentioned over 15,000 times in the pages of *The New York Times*. The prevailing American view of the United Nations in the war years is exemplified by a *Washington Post* report from mid-1943:

> The Flags of all the United Nations were flown in Moscow and in London as well as in Washington ... And to the banners of the respective nations were added a new flag, the flag of the United Nations. It is devoutly to be hoped that a precedent has now been established that will be followed regularly during coming years.[2]

When the 'Declaration by United Nations' was issued in January 1942, many of these nations were engaged in a fight for survival. Their prime concern was to win in battle, but to do so they needed hopeful ideas for the future, as well as weapons. The Declaration built on Roosevelt's 'Four Freedoms' speech of January 1941 and the Atlantic Charter he and Churchill had issued that August. This eight-point plan of political objectives for world peace set out the values that they asked people to fight for. These included human rights, free trade, social security, the rights of labour and a new system of international security.[3]

A few days after the Declaration was made, Roosevelt explained in his State of the Union address to Congress that,

> We of the United Nations are not making all this sacrifice of human effort and human lives to return to the kind of world we had after the last world war. We are fighting today for security, for progress, and for peace, not only for ourselves but for all men.[4]

Henry Stimson, US Secretary of War from 1940 to 1945, thought it was 'clear that American policy envisaged the development of the wartime United Nations into a peacetime organization'.[5] Sir Michael Howard, the eminent historian, has described how the United Nations developed from war making to peace planning. Nevertheless, the idea that the UN did not exist until the end of the war in 1945 has become a widespread belief.

The history of the United Nations between 1942 and 1945 demonstrates the effectiveness of liberal cooperative ideas in helping defeat Hitler, Mussolini and the Japanese warlords. These ideas helped hold the Allies together, generate public support for the war effort and create a spectrum of United Nations organizations and conferences to fight the war and sustain the peace. The organizational initiatives for peace encompassed global finance, economic development, post-war aid and reconstruction, war crimes, security of food supplies and, finally, global security, with the signing of the UN Charter at San Francisco in 1945.

Roosevelt had shown he could turn rhetoric into action at home through the 'New Deal', so his words inspired confidence among Americans. What the historian Elizabeth Borgwardt calls 'The New Deal for the World' reminds us of how the US contribution to the development of human rights had roots in domestic politics. But this understanding should not eclipse either the contributions of other states or the original military preoccupation of the United Nations.

Nowadays, we are taught that the Allies, mainly America, Britain and the Russians, won the war and that the UN was created in 1945. The lesson that is supposed to have been learnt is that the League of Nations having failed to stop Hitler and the Japanese, it is necessary to rely on national military power for security. In this way, the Allied victory in World War

II seems to have nothing to do with the United Nations. But the victory cannot be separated from the United Nations we know today because it was a United Nations victory, as this book demonstrates.

Roosevelt developed the United Nations from 1942 to avoid a repeat of the US refusal to join the League of Nations after World War I. He represented a desire of people in America and around the world to ensure that the failure to keep the peace after 1918 not be repeated. The means of preventing World War III emerging from the ruins of the Second, would be a regulated global economy, a better security system with enforcement powers and an inbuilt vested interest of the most powerful states in the UN through the veto on UN decisions, not reliance on national military might.

To this end, the United Nations had three interconnected purposes during the war: rallying American public support, keeping the Allies together, and building the post-war programme. By using the United Nations brand name to achieve all three objectives, Roosevelt made the brand pervasive, especially in the USA, so ensuring that the peace-building effort was not separated from the war effort until the post-war structure had been established.

This strategy helped defeat what were termed 'isolationists'. These were opponents of US involvement in foreign wars. The strategy succeeded in building Congressional support for wartime United Nations military and civil programmes, culminating in the Senate's ratification of the UN Charter in July 1945 by 89 votes to 2. A Gallup Poll found just 3 per cent of the American public opposed to ratification.

The Roosevelt Administration used the political argument of the value of the United Nations at every opportunity to convince the public and Congress to fund the supply of weapons to the Allies without their needing either cash or a loan. The USA sent huge quantities of weapons and other supplies to Britain and the Soviet Union under this Lend-Lease programme. These supplies helped prevent defeat and enabled the Red Army to beat the Germans as quickly and decisively as it did. It is hard to imagine the conservative and unilateralist Congress approving such largesse without public support. Unilateralists are those who then, as now, regard the best American policy as one where the US acts alone unencumbered by the Allies. The internationalist ideas coalesced around the idea that many nations were uniting for war and peace.

National governments did their best to show the importance of the new United Nations alliance by ensuring that the most prominent leaders were at the forefront of its activities. This was the reason that the teenage British Princess Elizabeth took part in the first global celebration of the United Nations. Her presence indicated the importance accorded to the event by the British government and her father King George VI.

1 United Nations Day Parade in London at Buckingham Palace, 14 June 1942.

On a June morning in 1942, the future British Queen joined her parents and younger sister to review a large parade in front of Buckingham Palace – a rare occurrence in wartime. The Palace windows were boarded up and it bore the scars of German bombing. The King and Queen were joined by the Kings and leaders of countries occupied by the Nazis, as well as by Churchill and the US Ambassador to Britain. Before them paraded the flags of all the United Nations, watched by cheering crowds of Londoners. At last, America was in it too. Similar events took place in communities and capitals across America and around the world.

Princess Elizabeth's presence symbolized both her own importance, that she was included, and the importance accorded to the event by the monarchy. It was part of a carefully prepared public relations programme by the Royal Family to show their relevance to the war effort. As the heir to the throne, Princess Elizabeth was already being given a public role. Since turning 16 in April 1942, she had combined traditional royal duties with involvement in public life, highlighting government programmes aimed at ordinary citizens. She was made honorary colonel of the Grenadier Guards and inspected the soldiers at Windsor castle. She went to government offices to register for work at the Labour Exchange, opened a bank account with the Post Office and sponsored an essay competition on recycling for

2 The future Queen Elizabeth II with her parents and other dignitaries review the United Nations Day Parade, London, 14 June 1942.

schoolchildren. The family's appearance at this showcase event shown at cinemas around the world reinforced the sense of unity with the simple innocence of children among the mighty.

International unity in the war effort was as hard to achieve as it was vital. We are so accustomed to the photos of Churchill, Roosevelt and Stalin at the wartime summits that, in retrospect, their alliance seems inevitable. But, amidst the uncertainties of war, the two Western Allies and Stalin were each concerned that the other might make a separate compromise peace with Germany.

Even more threatening than a separate peace was the possibility of a future war between Russia and the West. Without ideas for a new international order that met the interests of Russia as well as the West, 'the only alternative for the United States and the United Kingdom was most probably a quick shift from World War II to World War III. It could have happened somewhere in mid-Germany, when the armies of the West and East met', as an Associated Press reporter put it at the time.[6] The wartime United Nations served a key purpose in providing rhetorical and formal unity among the Allies so as to prevent the alliance collapsing. Such a continuing war was the last hope of anti-Bolshevik Germans envisaging an alliance with the Americans and British to expel the Russians from Europe in 1945. At the end of the war, General Patton, America's pre-eminent tank force general, expressed his enthusiasm for this idea.[7] Without the cohesion created by the ideas of the United Nations, such a war would have been more likely.

Mutual suspicion continued among the United Nations throughout the war and after, but all concerned were aware that it was vital to find new ways to work together for the future. Espionage and the decoding of intercepted radio transmissions were important features of the war and inter-allied relations. Broadly speaking, everyone was trying to spy on everyone else, with varying degrees of success. The Soviet Union had spies in America and Britain and the US was spying on the Soviet Embassy in the US capital, Washington, DC. US intelligence staff listened to the phone calls of the delegates to the San Francisco signing of the UN Charter, as Stephen Schlesinger has documented. It is beyond the scope of this book to review and engage with the topic. Many allegations need to be looked at critically. The Mitrokhin 'archive', for example, of supposed Soviet success in the West is not actually original material, while few stop to ask of Mitrokhin the obvious point that agents invent reports of contacts in a foreign government in order to justify their work. Christopher Andrew's history of the British counter-intelligence service, MI5, provides detail of Soviet infiltration of MI5 while its attention was focused on German activity. Some of Roosevelt's advisors and officials in the US Treasury department have been accused of being Soviet spies. While many certainly implemented the President's intention of sharing information to a similar degree to the relationship with Britain, on one topic the results indicate the opposite. Anti-communists assumed that a key objective of Stalin's was to divide the Americans and British, yet the efforts of officials such as Harry Hopkins and Harry White were vital to forging a lasting unity with the British in spite of many obstacles, not least from US isolationists. The existence of underhand behaviour does not show the United Nations' ideas to be no more than propaganda; rather they can be seen as Roosevelt explained them: aspirations that needed implementation, much like the values of the US Constitution.

The sometimes fragile diplomatic connections that kept the Allies together were reinforced by the United Nations framework. It was a framework on which Roosevelt began to weave agreements to reduce suspicion and build confidence among the Allies. These included food and other economic aid and assistance, but most importantly the free supply of weapons under the Lend-Lease programme. This task became urgent given the delay in launching D-Day: first anticipated for 1942, it was again postponed until 1944, delays which Stalin regarded as a betrayal.

The military cooperation between the British and Americans has been well documented, especially in British accounts of the war that emphasize 'the special relationship'. However, this is rarely placed in the context of the United Nations as a whole, although this is how it was described in the official documents of the time, as discussed in Chapter 2. The UK National Archives has over 400 files on the United Nations for the period 1942–4.

The political objectives and programmes for peace accompanied and enabled the military effort and shaped the international organizations that continue to exist in the twenty-first century. David Reynolds, a leading historian of Anglo-American relations, notes: 'The Four Freedoms [of speech and religion, from want and fear], the Atlantic Charter, and Declaration by United Nations of January 1942 became benchmarks for a new international order'.[8] These benchmarks set out the ground for the construction of global civilian organizations. During the war, their triple success in helping US public support for the war effort, high-level discussions between the 'Big Three' and international organizations for fighting the war and building the peace were mutually reinforcing.

From 1942 onwards, the US and its Allies used these benchmarks to put together United Nations conferences, some of which created formal UN institutions with internationally funded budgets and international staff. These encompassed public diplomacy, economics, security, aid and reconstruction, war crimes, food security, labour standards and education. Postwar reconstruction and war crimes investigation were the most important operational UN organizations. The United Nations Relief and Rehabilitation Administration (UNRRA) spent close to $4 billion by 1949, with a voluntary contribution from member states of 1 per cent of gross domestic product (GDP) for a year or more. The smallest operational body, the United Nations food commission, had a tiny staff in a rented house in Washington, DC.

But Roosevelt was not the most ambitious advocate of developing the United Nations. At home and abroad there were many who wanted a fully formed United Nations Organization in 1942 to improve the organization of the war as much as to prepare the peace. Similarly, promises of free elections and self-government were insufficient to satisfy the aspirations of the oppressed, whether in India, Alabama or the Soviet Union. And the United Nations War Crimes Commission constructed the foundations of modern international criminal law against the wishes of both the US State Department and the British Foreign Office.

The people who created these institutions saw themselves as implementing the United Nations ideals formulated in the Four Freedoms and the Atlantic Charter. Many were impatient for faster and more comprehensive progress.

Arthur Schlesinger, a historian and advisor to President Kennedy, has described how Roosevelt's policy was developed:

> He proceeded to lay the groundwork in 1943–45 with the same skill and circumspection with which he had steered the nation away from isolationism in 1937–41. The challenge of contriving a smooth transition from unilateralism to internationalism shaped Roosevelt's diplomatic strategy. He moved quietly to prepare the American people for a larger international role. By the end of 1944

a series of international conferences . . . established a framework for the world
after the war – an impressive achievement for a president whom historians
used to charge with subordinating political to military goals.[9]

The UN soon became much weaker than had been intended by
Roosevelt and other founders. After 1945, the most important states never
invested militarily or politically in making the UN the prime vehicle of
their international policies. Instead, their political disputes (for example,
the communist–capitalist divide and the control of the atom bomb) provided reasons and excuses for reducing the role of the UN system as a
whole. One long-term economic result of this was the diversion of the
original function of the International Monetary Fund (IMF) and the World
Bank away from the prevention of conflict through economic regulation
and policies promoting high employment. The very short engagement of
the Soviet Union with these financial bodies, until 1946, provides a further
example of an opportunity lost.

So why has the wartime United Nations been forgotten? This is partly
because some of the organizations it created, notably the IMF and the
World Bank, did not carry the UN name, though they were intended to
work alongside the UN organization created at San Francisco in 1945. The
new UN organization (UN) wanted a clean start unencumbered by the
wartime experience. As the war faded into memory, people knew the UN
organization had been created out of the ashes of the war; there was no
need to labour the point. The veto power of World War II's victors (the USA,
Britain, France, Russia and China) in the UN Security Council demonstrates
the UN's wartime origins; this has been seen by many, both at the time and
since, to be an inappropriate homage to the military victors. Many states –
losers such as Germany, Italy, Romania, Bulgaria, Hungary, Finland and
Japan, and neutrals such as Sweden, Portugal and Spain – that are active
in the UN today, along with the many new nations emerging from the
former British, French and Soviet empires, have little interest in looking
back. Perfectionists, seeking to place the UN on a pedestal of moral virtue,
were disinclined to mention its bloody beginnings.

Another reason for the eclipse of the wartime United Nations has to do
with the difficulties of retrieving data before the digital age. Today, online
searches can instantly list the hundreds of British government files with
United Nations titles during the war, or books written on the subject at that
time. And while early histories of the war, such as Charles Eade's collection
of Churchill's speeches published in the 1950s and Robert Sherwood's 1948
biography of Roosevelt and Harry Hopkins, his advisor, make mention of
the United Nations, in later works these fall away.

Overall though, in the United States, the reason for setting aside
the wartime United Nations was political. Roosevelt's 'New Deal' and
his internationalist foreign policy had bitter enemies at the time. The

confrontation with the Soviet Union that emerged rapidly after the war was accompanied by a far more conservative political strategy abroad and at home. Those who had opposed Roosevelt's depression-ending and war-winning politics came into the ascendancy, while the policies of the Four Freedoms, the Atlantic Charter and the UN were sidelined.

The Cold War and McCarthyism meant that both conservative Americans and anti-Americans in other parts of the world had a common cause in devaluing Roosevelt's radical contribution. In America, by the late 1940s, it had become politically and professionally suicidal to say that the Russians, British and Americans had been allies who had created the UN.

It is a cliché to say that history is written to meet the demands and needs of the present. The role of the United Nations in the political history of the war has been neglected. This is in part because politics has taken a back seat in those histories of the war which tend to concentrate on the main battles and leading personalities. Even the political interplay revealed in the correspondence between Roosevelt and Stalin has only been published recently. And the records of the wartime United Nations are unnoticed. Finally, the term 'Allies' was also in common use during the war and it was frequently used to describe the Western powers fighting alongside the Soviet Union, or Russians as they were commonly called. So the dropping of the formal United Nations term in favour of the word Allies was quite a natural thing to do, especially since the new UN organization had its own distinct identity after the wartime alliance collapsed in acrimony.

The absence of much of Roosevelt's wartime foreign policy, including his development of the United Nations, is an important loss of cultural memory, especially in the United States. Robert Kagan's thesis that 'Americans are from Mars and Europeans are from Venus', exemplified the attitude that America does not do global social work.[10] The reality of the effort in World War II was that US policy integrated 'social work' with the war effort and that Roosevelt, and those who thought like him, saw Mars and Venus as a complementary couple.

Joseph Nye has argued for the importance of integrating 'hard' (military and economic) and 'soft' (diplomatic and cultural) power, in contrast to the policy of President G.W. Bush, claiming that after World War II this combination of policies enabled success in the Cold War.[11] But the Marshall Plan and the operation of the Bretton Woods Institutions and the UN were stunted, Cold War-blighted versions of what had been prepared up to 1945.

The argument in this book is that Roosevelt and other leaders fighting Hitler and his allies were integrating 'hard' and 'soft' power during the war and did so with an agenda so much more far-reaching than those proposed at the start of the twenty-first century that they look inspired and gifted rather than merely smart. Roosevelt's policy in World War II

TABLE 1 World War II deaths for selected nations.

650,000	British Commonwealth and Empire
1,310,000	China (military only)
560,000	France
4,200,000	Germany
395,000	Italy
1,972,000	Japan
5,800,000	Poland
18,000,000	Union of Soviet Socialist Republics
298,000	United States of America
1,505,000	Yugoslavia

Source: *Encyclopaedia Britannica* 2010 and the UK.

employed a full spectrum of military, economic and political measures to create a winning progressive synergy.

This book is concerned with the politics of war, but it is important not to lose sight of the human cost which motivated leaders and publics alike to try to prevent further conflict by building the United Nations. The above table presents in a summary of numbers the reasons why in so many countries it is felt important to continue to remember the war more than 70 years later.

These data are intended as a guide and not as a definitive account, a point the *Encyclopaedia Britannica* is at pains to make itself.[12] China's figure does not include deaths among communist forces or civilians; the latter are sometimes numbered at over 20 million. The six million Jewish deaths are encompassed in the national totals, while a commonly accepted figure for Soviet deaths is 27 million.

CHAPTER 1

America before Pearl Harbor: ostrich or owl?

I n the years before Pearl Harbor, many Americans were in furious disagreement over whether or not to resist Hitler; a disagreement that continued earlier arguments over participation in World War I and the League
of Nations. From 1920 until 1932, successive Republican Presidents pursued a policy of keeping America isolated from international organizations and conflict. In contrast, Roosevelt, elected President in 1932, had
supported President Woodrow Wilson and the League of Nations. He introduced policies of free trade and tried to use economic and military means
to counter what he saw as the growing threat from Hitler and Mussolini,
and the Japanese in Asia. To persuade Americans to get involved abroad,
he put forward a positive agenda of international cooperation as values for
which Americans should be prepared to stand up for. After Pearl Harbor
they were formalized in the Declaration by United Nations.

One reason the ideas of the United Nations during the war have been
forgotten is that as US politics became more conservative during the Cold
War when Roosevelt's liberal policies were attacked successfully. As part
of this process, the liberal political ideas he had used to underpin the war
effort were discarded. In life, Roosevelt defeated conservative resistance
to a radical internationalist policy. In death, the conservative ascendancy
has seen his role in the war effort marginalized along with the ideas he
championed.

From 1946 his face has been on US ten cent coins. Nevertheless, he
has been neglected by the US military. One might expect that, given his
track record in leading what Americans now call 'the Greatest Generation',
Roosevelt would be revered by America's national security institutions as
a strategic genius. Indeed, he built most of the military, industrial and
bureaucratic organizations that are so influential today, as the historian
Alan Henrikson (2008) has demonstrated.

Nevertheless, there are no significant US Army, Air Force or Marine
Corps facilities that bear Roosevelt's name. And he has only one of the
US Navy's smallest ships named in his honour, while Gerald Ford, Presi-
dent for just two years, has a new generation of aircraft carriers, the most

prestigious type of warship, named after him. Only in the 1990s was a major memorial built for Roosevelt in Washington, DC, and this seems to have been an isolated act.

Certainly, conservatives who associate themselves with the aura of victory over Hitler, and opposition to anything they can call appeasement, do not mention him, or the policies he led, in favourable terms, despite his leadership in opposing appeasement. President George W. Bush used the 'Axis of Evil' terminology as a means of comparing Iran, Iraq and North Korea to Hitler and his Axis allies,[1] without any mention of the President who led the resistance to Hitler. The ostensible reason for neglecting Roosevelt as a military leader is his alleged appeasement of Stalin. Whatever the reality, this should not detract from his greatest success, the defeat of Hitler, Mussolini and the Japanese warlords.

Roosevelt himself regarded these critics of his policy towards Stalin as part of a general smear campaign. However, as we shall see, Roosevelt's success in mobilizing America required him to defeat conservative 'anti-communist' smears within the United States in the 1920s and 1930s and throughout the war. As Roosevelt put it, 'Labor-baiters, bigots, and some politicians use the term "Communism" loosely, and apply it to every progressive social measure and to the views of every foreign-born citizen with whom they disagree'[2] – a practice still familiar almost a century later.

Roosevelt brought to politics a strand of progressive Protestant values of part of the New England elite. These included a belief in public service and helping the unfortunate in society instilled in him by Endicott Peabody, his headmaster at Groton School. These ideas were suited to an age when economic disaster afflicted many Americans. When he became President he had already the experience of high office as Navy Secretary in World War I and as Governor of New York. He had also had to steel himself to overcome an inability to walk caused by the disease poliomyelitis.

Roosevelt gave his own assessment of the political struggle up to Pearl Harbor in a speech he gave in 1944 when victory in World War II was in sight.[3] In a radio broadcast made before 2,000 people at the Foreign Policy Association in Manhattan, Roosevelt reminded his listeners that it was the Republican Party that had opposed the League of Nations, so dooming that organization. He accused the Republicans in Congress of obstructing his efforts to prevent the rise of Hitler and warned that if they were returned to power they would destroy his efforts at building the peace. And he particularly attacked their past refusal to recognize the existence of the Soviet Union.

He also, though, took care to praise the internationalist section of the Republican Party whose votes he wanted and some of whom had senior positions in his Administration. Turning to his own time as President,

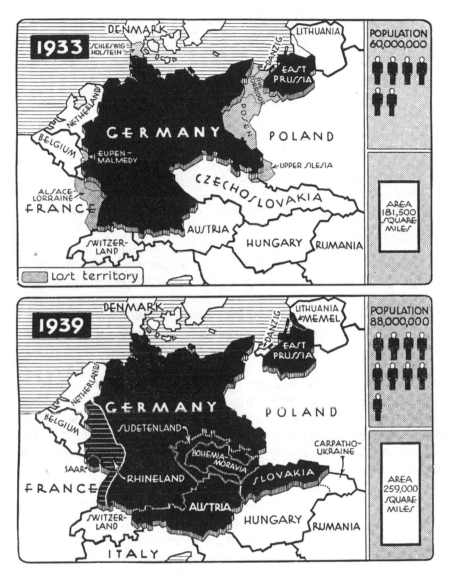

1 The expansion of Germany from 1933 to August 1939.

Roosevelt intensified the attack on the trade and security politics of his political opponents:

> We know that after this Administration took office, Secretary [of State, Cordell] Hull and I asked that high tariffs be replaced by a series of reciprocal trade agreements under a statute of the Congress. The Republicans in the Congress opposed those agreements – and tried to stop the extension of the law every three years. I am just talking about their votes [in Congress]. In 1937, I asked that aggressor nations be quarantined. For this, I was branded by isolationists in and out of public office as an 'alarmist' and a 'war-monger'. From that time

on, as you well know, I made clear by repeated messages to the Congress of the United States, and by repeated statements to the American people, the danger threatening from abroad – and the need of re-arming to meet it.

And it was made plain to Mr Hull and me that because of the isolationist vote in the Congress of the United States, we could not possibly hope to obtain the desired revision of the Neutrality Law. In 1941, this Administration proposed and the Congress passed, in spite of isolationist opposition, the Lend-Lease Law, the practical and dramatic notice to the world that we intended to help those nations resisting aggression.

The majority of the Republican members of the Congress voted – I am just giving you a few figures, not many – against the Selective Service Law [selective compulsory military service] in 1940; they voted against repeal of the Arms Embargo in 1939; they voted against the Lend-Lease Law in 1941; and they voted in August 1941 against extension of the Selective Service – which meant voting against keeping our Army together – four months before Pearl Harbor.[4]

Roosevelt's argument was that the Republicans had prevented the development of global security organizations and free trade, alienated allies, built up Germany and tried to prevent all resistance to the dictators. His critics argued that Roosevelt needlessly provoked the Germans and Japanese and had responsibility for the failure of an international economic conference in 1932 supposed to revive international trade.

His argument about the difficulty of getting Republican support to stop Hitler becomes clearer when we look in more detail at America's reaction to Hitler's successes in 1939 and 1940. In March 1939, Hitler attacked that part of Czechoslovakia he had not been given at Munich six months before. Poland joined Hitler in carving up Czechoslovakia by seizing the area around Techen. In Spain, Franco finally defeated the democratic government. Then, in July, discussions between Britain, France and the Soviet Union on a military alliance against Hitler collapsed – the Western Europeans showed little interest in working with the communists. Stalin cut his losses and stunned the world by making an alliance with his ideological arch-enemy, Adolf Hitler: in August 1939 they announced their pact. A few weeks later, in early September, Hitler attacked Poland from the west. Stalin then moved into Poland from the east, overrunning the country. The British and French, having declared war on Germany, declined also to go to war with Russia, accepting the Soviet explanation that they were protecting people from the Nazis. People soon began to suffer under the Nazi and Soviet occupations, and by the summer of 1940, Stalin had moved to take over the Baltic States.

In response to these events, Roosevelt at last felt able to ask Congress to repeal America's Neutrality Act, which banned sending help to states at war. After six weeks deliberation, Congress voted to allow Britain and France to buy US weapons for cash, but took away authority for them to be transported on US ships, something that had been legal, thereby giving

3 Adolf Hitler and Benito Mussolini.

help in one way while restricting it in another. This extraordinary restriction may have been designed to keep the US out of the war, but it was of direct help to Hitler, who no longer hard to worry that the weapons would be carried on American ships which he could not sink without going to war with the US. The Allies could now buy US weapons, but could they get them across the U-boat infested Atlantic?

Too little, but not quite too late, Congress began to pay for more weapons for US forces. In 1940, Americans were still spending less on

4 The Dutch city of Rotterdam after German bombing in May 1940.

the military as a proportion of national wealth than they had in 1932, in the depths of the recession. In 1938, Roosevelt had sought increased spending for the production of 20,000 warplanes, but had been rebuffed in Congress.[5] Only in 1941 did spending increase substantially, including an order for a dozen aircraft carriers.

Legislators failed to take advantage of one of Roosevelt's most far-sighted and least-remembered preparations for war. In 1933, he requested the defence industry to offer a range of the latest high-tech weapons. Of these, one of the most famous was a bomber aircraft – the B-17 Flying Fortress – built by the Boeing aircraft corporation as early as 1935 to meet a War Department specification which resulted from Roosevelt's 1933 request.

In the summer of 1940, however, the US had few modern weapons and few trained men – the army had just a few hundred thousand compared to millions in those of Germany, Britain, France and the Soviet Union. Only after Dunkirk, when it appeared Britain could fall to the Nazis, did Roosevelt think it possible to get a law past Congress compelling young men to register for compulsory selection for a year's military service. At this point in the war, Hitler's tanks and warplanes had destroyed the British and French armies in Europe and bombs were falling on London and other cities. Britain stood alone, expecting Hitler's invasion fleet of air- and seaborne forces and braced to fight another battle at Hastings, where the English had lost 900 years earlier to the Norman conquest.

In America by 1940, there were two main political movements vying for the support of the American people in relation to the war in Europe. These were America First and the Committee to Defend America by Aiding the Allies (CDAAA).[6]

America First was a broad alliance or a ragbag of misfits depending on one's point of view. It contained pacifists, communists, those who favoured fascism and feared communist revolution at home and abroad, those who hated British Imperial domination from Ireland to India, and those who believed that America could get along fine protected by its navy and the wide Atlantic and Pacific oceans.[7] The CDAAA leaders were William Allen White of the Kansas City *Emporia Gazette* and Clark M. Eichelberger of the League of Nations Association. The Committee to Defend America sought to link the need to help those fighting to the ideas that this was a fight for freedom against tyranny and that victory would be accompanied by a better world.

Both groups sought to influence the 1940 presidential election. Then, as now, the nomination and election campaigns were a long-drawn-out affair. When the Democrat and Republican Party conventions met in the summer, it was after Dunkirk. Gallup polls showed that American public opinion had swung towards fighting alongside Britain if this was essential to stopping Hitler from winning.

The Republicans were focused on attacking Roosevelt's economic New Deal, including financial programmes to support the elderly and unemployed and nationalization of businesses. Front runners were the gang-busting New York state prosecutor Thomas Dewey and Senator Arthur Vandenburg. The convention in Philadelphia that July ended up choosing neither of them. Wendell Willkie, a charismatic lawyer and lobbyist for the electric power and other private utilities, came in as an outsider. One of his advantages was that he had no record of opposing involvement in the European war. At this time the Republicans needed a candidate untainted by isolationism but likewise not bent on war, and Willkie was the only contender to fit that specification. The Republican platform blamed Roosevelt for the failure to resist Hitler and gave a commitment to 'all peoples fighting for liberty, or whose liberty is threatened, of such aid as shall not be in violation of international law or consistent with the requirements of our own national defense'.[8]

The vagueness was satisfactory to the competing factions in the party, but barely edged the party towards intervention. Willkie, who had spent most of his life as a supporter of the Democrats, had little difficulty in working with Roosevelt as an ardent supporter of internationalism soon after he had lost the election. Republicans Frank Knox and Henry Stimson joined the Administration as Secretaries of the Navy and War respectively in the summer of 1940, shortly after Dunkirk. Their effort at providing a bipartisan character to the Roosevelt Administration was cut down when Stimson was promptly expelled from the Republican Party.

Republican resistance to helping Britain came to a head over what became known as the 'Destroyers for Bases' deal became a political focus during the presidential campaign. Following Dunkirk, Churchill had made increasingly desperate pleas to Roosevelt for warships to stave off the Nazis. After lengthy debate, Roosevelt eventually found enough legal and political support for sending 50 World War I vintage vessels in return for leases on bases in the British Caribbean Islands.[9]

Even after his unprecedented re-election for a third term as President in November 1940, Roosevelt still had a huge task in persuading the American people and Congress to resist Hitler. In the winter of 1940–41, Roosevelt began to combine the argument for military strength to resist Hitler with ideas for a progressive international New Deal to inspire the American people to engage with the enemy. This international strategy was outlined in successive speeches on the 'Arsenal of Democracy' and the 'Four Freedoms'; and then with Churchill in the eight-point Atlantic Charter of August 1941.

The speeches on the Arsenal of Democracy, on 29 December 1940, and on the Four Freedoms, in his State of the Union Address to Congress on 6 January 1941, reinforced each other. The weapons that the US arsenal was to supply were for the political and moral purpose of defending democracy. The Four Freedoms spelled out the democratic values that needed to be defended abroad. In American politics a call to supply weapons to those opposed to Hitler would have met with less response from the public if it had been presented solely as a means of defending the USA. It was necessary to spell out what was so odious about Nazi ideology and what was so beneficial about democratic values. Roosevelt's officials organized publicity campaigns linking the two speeches.

But for those already suffering under Nazi occupation in Europe and under their bombs in London, the speeches offered no immediate help. Londoners experienced the most intense aerial bombardment the world had yet seen on this same night of 29 December 1940.[10]

The battle of political ideas in America over whether to resist Hitler dragged on. It was not until March 1941 that the Lend-Lease Act was passed by Congress. The Lend-Lease Act was the most important decision taken by the USA in favour of the Allies prior to Pearl Harbor. It was used initially to spend some $7 billion of US taxpayers' money on weapons for the British. The Act was passed three months after, on 17 December 1940, Roosevelt had first spelled out at a press conference the case for helping one's neighbours in a crisis:

Well, let me give you an illustration: Suppose my neighbor's home catches fire, and I have a length of garden hose four or five hundred feet away. If he can take my garden hose and connect it up with his hydrant, I may help him to put out his fire. Now, what do I do? I don't say to him before that operation, 'Neighbor, my garden hose cost me $15; you have to pay me $15 for it'.[11]

These 'firehose' remarks were soon followed by the Arsenal of Democracy speech and then by the Four Freedoms which laid out the global political policies to accompany the argument for military supplies:

In the future days, which we seek to make secure, we look forward to a world founded upon four essential human freedoms. The first is freedom of speech and expression – everywhere in the world.

The second is freedom of every person to worship God in his own way – everywhere in the world.

The third is freedom from want – which, translated into world terms, means economic understandings which will secure to every nation a healthy peacetime life for its inhabitants – everywhere in the world.

The fourth is freedom from fear – which, translated into world terms, means a world-wide reduction of armaments to such a point and in such a thorough fashion that no nation will be in a position to commit an act of physical aggression against any neighbour – anywhere in the world.

That is no vision of a distant millennium. It is a definite basis for a kind of world attainable in our own time and generation. That kind of world is the very antithesis of the so-called new order of tyranny which the dictators seek to create with the crash of a bomb. To that new order we oppose the greater conception – the moral order. A good society is able to face schemes of world domination and foreign revolutions alike without fear.[12]

His opponents resisted the attempt to make the US an arsenal for democracy and create a new moral compass. Indeed, within conservative America and within business there was active support for Hitler. Critically, US automobile makers Ford and General Motors (GM) increased their role as an arsenal for Nazism, while resisting the US Government's request to convert to war production. According to a 1998 report in *The Washington Post*,

In certain instances, American managers of both GM and Ford went along with the conversion of their German plants to military production at a time when US government documents show they were still resisting calls by the Roosevelt administration to step up military production in their plants at home.[13]

While Roosevelt tried to get a tougher line from Congress, the war did not wait. Britain was under siege in early 1941 and Axis victories in Africa and Greece were followed by Hitler's attack on the Soviet Union.

Britain's ships were being sunk by German submarines at such a rate that the country was fast running out of food and ammunition. A total of 1,300 British and Allied ships were sunk that year – two a day in the

Atlantic during June 1941[14] – far faster than they could be built. US ships were also sunk but there was no media or political outcry to take on Hitler. Roosevelt ordered the US Navy to protect shipping further and further out into the Atlantic from the East Coast, occasionally fighting U-boats by mid-1941.

With Britain contained but not crushed, Hitler switched his attention to the Soviet Union. In June 1941, he ordered millions of men to attack, and the Panzers raced for Moscow. Soviet armies and cities fell before them seemingly every day. The German SS followed behind, exterminating or imprisoning every Jew they could find.

In Washington, Congress debated the draft and Roosevelt sought further ways to help Britain and the Soviet Union. Senator Harry S. Truman made the front pages with his recommendation: 'If we see that Germany is winning we ought to help Russia and if Russia is winning we ought to help Germany and that way let them kill as many as possible'.[15]

That July, America managed to build just two bomber planes.[16]

Despite Hitler's triumphs, large parts of the US public remained opposed to the war. In Congress, Republicans nearly succeeded in disbanding a key part of the military preparations that had finally begun to be made after the fall of France. As part of his desire to overcome this isolationist opinion, Roosevelt expanded his ideas for a global political programme.

Within the US political system, matters came to head in early August 1941. The House of Representatives considered whether to extend the draft. *The Oakland Tribune*, in a front page report on 8 August, stated that a leading opponent, Representative Dewey Jackson Short of Missouri, argued that keeping men in uniform would be a breach of faith with the undertaking that the draft was for just one year and that keeping the men on would fatally undermine morale.[17]

Former President Herbert Hoover and 14 other Republicans asked that 'Congress put a stop to the step-by-step projection of the United States into an undeclared war', attacking what it called unauthorized aid to Russia as undermining democratic government. They rejected the idea that the war was a battle for freedom because Churchill's alliance with Stalin 'has dissipated that illusion'.[18]

There were also rumours in the press of a meeting between Churchill and Roosevelt alongside the false lead that Roosevelt was on a boating trip. The papers reported that none of the leading members of the Roosevelt Administration could be found in Washington, increasing the speculation. The next day, 9 August 1941, people read local papers anxious to see if their sons, brothers and fathers would be drafted. In a typical report, *The Paris News* in Texas spoke of an attempt to find a compromise on the draft.[19] Almost all Republicans were thought to oppose any extension of the draft at all, with 20 of their 170 needed to get the law passed.

What happened next is told by Karl Bendetson, a veteran of World War I. He had come to Washington on his own initiative to lobby Congress to resist Hitler. By 1941 he was an official working in Congress for the Administration. Here is his account of the crisis in the House of Representatives:

> The Selective Service Act of August 16, 1940 would expire on August 16, 1941 if not extended by congressional action. The Senate had voted for extension in a relatively close vote. In the House there were great pressures to let the Act die. Most people have probably forgotten how some of the draftees and many others were behaving in those days. Draft cards were publicly burned. There were riots. There was a concerted effort to end the draft. It was a 'rehearsal' for the anti-Vietnam demonstrations [. . . .]
>
> The bill came to the floor of the House for debate a very short time before it was due to expire, about seven days as I recall [. . . .]
>
> An hour before the final vote, Mr. Rayburn [Sam Rayburn, the speaker of the House] told us that a compromise had been proposed which would assure passage if agreed to. He then outlined the compromise. He stated that the extension Act would limit the total length of service of each draftee to 12 months; prohibit service outside the Continental limits of the 48 states; and require the immediate redeployment of each individual draftee then serving beyond these territorial limits, such as for example: Puerto Rico, the Canal Zone, Hawaii, the Philippines and Alaska. 'What do you think of the compromise?' he asked.
>
> Bendetson told him, 'It's untenable, unworkable. It will intensify the crisis that we already face. This compromise will make it impossible adequately to train, deploy and replace our soldiers'. He then asked [his fellow officer], 'Jerry, what do you think?' He said, 'I think we're caught up with an unacceptable proposal'.
>
> The Speaker said, 'Well, so do I'.
>
> It was a critical situation. Jerry and I made our telephone calls to the Chief of Staff and the Secretary of War. After 20 or 30 minutes, we were instructed to advise the Speaker that the Secretary and the Chief of Staff 'cannot, in deference to our accountability for the preparedness of the nation, agree to such a compromise'.
>
> The Speaker said, 'We will see what happens. I can't predict the result'. He handled the situation masterfully. A final vote was soon taken. It was then to become the famous vote of 201 to 200 in favor. Mr. Rayburn banged the gavel at a critical moment and declared the Bill had passed. If he had not banged it at the precise moment he did, the vote would have been reversed in the next few minutes. The fainthearted Congressmen who had voted 'aye' would have switched their votes when they realized that there were 200 votes against. The Speaker sensed this and he knew his parliamentary rules full well. If the nation owed anyone a debt, it was to him for that forthright action. He later told us in his office that as he raised the gavel, he saw five 'doves' on the way to the floor of the House. He knew they would sink the extension! Still later, we all went over to see Senator Truman who invited us to Les Biffle's office (The Secretary of the Senate) where we raised a toast with a small splash of bourbon![20]

The Bill had to face further votes in Congress and these were carried with the help of a new internationalist initiative from Roosevelt. This was the Atlantic Charter. Looking back at the publication of the Atlantic Charter, one of America's pioneering women reporters, The Associated Press's Sigrid Arne, put it this way:

> Too few knew what the shooting was about. And since the United States was not at war, the question was, 'for what kind of peace is England fighting? Is it the kind we want?' An acceptable answer to that question might mean higher war production in Camden, Pittsburgh, Detroit, Los Angeles, Seattle.
>
> Then one August Thursday – the 14th– Britons and Americans, buying their afternoon newspapers, were electrified to read that their chiefs of state had met 'at sea' – notwithstanding the constant danger from German planes and German submarines. . . . The meeting on the Atlantic can be called the birth of the United Nations.[21]

Arne's 1945 *United Nations Primer*, from which this quote comes, gives a freshness to the history of the international meetings discussed throughout this book. She went on to become President of the American News Women's Club.

A great deal of preparation had gone into this first summit between Churchill and Roosevelt. Roosevelt had sent a team to London in preparation for the meeting. Among them were his personal ambassador, Harry Hopkins, and military officers. The officers warned the British to expect 60,000 Nazi paratroopers to land in southern England at any time.[22] The American generals were dismayed that the British were still sending men and scarce tanks and planes to hold onto Egypt and support Russia when they were in so much peril at home.

Hopkins, with great personal courage and accompanied by two army officers, flew on to Moscow to meet Stalin. While in London he had discovered that the British had opened up an experimental air route to Russia involving a 2,000-mile round-trip from Scotland aboard a 100-mile an hour seaplane. He took the twin-propeller Catalina from the Scottish islands up around the North Cape of Norway to the Arctic city of Murmansk in Russia. The plane risked being shot down by the Luftwaffe but at least it was big enough for his lanky frame. Both the seaplane and the Russian aircraft that took him between Murmansk and Moscow were among the items he had organized to be supplied by the USA.

In Moscow, Stalin discussed the capabilities of Russian weapons in great detail with him. Hopkins offered as much military support as the USA could produce and came away more confident that the Russians would fight on.

Back in Britain, with this fresh news, Hopkins joined Churchill for the voyage aboard the British battleship *HMS Prince of Wales*. The ship was still showing scars of shell explosions from its fight with the German battleship *Bismarck* that March. (Later that year most of the crew were killed when it was sunk by the Japanese.) The *Prince of Wales* met up with US warships accompanying Roosevelt at Placentia Bay, off Newfoundland.

5 Josef Stalin and Harry Hopkins in Moscow, July 1941.

The document produced by the two leaders is a model of both vision and caution. It is evidence of the importance that the two leaders placed on politics as a tool of military victory, that they set out a far-reaching agenda – an agenda that, in twenty-first century terms, is one of liberal social democracy. The other countries fighting the Axis soon declared their support. And what rapidly became known as 'The Atlantic Charter' is

6 The church service at the Churchill–Roosevelt Atlantic Charter meeting.

listed as the first 'basic' or 'antecedent' document in the archives of both the UN and the North Atlantic Treaty Organization (NATO).[23]

The Charter provided a political basis for countering Nazi ideology and, for Roosevelt, of defeating the isolationists at home. It is easy to be cynical about it, given Churchill's pugnacious defence of the British Empire and Roosevelt's interest in expanding US influence,[24] but consider Nelson Mandela's recollection:

> Change was in the air in the 1940s. The Atlantic Charter of 1941, issued by Roosevelt and Churchill, reaffirmed faith in the dignity of each human being and propagated a host of democratic principles. Some in the West saw the charter as empty promises, but not those of us in Africa. Inspired by the Atlantic Charter and the fight of the Allies against tyranny and oppression, the ANC [African National Congress] created its own charter, called African Claims, which called for full citizenship for all Africans, the right to buy land and repeal of all discriminatory legislation.[25]

The Atlantic Charter

> Joint declaration of the President of the United States of America and the Prime Minister, Mr. Churchill, representing His Majesty's Government in the United Kingdom, being met together, deem it right to make known certain common principles in the national policies of their respective countries on which they base their hopes for a better future for the world.
>
> First, their countries seek no aggrandizement, territorial or other;

Second, they desire to see no territorial changes that do not accord with the freely expressed wishes of the peoples concerned;

Third, they respect the right of all peoples to choose the form of government under which they will live; and they wish to see sovereign rights and self government restored to those who have been forcibly deprived of them;

Fourth, they will endeavor, with due respect for their existing obligations, to further the enjoyment by all States, great or small, victor or vanquished, of access, on equal terms, to the trade and to the raw materials of the world which are needed for their economic prosperity;

Fifth, they desire to bring about the fullest collaboration between all nations in the economic field with the objector securing, for all, improved labor standards, economic advancement and social security;

Sixth, after the final destruction of the Nazi tyranny, they hope to see established a peace which will afford to all nations the means of dwelling in safety within their own boundaries, and which will afford assurance that all the men in all the lands may live out their lives in freedom from fear and want;

Seventh, such a peace should enable all men to traverse the high seas and oceans without hindrance;

Eighth, they believe that all of the nations of the world, for realistic as well as spiritual reasons, must come to the abandonment of the use of force. Since no future peace can be maintained if land, sea or air armaments continue to be employed by nations which threaten, or may threaten, aggression outside of their frontiers, they believe, pending the establishment of a wider and permanent system of general security, that the disarmament of such nations is essential. They will likewise aid and encourage all other practicable measures which will lighten for peace-loving peoples the crushing burden of armaments.

FRANKLIN D. ROOSEVELT
WINSTON S. CHURCHILL

The eight points fill barely a page, in contrast to the volumes that pour from the word-processors at twenty-first century summits. And it was a set of goals not an operational plan. Arne was pretty sharp about its limitations:

> This is as good a place as any to put a sort of intellectual leg iron on the average hasty, generous, read-as-you-run American. Even commentators who should know better fell to discussing the Atlantic Charter as if it were a fait accompli. It was in fact a set of ideals to aspire to ... anyone who had read it thoroughly, and understood the limited freedoms placed on any leader in a democracy, would have known that ... raising the prospect of social security, free trade, better labor rights, free trade, free speech, elections and a more effective version of the League of Nations.[26]

In public, each leader was speaking to a political audience to build the domestic and international coalition to fight the war. They knew that without the will of men to pick up weapons and risk death, weapons by themselves were of no use. In private, the two leaders and their military staff were working out the best way to win, if and when the USA went to war.

In the USA, Roosevelt's critics speculated on what secret deals had been made and were scathing about the high-toned language in the Charter. America First quibbled that the first point on limiting further imperial acquisitions did not apply to the Dutch, Australians, Canadians and Russians.[27] The Hearst Press, not a notable supporter of democratic rights for 'coloured' people, charged that the Atlantic Charter would not apply to India, Persia, Egypt and a host of other peoples under colonial rule.[28]

The coded reference to British Imperial trade taxes – tariffs – in the phrase 'existing obligations' in point 4 of the Charter implied support for the Empire. The ideas of disarmament, and the implication that there might be a new League, drew special opposition.[29] Congressman George Holden Tinkham thought that a charge for treason was in order against Roosevelt as the eight points amounted to a declaration of war made aboard a British warship.[30]

The private discussions aboard ship between the leaders went deep into post-war issues. Sumner Welles, the Assistant Secretary of State, noted a talk with Roosevelt that provides the first sketch of a council of the powerful sitting with a wider general assembly. At the time, the working assumption was that the Soviet Union would collapse, but then as the Red Army's resistance grew, the Soviet Union would become a more viable partner. In a form of enlightened dictatorship, the victorious powers would rule in consultation with a wider group of small states whose negligible power encouraged Roosevelt to ignore altogether:

> I [Sumner Welles] said I also had been surprised and somewhat discouraged by a remark that the President had casually made in our morning's conference (with Churchill) – if I had understood him correctly – which was that nothing could be more futile than the reconstitution of a body such as the Assembly of the League of Nations. I said to the President that it seemed to me that if he conceived of the need for a transition period upon the termination of the war during which period Great Britain and the United States would undertake the policing of the world, it seemed to me that it would be enormously desirable for the smaller Powers to have available to them an Assembly in which they would all be represented and in which they could make their complaints known and join in recommendations as to the policy to be pursued by the major Powers who were doing the police work. I said it seemed to me that an organization of that kind would be the most effective safety valve that could be devised.
>
> The President said that he agreed fully with what I said and that all that he had intended by the remark he made this morning was to make clear his belief that a transition period was necessary and that during that transition period no organizations such as the Council or the Assembly of the League could undertake the powers and prerogatives with which they had been entrusted during the existence of the League of Nations.
>
> I further said that while from the practical standpoint I was in agreement that the United States and Great Britain were the only Powers which could or would exercise the police trusteeship and that it seemed to me that it would be impossible if such a trusteeship were set up to exclude there from the other

American republics or for that matter the countries at present occupied such as Norway, the Netherlands, and even Belgium. The President said that he felt that a solution for this difficulty could probably be found through the ostensible joining with Great Britain and the United States of those Powers, but it would have to be recognized that it would be ostensible since none of the nations mentioned would have the practical means of taking any effective or, at least, considerable part in the task involved.[31]

The ideas that were made public in the Atlantic Charter provoked intense and continuing international debate throughout the rest of the war and on into our own time. Nowadays, academics who teach would-be policymakers argue whether 'hard' (military and economic) or 'soft' (ideological and cultural) power is more important. And they discuss 'public diplomacy' as an innovation. It is clear in the text of the Atlantic Charter, and in the context of the time, that power should be considered as a whole, where the balance and strength of all elements need to be considered, while the Charter is an example of using public diplomacy for domestic and global purposes.

The Altantic Charter was soon adopted by the countries at war with the Axis. Today, St James's Palace, just below London's Piccadilly, houses the offices of the English Princes, William and Harry. In September 1941, it hosted the first main political meeting of the Allies fighting Hitler. They all, including the Soviet Union, publicly endorsed the Atlantic Charter.[32]

That autumn, America was edging closer to war through naval action, military supplies to Hitler's foes and this Charter. Whether America would ever get into the fight was still an open question, as the reluctance of the Congress to either endorse the draft or supply those already in the fight indicates.

At this time the Japanese were moving into French Indo-China (now Cambodia, Laos and Vietnam), having already occupied parts of China. The Vichy French government offered no resistance. The Japanese looked to take advantage of the weakness of the British, Dutch and French Empires by taking power in South East Asia. But the Japanese came under pressure as Roosevelt stopped American companies selling them oil, of which they had none themselves. Their military appeared ready to seize oilfields in the Dutch East Indies (today's Indonesia).

Roosevelt ordered the US Navy in the Pacific to prepare for war. He and his advisors thought that the Japanese would leave the US alone and concentrate on the almost defenceless territories owned by the Europeans. In fact, in what Roosevelt called 'a day that will live in infamy', Japanese naval warplanes attacked the US fleet at Pearl Harbor, its port at Hawaii, on 7 December 1941. They missed the fuel storage tanks and aircraft carriers. Had the Japanese fliers done a more effective job that day, it is more likely that Japanese forces would have reached into India and the US West Coast.

II The growth of Japanese influence.

The political arguments against American participation in the war were now put aside as everyone rallied to defend America. Justus Doenecke, historian of the anti-interventionists, provides a useful conclusion:

> In the end the anti-interventionists were defeated at every point. With consummate skill, Franklin Roosevelt set the agenda, defined the issues, and chose his timing well. Besides, noninterventionists were far too diverse to offer any unified alternatives of their own, and even too divided to offer any alternative vision of a positive international order.[33]

Their anti-communism meant that 'it would hardly be exaggerated to find in the anti-interventionist posture a kind of rehearsal for the Cold War'.[34]

Forty-eight hours before Pearl Harbor, Hitler's armies began to retreat from Moscow under an icy onslaught from the Red Army. Notwithstanding this, the Führer declared war on the United States on 10 December. In so doing, he removed the last hope of those Americans content to leave the European war to the Europeans.

Stalin, encouraged by his victory at Moscow, told his generals that they could win the war in 1942 and set about planning the march to Berlin.[35] He had already publicly praised the help from Britain and the USA as making victory inevitable. And in private meetings with Anthony Eden, the British Foreign Secretary, he tried to get British agreement on post-war European spheres of influence. This would have involved the Soviet Union keeping the Baltic states and certain Ukrainian inhabited territories in Poland it had obtained under the Molotov-Ribbentrop Pact. With Roosevelt's encouragement, the British refused to deal on post-war frontiers.

But now it was finally at war, the key issues were how would the USA choose to fight and how would it cooperate with the British and Soviet Union? These became an immediate preoccupationof everyone concerned with the war.

CHAPTER 2

America goes to war: the creation of the United Nations

C hurchill rushed to Washington after Pearl Harbor, arriving on 22 December. He needed to plan with Roosevelt how to win the war in coordination with Stalin, Chiang Kai-shek, the Chinese leader, and smaller nations.

Under the headline 'United Nations', *The Economist* described the outcome of their meetings thus:

> The details were made known on Tuesday of the most comprehensive system of international association the world has yet seen. The students of post-war leagues and federations would do well to study it; the Axis states no doubt are already giving it their close attention. The problem is to mobilise the resources of all the United Nations.[1]

Over New Year 1942, the two leaders made their military and political plans. These laid the foundations for victory and for the post-war institutions, including the UN we know today. The military plans were necessarily conducted in secret. The political plans though had a vital public dimension in rallying domestic and international support for the war effort. In June 1942, the political effort was reinforced when Roosevelt led political celebrations organized by governments around the world at national and community level. As a result, the ideas of the United Nations became embedded in wartime civilian culture, especially in the USA.

The creation of military planning systems and political goals were more enduring than the immediate battle plans they made. As Churchill and Roosevelt and their military staff set about preparing to liberate Europe and defeat the Japanese, they had to cope with another round of catastrophic defeats on the battlefield. For it was the Axis that was still winning the war, with new victories in early 1942 in Libya, Singapore, Malaya, Java, Sumatra, New Guinea, Russia and Ukraine. Nevertheless, these disasters did not make Churchill and Roosevelt change their most vital military decision, which was to contain the Japanese while defeating Germany first. This secret priority had been set earlier in 1941 during Anglo-American military staff discussions.

The political and organizational results of the White House meeting that winter answered several questions. How could the peoples fighting the Axis be united around a cause to fight for? How would the various national military and industrial resources be combined? And when and where were these resources to be used to defeat the enemy?

The first priority was to create a political alliance among the states at war with the Axis.[2] In World War I, poor coordination between the Allies had hindered the war effort. Britain and America were determined not to repeat those mistakes. Britain already had a series of agreements with the countries Hitler had attacked, while the USA had Lend-Lease agreements with the British, the Soviet Union and the other Allies. But there was nothing that bound everyone together or that brought in wavering nations.

At the State Department, Cordell Hull, despite suffering from tuberculosis, oversaw the preparation of two documents designed to solve these problems. He prepared both a draft political agreement of Associated Powers and the structure of a Supreme War Council of all the allied nations. The first of these was intended to answer the question of how to cooperate politically and the second, the question of military cooperation. For the USA, these documents were revolutionary and a huge advance on the process of World War I when the USA had refused to engage in any formal alliance.

The Anglo-American talks at the White House on these and other military and war industry plans were conducted in a sociable atmosphere (along corridors filled with the Roosevelt family's Christmas presents) and continued through to mid-January. Churchill took up residence in the White House, aside from a brief vacation in Florida and a visit to Canada. The two leaders and their staffs dined and chatted together at length and often far into the night. Roosevelt inflicted whisky/vermouth cocktails on Churchill, who was not averse to disposing of them discretely, pending supplies of his preferred champagne or whisky. Churchill was rarely without a cigar and Roosevelt a cigarette.

Four days into their talks, on the night of 28 December 1941, Roosevelt had the idea of using the term 'United Nations' rather than Associated Powers to describe the political alliance. His companion, Daisy Suckley, recorded in her diary the historic event:[3]

> F.D.R. got into his bed, his mind working & working...Suddenly, he got it – United Nations! The next morning, the minute he had finished his breakfast, he got onto his chair & was wheeled up the hall to W.S.C.'s room. He knocked on the door, no answer, so he opened the door & went in & sat on a chair, & the man went out & closed the door – He called to W.S.C. & in the door leading to the bathroom appeared W.S.C.: 'a pink cherub' (FDR said) drying himself with a towel, & without a stitch on! F.D.R. pointed at him and exploded: 'The United Nations!' '*Good!*' said W.S.C.

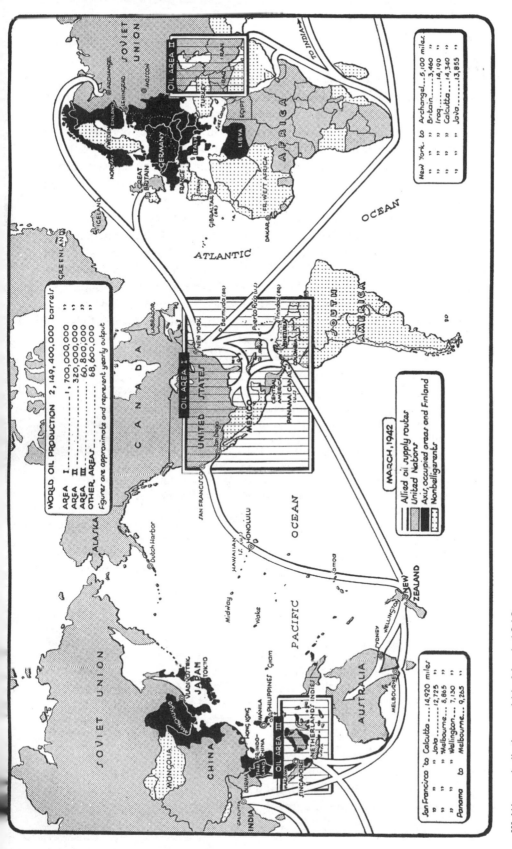

III War and oil, the world in March 1942.

The detail in her account indicates that she may have been alone in the room with the two men at the time. Apparently part of the furniture, Suckley was an almost daily companion of Roosevelt's from the early 1930s. Only after her death was her diary found in a trunk under her bed. It contains numerous insights into events of the time that tend to support the accounts given by Roosevelt's son Elliot and by his speechwriter Robert Sherwood. Harry Hopkins had always told the tale of the President and the gleaming Prime Minister – Suckley provides even more detail.

Sherwood traced a document which shows that 29 December was 'the day when the United Nations was formally given its name', when, having agreed the term with Churchill, Roosevelt struck out the phrase 'Associated Powers' and replaced it with 'United Nations' in a draft paper on China sent in by General George C. Marshall, the US Army's Chief of Staff.[4]

The text of the Declaration and the choice of who would sign was determined in the next 48 hours. The resulting document was a fusion of the military and the political; of a vision for human rights for the world and of compromises forced by the realities of power:

> A Joint Declaration by the United States of America, the United Kingdom of Great Britain and Northern Ireland, the Union of Soviet Socialist Republics, China, Australia, Belgium, Canada, Costa Rica, Cuba, Czechoslovakia, Dominican Republic, El Salvador, Greece, Guatemala, Haiti, Honduras, India, Luxembourg, Netherlands, New Zealand, Nicaragua, Norway, Panama, Poland, South Africa, Yugoslavia. The Governments signatory hereto, Having subscribed to a common program of purposes and principles embodied in the Joint Declaration of the President of United States of America and the Prime Minister of the United Kingdom of Great Britain and Northern Ireland dated August 14, 1941, known as the Atlantic Charter.
>
> Being convinced that complete victory over their enemies is essential to defend life, liberty, independence and religious freedom, and to preserve human rights and justice in their own lands as well as in other lands, and that they are now engaged in a common struggle against savage and brutal forces seeking to subjugate the world,

Declare:

1. Each Government pledges itself to employ its full resources, military or economic, against those members of the Tripartite Pact [the Axis] and its adherents with which such government is at war.
2. Each Government pledges itself to cooperate with the Governments signatory hereto and not to make a separate armistice or peace with the enemies.

> The foregoing declaration may be adhered to by other nations which are, or which may be, rendering material assistance and contributions in the struggle for victory over Hitlerism.

For Sherwood, the Declaration by United Nations was a 'prelude to a new world symphony'.[5] It is a legal foundation of the UN today as its signatory states became the first founders of the UN according to the Charter signed in 1945, which states in Article 3 that 'The original Members of the United Nations shall be the states which, having participated in the United Nations Conference on International Organization at San Francisco, or having previously signed the Declaration by United Nations of 1 January 1942, sign the present Charter and ratify it in accordance with Article 110'.

The military component of the Declaration was a pledge to fight on until victory. No nation was to make a separate peace agreement. It was carefully worded so that states did not have to fight members of the Axis they were not already at war with. To this end, the Declaration had been redrafted by Stalin and his Ambassador in Washington, Maxim Litvinov.[6] They wanted to make sure that Japan could find no excuse to attack the Soviet Union in Siberia. Thus, the term Hitlerism was used rather than some broader term such as 'Fascism'. The provision also conveniently allowed the USA not to go to war with some European states, including Finland, that it was not fighting at the time.

The Americans, British and Russians also had a brief but intense discussion about the political content of the Declaration, although all concerned already supported the Atlantic Charter. Churchill telegraphed the draft back to London for consideration, where the War Cabinet sought to increase the importance of social security. Roosevelt regarded the statement in the Atlantic Charter on the issue as sufficient. The atheistic Soviet leadership baulked at signing up to freedom of religion, but Roosevelt was adamant. It was a basic American value and was one of his vaunted Four Freedoms. In the end, the Soviets were convinced by the argument that freedom of religion could include no religion at all. The practical impact of ideas such as these is hard to assess. As discussed later, many of the specific items in the Atlantic Charter and this Declaration became starting points for important global programmes, not least in economic and financial matters and for the UN itself.

The role of religion is worth discussing for a moment since it is easy to dismiss Stalin's commitment as without substance. In the USA, churches, especially the Catholic Church, continued their anti-communist crusade, anxious to minimize help to the godless Red Army. But while officially so, the Red Army was in fact not totally 'godless'. On the contrary, during the war Stalin permitted a significant re-establishment of the Russian Orthodox Church to its traditional role as defender of Russia and its rulers. By the end of the war some 10,000 churches had re-opened, though Stalin claimed it was 50,000. According to an Irish observer and Soviet documents,[7] there was a widespread belief in the Soviet Union that the public celebration of Easter in 1942, and the general relaxation of constraints on religion, was a result of Stalin seeking to please England and America. Some consider that this was a condition of US military supplies to Russia.[8] Although the conventional explanation is that it was an attempt on Stalin's part to use any device to rally opposition to the Nazis, by September 1943 Stalin had re-established the Patriarch, Synod and a training academy for priests for the Orthodox Church.

With the text finalized by the Big Three, the Chinese were invited to sign, and then the other Allies. In a presage of things to come, the British had sought to list their Commonwealth partners next, after themselves, but Roosevelt put the Commonwealth back into the alphabetical listing and raised the Soviet Union and China into the big four, establishing a public order of importance of the nations.[9]

The Poles, Canadians and others complained that they had not been included in the drafting. The Norwegians argued that the Danes not be allowed to sign as they had not fought the German invasion, and the Czech Ambassador was so nervous he could not sign for several minutes.[10] According to Roy Jenkins in his biography of Churchill, 'What the ceremony and the declaration did, without formal proclamation, was to accept Washington's position as the imperial capital of the Allied war effort, although with Stalin maintaining a semi-independent position as Emperor of the East'.[11]

From this point on, the United Nations concept combined an old-fashioned alliance of convenience with an alliance that deemed it essential to have in its core mutual aid. This mutual aid was to continue after the war as a global order in which national interests could best and sometimes only be met in a supranational body.

The United Nations term remained in formal use throughout the war. The question 'what is meant by the term "United Nations" and how does it differ from the term "Allied Nations?"' immediately comes to mind. The British Foreign Office provided a formal answer to this precise question in an internal memo of June 1942. Their official answer was that,

> The phrase 'United Nations' was coined by President Roosevelt specifically for the joint declaration at Washington on 1st January 1942. In this, its first official use, it means the twenty six [that signed the declaration].... The term 'Allied Nations' is used to some extent for oratorical purposes to describe the nations that are at war with the common enemy.[12]

Article 38 of the Italian Instrument of Surrender of 29 September 1943 provides an example of this dual usage definition, with the term United Nations being the formal, superior and all-encompassing term: 'The term "United Nations" in the present instrument includes the Allied Commander-in-Chief, the Control Commission and any other authority which the United Nations may designate'.[13] As an example of wartime practice, the wartime index of newspaper cuttings by the London think-tank Chatham House and managed by the British Library directs the reader who looks up 'Allied Forces' to seek them under 'United Nations: Allied Forces'.[14]

With the Declaration finalized and the ceremony concluded, there was the problem of what to do with those who had not been allowed to sign. The balance of aspiration to support human rights was tempered by the refusal of the UK and USA, on Russian insistence, to allow in representatives of the Baltic states which had been occupied by the Soviet Union in 1940. De Gaulle's Free French were also refused admission to the United Nations. Roosevelt disliked De Gaulle and continued to recognize the Vichy Regime until the liberation of France in 1944. While the USA resisted demands from non-governmental groups such as the 'Free Germans' to be formally included, they were permitted to express their adherence.

The inclusion of the Latin American states was not obvious as they were not at war with Germany. The military reasons for their inclusion also serve as an introduction to the strategic problem the United Nations leaders faced in choosing the weapons, place and time to attack the Axis.

It is usual to think of Latin America as entirely dominated by the USA and if the question of German influence comes up, it is in connection with Nazi fugitives after the war. In reality, the Germans and Italians were challenging the USA in the region in the 1930s, especially through the development of airlines which had special political importance in the region given that its vast distances were difficult to cross by road or rail.

Had South American states joined the Axis, they would have threatened to link across the narrowest part of the Atlantic Ocean with Axis advances in West Africa. As is discussed in the next chapter, British and US planners could not assume that the Germans would fail to produce effective long-range bombers or ramp up weapons production as rapidly as their enemies. Indeed, the experience up to this point was of unexpected enemy successes. An Axis air force or naval presence in South America could negatively influence the submarine battle in the Atlantic. D-Day, when it came in 1944, was only possible because American armies were safely shipped to England across seas cleared of U-boats. Consequently, securing Latin America from enemy influence was a necessary foundation for liberating Europe.

Some states in the region, notably Argentina, were strongly sympathetic to the Axis up to 1945. US military planners expected a German attempt to reach as far as Brazil through North West Africa and the Atlantic Islands. This could have been facilitated by Spain and the Vichy French colonies in North Africa. In fact, Spain stayed out of the war, and despite his brutal actions, its dictator, Franco, remained in power until the 1970s.

In consequence, the British and Americans took preventive measures. The US Army arranged to send forces to defend North West Brazil. In London on 3 January 1942, General Alan Brooke, Chief of the Imperial General Staff, argued that the Japanese were 'likely to step in' and occupy the Falkland Islands in the South Atlantic.[15] Such a concern could only be based on the fear that the Japanese had the ability to sail around Cape Horn at the southern tip of South America and link with the German fleet and air force.

The US official history of the period up to Pearl Harbor in Latin America describes in some detail both German plans to march down the coast of Africa and the competition played out in South America: 'A struggle for control ... was ... waged during the pre-war period ostensibly by private commercial interests but in reality between US and the Axis'.[16] After the fall of France, the German-controlled Ecuadorian airline SEDTA tried to start flights out into the Pacific to the Galapagos Islands. The Colombian airlines threatened the Panama Canal, while the Italian airline LATI operated the only transatlantic route in 1941, flying from Europe via Cape Verde and Natal to Rio. These airlines had airfields with radio transmitters and weather forecasting stations to aid U-boats. And both Condor and LATI planes spotted ships for U-boats to sink. Pan Am (Pan American World Airways) helped buy up the airlines of the Axis in Brazil, Colombia and Ecuador.

The military and political alliance that constituted the United Nations of the war years was effective in eliminating the Axis threat in the region in 1942 and then in helping mobilize its resources for the war effort. The Latin American states were also a source of shipping and supplies with which to meet the requirement to get more weapons and supplies into battle. The successful inclusion of most Latin American states in the United Nations was exemplified by a military contribution from South America: a 25,000-strong Brazilian Expeditionary Force fought in Italy from 1944.[17]

Bringing as many Latin American states as possible into the January 1942 Declaration by United Nations was part of an inclusive international strategy pursued by Roosevelt. Merely bothering to include smaller states sent a signal that they would also have their say after the war and provided some legitimacy for the claim to be acting for humanity as a whole.

Roosevelt's early encouragement of anti-colonial movements around the world can be seen in the signature of India as a separate state. Churchill was in no position to object. Roosevelt and the American public sympathized with the vociferous independence campaign led by Gandhi and were concerned that Japanese anti-Western rhetoric would resonate in India. But Roosevelt's need for the military relationship with Churchill took priority, so that Indian inclusion as a separate entity in the multilateral wartime conferences was as far as he was prepared to go publicly. However, as is discussed in the following chapter, he continued to press Churchill to dismantle the British Empire.

In parallel with the political process of the Declaration, the British and American officials in Washington that winter began to find answers to the question of how to organize their military forces. They rejected Hull's Supreme War Council in favour of Anglo-American Committees: 'The Army planners apparently expected that, after the preliminary British-American meetings, the scope of the military conversations would be extended to include the representatives of Australia, China and the Soviet Union. But the military conversations at ARCADIA [the code name for the summit] – unlike the political conversations, which led to the drafting and signing of the Declaration of the United Nations – involved only the British and American staffs'.[18] The political and organizational problems associated with creating a joint military staff with the Soviet Union were simply too great to contemplate. At the time, US public opinion was ahead of the decision makers. In a poll taken at the end of December 1941, Gallup found 68 per cent in favour of US forces coming under the control of an American, British, Soviet and allied 'Joint War Council'.[19]

Roosevelt repeatedly sought a meeting with Stalin but this was not arranged until the end of the following year. The main and usual reason given was the need for Stalin to keep personal control of the war. Stalin was hard to get to a meeting.

Nevertheless, even without the day-to-day involvement of other powers, the terms of reference for the Anglo-American Combined Chiefs of Staff Committee state that it was to operate 'under the direction of the heads of the United Nations'.[20] The British official history of the organization of supplies from America explains that,

> The United Nations, first launched as a symbol but soon to acquire a corporate identity, made the combined British-American machinery [which neither military envisaged on embarking on Arcadia] more palatable to American public opinion. It parried the traditional American distrust of exclusive alliances, particularly an alliance with the United Kingdom... ranging the free nations of the world behind the Great Powers.[21]

This framework was laid out in public when the British Government published White Papers on Defence in 1942. The 'Co-ordination of the Allied War Effort' dealt with the agreements made between Churchill and Roosevelt. This White Paper explains how, 'To further co-ordination of the Allied War Effort, the President and Prime Minister have set up bodies to deal with Munitions Assignments, Shipping, Adjustment and Raw Materials... These bodies will confer with representatives of the USSR, China and others of the United Nations as are necessary to attain common purposes and provide for the most effective utilization of the joint resources of the United Nations'.[22] In this description, major policy was determined by the major powers and the United Nations served both as a legitimating title and a device for engaging other states, large and small, in the war effort.

Consequently, numerous classified documents, never intended for public view, carried United Nations titles: for example, a Report of the

Vandenburg Committee of the Joint Chiefs of Staff on the Aircraft Situation of the United Nations, May 1942;[23] Rapid Military Communications of the United Nations, July 1942;[24] United Nations [Oil] Refinery Production 1942–1945;[25] and United Nations Plan of Campaign in 1943.[26]

The British White Paper on 'The Organization of Joint Planning' provided a detailed breakdown of the headquarters staff arrangement amongst British forces. It included an explanation of the use of the word 'Joint': 'To avoid confusion, the terminology agreed by the United Nations is that the term "Joint" should be used to denote the Inter-Service collaboration of one nation; and the term "Combined" should be used to denote collaboration between two or more of the United Nations'.[27] It is worth emphasizing the point that here, in a formal British White Paper of 1942, a decision is recorded as having been made by the United Nations that is followed to this day in United Nations and NATO operations. In New York, the Foreign Policy Association published a summary of what was known publicly as 'Machinery of Collaboration between the United Nations'.[28]

From January 1942 onwards, military communiqués were studded with references to the United Nations. Within a week of the Declaration, newspapers carried announcements such as 'General Brett named Deputy Supreme Commander of all United Nations Forces in the South West Pacific'.[29] On 3 February 1942, *The Times* reported 'from the headquarters of the United Nations in the south-west Pacific, it was announced that United States bombers had scored another success yesterday'. Nevertheless, it was, of course, also normal for forces to be named by country or as Allied.

The Combat Chronology of US Army Air Forces in the World War II entry for 17 March 1942 states: 'Gen MacArthur arrives in Australia to assume cmd [abbreviation in the original]; of United Nations forces in SWPA [South West Pacific Area] actually assumed command on 18 Apr'.[30] Henry Stimson, US Secretary of War, in an explicit comparison with the arrangements in World War I, explained: 'MacArthur's command closely approximates to that which the United Nations gave to General Wavell in much the same area. It is also the same type of command as the allies in the Great War finally entrusted to Marshal Foch in 1918'.[31]

Churchill made the importance of the new alliance clear when he returned from Washington to face a vote of no confidence in the House of Commons at the end of January 1942. This resulted from a series of military disasters in Africa and the Far East. He replied to the motion with a detailed justification of his conduct of the war, including his recent meetings with Roosevelt. Churchill explained to a packed chamber that '... we [Roosevelt and Churchill] formed the league of twenty-six United Nations' and described '... the bonds which unite us with the rest of the twenty-six United Nations'. Churchill went on to outline the coordination of military operations in the Far Eastern war theatres by means of international councils and the intention 'to extend that system to all areas in which the forces of more than one of the United Nations – for that is the term we have adopted – will be operating'.[32] Churchill ended his speech by saying, 'I make so bold now as to demand a declaration of confidence of the House of Commons as an additional weapon in the armoury of the United Nations'. For him to close his remarks in this way indicates both the importance he gave to the United Nations alliance and the appeal that he thought reference to it would have in the House of Commons, in the country and with Roosevelt. Only a handful of MPs voted against him.

General George C. Marshall, lecturing at Columbia University in New York in 1942 on the Unity of Command of the United Nations, remarked, '... despite all of these difficulties the most heartening factor of the war to date, in my opinion, is the remarkable success which thus far has been achieved in coordinating and directing the military and allied interests of the United Nations'; his colleague Admiral Ernest J. King wryly advised the same audience that it could 'busy itself for some time with the political relationship among the United Nations of which there are now some thirty'.[33] In this way King reflected the impatience of the powerful in having to manage relations with many small and weak states.

Later in the war, the public and secret discussions of D-Day were, naturally enough, studded with references to the United Nations. General Dwight D. Eisenhower's orders to prepare D-Day told him: 'You will enter the continent of Europe and in conjunction with the other United Nations, undertake operations aimed at the heart of Germany and the destruction of her armed forces'.[34] For those with a penchant for military insignia, the description of the unit shoulder-patch of his Supreme Headquarters Allied Expeditionary Force states that: '... The heraldic chief of azure (BLUE) above the rainbow is emblematic of a state of peace and tranquillity the restoration of which to the enslaved people is the objective of the United Nations'.[35] This may be the first association of light blue with the United Nations. Eisenhower reminded his troops as they embarked for France that '... the United Nations have inflicted upon the Germans great defeats, in open battle, man to man'.[36] He had crossed out the word 'Allies' in the draft prepared for him by his staff and written in 'United Nations' himself.[37] *The Times* editorial marking the landings described how '... four years after the rescue at Dunkirk of that gallant defeated army without which nucleus the forces of liberation could never have been rebuilt, the United Nations returned yesterday to the soil of France'. A contemporary Canadian official history stated, 'The sector held at the end of July by First Canadian Army, and in particular by 2 Canadian Corps, was in a strategic sense undoubtedly the most important part of the entire United Nations line in Northern France'.[38]

7 A typical US newspaper headline from early 1942.

Despite all this organizational progress it would be a fundamental mistake to think that the war was organized smoothly. There were major disputes over where and when to attack Germany and Japan. In addition, the Washington bureaucracy was publicly criticized as ineffective, over-lapping and conflicted. Oliver Lyttleton, the British production minister, sent his Cabinet colleagues an assessment of a visit made just after the 1942 mid-term elections when the USA had been at war for a year:

> Although the President and Mr Hopkins seem to get the big things right [Lend-Lease], the Secretariat at the White House appears to the outsider to be quite unequal to the task of sifting the multitudinous subjects which must

be presented every day to the President for decision... Even a single metal like copper is controlled by five different agencies... Even the Joint American Chiefs of Staff hardly work as a team, and the joke which is bandied about Washington is that General Marshall read about the Solomons expedition [in the Pacific] only in the newspapers is too near the truth to be repeated by a foreigner.[39]

In the midst of the war planning of early January 1942, Roosevelt delivered his annual State of the Union address to Congress. He needed to give his listeners in America and around the world inspiration and confidence in military and political success, as well as match Churchill's soaring rhetoric when he had addressed the same audience a few days earlier.

Roosevelt's address had two positive themes, his shopping list for weapons and his aims for the post-war world. With confidence in the power of American industry, he announced orders for tanks and planes on a prodigious scale – 60,000 warplanes and 45,000 tanks for delivery in 1942 topped the list. His objective was not to match the Axis but to completely overwhelm them.

Raymond Clapper, a syndicated newspaper columnist, noted the second, political, message:

Mr. Roosevelt referred frequently to the united nations, and to the hope of establishing security after the war. With the military strength that the united nations will possess after this war, with American military strength alone unmatched in all history on the basis of the program just outlined; the united nations will have in mind the force with which to establish security, and to insure that no butcher regimes can ever get started again. This time, maybe we won't be so stupid as to throw it away as we did before. This time, maybe, even the senate will be smart enough to see that it is better to keep the united nations together and have peace than to fall apart and have another world war. The road Mr. Roosevelt shows us is hard. But at its end is offered, for a second time, the great opportunity which is ours for the taking.[40]

The grand vision of the United Nations, the Atlantic Charter and the Four Freedoms had the purpose of building confidence at home and abroad and deflecting attention from the vulnerability and lack of preparedness across America that winter. There was a rush of demand for steel helmets and fire hoses, even in the Midwest. The movie *1941* parodies the panic across government and much of the public on the West Coast. At the time, people feared that the fleet that had attacked Pearl Harbor would appear off the coast of California, wreaking havoc from Seattle to San Diego.

The dictators' successes were built on a bold and savage use of military force. The war had already seen a sea battle in the South Atlantic off Argentina between a German pocket battleship, the *Graf Spee*, and British warships in the Battle of the River Plate. In this climate of unpleasant shocks, Japanese attacks on the West Coast seemed quite conceivable. In those days, there was no long-range radar, let alone satellites, to find the Japanese battle fleet. The two years of war up to Pearl Harbor had shattered conventional wisdoms of what was possible militarily. At the time, the risk was real that both US coasts could have been put under sustained attack, keeping the USA hemmed into its own borders. As the US official history of the war in the Pacific put it,

> After Pearl Harbor it seemed, at the outset, that this barrier [the Pacific Fleet] had been broken and that the 1,300 mile length of the west coast could be attacked by the Japanese in strength and almost at will. The most vital installations along this coast were military aircraft factories that had sprung up during the prewar years at Los Angeles and San Diego in the south and at Seattle in the north. In December 1941 nearly half of the American military aircraft production and almost all the heavy bomber output was coming from eight plants in the Los Angeles area. The naval yards and ship terminals in the Puget Sound, Portland, San Francisco Bay, Los Angeles and San Diego area, and the California oil industry were of only slightly less importance to the future conduct of the war. In the first two weeks of war it seemed more than conceivable that the Japanese could invade the coast in strength, and until June 1942 [when the US Navy sank Japanese aircraft carriers] there appeared to be a really serious threat of attack by a Japanese carrier striking force.[41]

The US had only a few hundred fighter planes to defend the whole of the West Coast in early 1942, with only ineffective radar installations to direct them. The fear was that the Japanese could conceal their approach behind one of the many rainstorms that travel East across the Pacific onto the American continent. And by keeping radio silence, neutralize the advantage the US has gained by breaking the Japanese Navy's signal code, JN25.

The British and Americans assumed that Tokyo and Berlin were working to a common plan of military conquest and tried to plan accordingly. Thus it was feared that the two main Axis powers aimed to link up in two ways. First, through the Middle East and India, and second by harassing the US from bases established in Brazil and Hawaii. Fortunately, there was no such coordination, something that horrified military officers in the two enemy countries.[42]

Nevertheless, the war continued to go badly for the United Nations through the spring of 1942. The Japanese were bombing northern Australia, the east coast of India was threatened and they had overrun the Philippines, the Dutch East Indies and Malaya. In Russia, the Germans had crushed Soviet counterattacks, and in the Atlantic, the U-boats still seemed unstoppable.

Roosevelt saw a need to try to boost morale. In the 1930s, he had used parades as a means of getting across the idea that his economic reform was getting people back to work. He used a similar approach on a global scale in 1942.

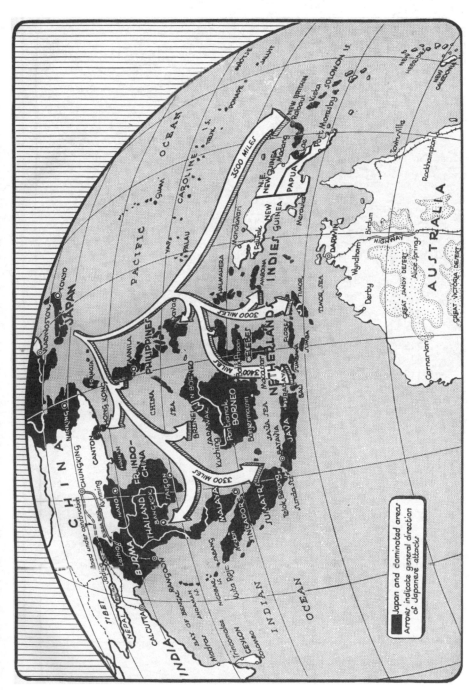

IV Japan's conquests by 1942.

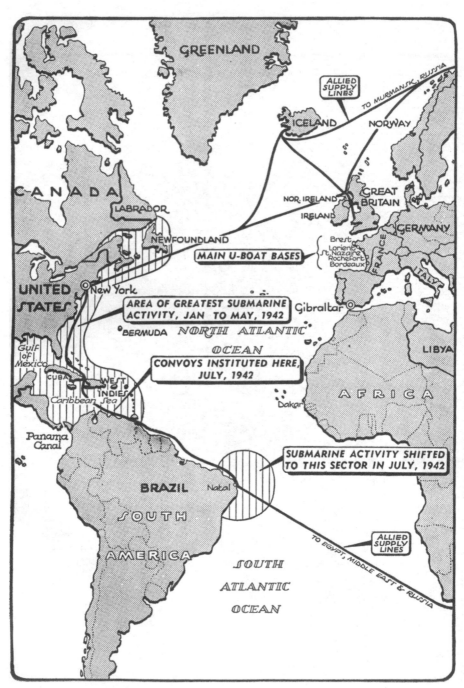

V The U-boat war in the Atlantic, 1942.

Lord Halifax, the British Ambassador in Washington, told London in April,

> The Administration is seeking ways and means of bringing home to American people the existence of United Nations of which this nation is but a part, and it is in our interest that such a campaign should succeed, for with the exclusion of China, Australia and perhaps Russia, we and other nations are apt to be left in the background and even our successes are often attributed in the press to the assistance which we obtain from American participation. It is reliably stated that the President is considering announcing the fact that June 14th normal celebration as Flag Day shall be observed this year as United Nations Day with appropriate celebrations, broadcasts etc.[43]

Halifax explained that the Chinese were already supportive and that Washington wanted the involvement of the British and other Allies. Nowadays, talk of a political event with simultaneous events around the world might mean something organized by Bono to help people in poverty. Sigrid Arne tells how 'Six months after the United Nations were formally allied through the Declaration there was a world celebration to dramatize the union. The notion of the United Nations was taking hold'.[44]

The response to Roosevelt's initiative was huge, in America and around the world. Radio, newspapers and newsreels carried stories of local, national and international events, providing a much needed sense of solidarity. In America countless communities held events. In Washington, DC they centred on Union Station, with parades and concerts at the Water Gate on the Potomac River.[45] In Chicago the main parade went down Michigan Avenue.[46] And in New York,

> The greatest parade in New York's history moved up Fifth av. hour after hour Saturday and Saturday night with more than 500,000 men and women joining in a tremendous demonstration of the nation's will to win.
> The parade was more than twice as big as any ever held here. The fighting men and the men and women from the factories and behind-the-front organizations stepped briskly past miles of close-packed spectators estimated at more than 2,000,000. There were jeeps and tanks and field guns on the ground and flying fortresses, pursuit ships, overhead. From stands along the line, broadcasters sent the stirring story in seven languages around the world. Floats told the tale of what New York and the entire nation had pledged as a fight to the finish.[47]

US Government agencies ensured that organizations as diverse as the American Legion of veterans and peace groups were mobilizing. A typical preview newspaper report focused on civil society mobilization for United Nations Day. This was at a time when the name was brand new, and people's attention was focused on the fighting. Under the headline, 'Urges Observance of United Nations Day' (Sunday 14 June), the story quotes at length from a letter of Roosevelt's that explained the purpose of the event:

> President Roosevelt, in a letter wishing 'every success' to the six weeks' nationwide program in support of the United Nations and the Atlantic Charter, said:

'Nothing could be more important than that people in the United States and of the world should fully realize the magnitude of the united effort required for this fight'. The letter was written by the President to Clark M. Eichelberger, Chairman of the United Nations Committee, and has just been released by the national headquarters of the committee in New York. 'I have read with interest of your plan to inform our people of the United Nations' aspect of the struggle', the President wrote. 'With the vital contribution toward winning the war that has been made, is being made, and will be made, by each of our Allies, we shall be successful in our struggle against Axis domination of the world by force of arms'. The nationwide program centered on the United Nations and the Atlantic Charter will extend over the month of May and the first two weeks in June. This program is planned to lead up to a national observance on June 14, which it is expected, a presidential proclamation will soon set aside as 'United Nations Day'. Closing the campaign, there will be simultaneous mass meetings all over the country on the evening of June 13.

In the time intervening there will be United Nations radio features, special United Nations programs by clubs, churches, labor unions and other organizations. The United Nations Committee is urging that all the organizations holding regular meetings during the month of May and June devote one of the meetings to a discussion of the United Nations to win the war and, on the basis of the Atlantic Charter, to win the peace. In a letter supporting this program, Archibald MacLeish director of the Office of Facts and Figures declares: 'It is naturally of the utmost importance that all the people of these nations engaged in the struggle against slavery shall understand each other to the greatest possible extent. To that end, it is desirable that as many civic organizations and other bodies as possible, will, during May and June of this year and also during months that follow stage celebrations which will heighten the understanding among the United Nations'.[48]

By mid-June, a Gallup poll suggested that 73 per cent of the public now supported a post-war League of Nations – despite the use of the discredited organization's name in the title – up from 51 per cent in May 1941.

When the big parades took place there was more of substance to feel good about. US naval aircraft had sunk elite and irreplaceable Japanese aircraft carriers off Midway Island in the Pacific. Britain and the Soviet Union had signed a Treaty of Cooperation. And in Washington, following a series of planning meetings with V. M. Molotov, the Soviet Foreign Minister, there was anticipation that D-Day would come soon. A joint communiqué issued on 11 June stated, 'Full understanding was reached with regard to the urgent tasks of creating a Second Front in Europe in 1942'.[49] British and senior US officials, including General Marshall, did not think that their forces were strong enough to do anything more than make a suicidal attack on the French coast to divert German troops from Russia, if it looked like the Soviet Union would be defeated. But the public impression was created that the liberation of Western Europe was at hand.

The United Press report of the worldwide events ran,

United Nations Celebrations Held Throughout Allied World, OLD GLORY HONORED PLACE IN MANY CAPITALS, Mexico and Philippines Join In

Vast Combination to Beat Axis, Twenty-eight nations were pledged today to successful prosecution of the war after colorful United Nations day celebrations in every capital. The Stars and Stripes held honored positions throughout the world yesterday on the anniversary of its creation and military parades, public demonstrations and prayers marked the observance.

In Washington, President Roosevelt welcomed two new signatories [Mexico and the Philippines] to the United Nations declaration. In London, crowds broke through police lines to cheer the King and Queen and Prime Minister Churchill. In Moscow, American and British flags flew with the Red Banner on the Kremlin spires.

The observances generally reflected a unified determination to beat the Axis. Wildly cheering crowds outside Buckingham palace climaxed Great Britain's celebration. As King George and Queen Elizabeth both left with the Prime Minister Winston Churchill and Allied dignitaries after reviewing a parade presenting a cross-section of the empire at war, the crowd swept aside mounted police to climb the palace fence and cheer. They shouted at Churchill, 'Give 'em hell Winnie'.[50]

Throughout the Empire, prayers for the United Nations were offered and pastors read a message from Churchill: 'In this ceremony we pledge to each other not only support and succour until victory comes, but that wider understanding, that quickened sense of human sympathy, that recognition of the common purpose of humanity without which the suffering and striving of the United Nations would not achieve its full reward'.

Moscow: Russian, American and British flags fluttered from the Kremlin while public lectures, concerts and exhibitions emphasized the strengthening of bonds among leaders of the three leading United Nations. Two book-shows were devoted to British and American literature and critics reviewed contemporary works of English language writers. Shops displayed commentaries by democratic authors on the power of the Red army. The government ordered the Russian flag flown throughout the Soviet Union in honour of United Nations day.

Chungking: a mass meeting heard a message from Nelson T. Johnson; American minister to Australia expressing gratification that the United States and China were allied 'in this great fight against primitive despotism'. It replied with a resolution: 'Today the people of China's wartime capital are flying the flags of all nations as an expression of a sense of comradeship with the Allied nations. We are confident of our ability to persevere in our duty to the fullest and, we trust, you also will do all in your power to bring about a common victory over the Axis'.

Melbourne: Australian cities were flag-bedecked but there were no formal observances except in churches. . . .

New Delhi, India: The Viceroy, the Duke of Gloucester and Gen Sir Archibald Wavell took the salute of Indian troops outside the Viceroy's palace. American, British, Russian, Chinese, and Dutch flags were displayed and bands played the national anthems of these countries.[51]

In Moscow, the Soviet newspaper Izvestia explained editorially that 'the United Nations chose the day of June 14 for their international demonstration in connection with the fact that for many years June 14 has been annually observed in the United States of America as the day the American flag was consecrated by the traditions and struggle of the American people for independence and liberty'. The celebration of United Nations Flag Day, the paper continued, coincided with the 'truly historic events opening a new chapter in the annals of the war of liberation against the Fascist hordes – the signing of the agreement between the United States, Russia and Britain'. Flags were flown from all public buildings.[52]

As an example of the profile of the event in the British sphere of influence, the paper in Kingston, capital of the British Colony of Jamaica, carried three front-page stories on United Nations Day, covering events in London, Washington, a global survey and local events including a church service and military parade led by the Governor: 'United Nations Day was celebrated in Britain today – as in all parts of the free world. Every town and village in the Kingdom, many of which have suffered the Nazi air blitz, are flying flags in honour of the occasion'.[53] An official British film from June 1942 describes how,

> In London, the Royal Family is joined by the exiled heads-of-state of Norway, Yugoslavia, Poland and Czechoslovakia on the stand [at Buckingham Palace] to review a parade of Civilian Defence Service contingents, workmen and women, merchant seamen, Royal Navy, RAF, Commonwealth troops, Home Guard and British Army; in Aylesbury, the Lady Mayoress (Mrs Olive Paterson) reads the Prime Minister's proclamation adopting President Roosevelt's idea that June 14th (previously marked in the USA for honouring the national flag) should be a day of honouring all of the flags.[54]

Public momentum for the political-military United Nations increased as the war progressed, with varying degrees of encouragement from the allied governments. The first multinational United Nations organization with an international staff and budget was formed in mid-1942: this was the UN Information Board, based on 5th Avenue in New York. Its function was information, propaganda or, in modern parlance, public diplomacy. Its archives occupy 50 feet at the UN in New York.[55]

In Washington, a private group, the Four Freedoms Committee, debated the need for a UN flag with representatives of national governments. Its members included officials from the American Legion, Veterans of Foreign Wars and Elizabeth Mallett Barnes, chairman of the 'Correct Use of the Flag Committee' of the Daughters of the American Revolution. The outcome came in March 1943 at a time when the Administration was beginning discussions with the Senate and the Allies on a draft United Nations Plan for the Peace. *The Washington Post* of 17 March 1943 reported on the Committee's

> 8 page color 'United Nations Flag' Manual distributed internationally. Produced a flag representative of all the UN after 5 months of study. Four vertical colored bars 'are to stand for freedom in any place in the world and the flags of the Four Freedoms will be white with four upright red bars emblazoned upon them. The new flag is never to be flown alone but alongside or beneath the flag of the country in which it is flown'.[56]

8 George C. Marshall and Henry L. Stimson.

The flag design was the brainchild of Brooks Harding, a New York industrialist.[57]

The British Ambassador telegraphed London for advice on the proposed flag, reporting to London that several US Government agencies were producing United Nations symbols, some were being attached to supplies headed for Africa, and that at a meeting of the United Nations Information Board there was general support for the idea.[58] Protocol being what it is, the flag failed to get formal approval – but fly it still did.[59] Even then, some Americans were opposed.[60] The UN flag we know today was developed separately after the signing of the Charter, and the wartime United Nations flag has since been forgotten.

In 1943, the British Cabinet was sceptical about a repeat of United Nations Day that year, claiming even that there were not enough troops left in the country to mount parades nationwide, so celebrations were limited to London, Edinburgh and Cardiff. In the same year, a British film of United Nations Day featured the United Nations parade in Cairo.[61] The idea had taken sufficient root that it was marked by Haile Selassie, Emperor of Ethiopia, newly restored to his throne in Addis Abbaba.

By 1944, British celebrations were in the hands of the United Nations Day Committee, of which Brendan Bracken, Minister of Information in Churchill's government, had become Honorary President.[62]

9 United Nations flag, 1944.

The USA and the Soviet Union both produced postage stamps marking the United Nations, the Soviet stamps were dedicated to the 14 June United Nations Day in 1944.[63]

Without the benefit of satellites and television, these United Nations Days were global expressions of political will unmatched before or since. The UN Days and the continual references to the United Nations fighting the war were reinforced in propaganda, which had a strong resonance in wartime society through the rest of the war. From 1942 to 1945, the United

Nations had a significant place in commercial advertising, religion and literature.

Rolls Royce advertisements for the Merlin engine which powered the Spitfire fighter planes claimed that 'It has played a more consistently conspicuous part than any other type in the United Nations establishment of air supremacy'.[64] Later on, Rolls Royce proclaimed, 'The first and so far the only Jet-propelled Aircraft of the United Nations to go into action against the enemy is the Gloster Meteor ... powered with Rolls Royce Engines ... more efficient and of longer life than the Jumo Engine of the German M.E. 262'.[65]

In 1943, Simpson's of Piccadilly proclaimed, 'Piccadilly Circus has been called the hub of the universe. Half a minute away from it is a hub of the United Nations ... a warm welcome to all officers, men and women of the United Nations'.[66]

The *Daily Express*, with a relish familiar to readers of today's tabloids, held a 'Panorama of the United Nations at war' featuring images of the Germany city of Essen – 'Essen Aflame' – at the Royal Academy in the autumn of 1943.[67]

Publishers were keen to find new talent suppressed by the war. In 1943, the London-based publisher Hutchinson & Co. announced prizes amounting to $10,000 for a 'United Nations Literary Competition' and amongst the judges were Rebecca West and Sir Max Beerbohm.[68] As the war drew to a close, Harrap, Thomas Crowell and Columbia Pictures offered a £1,500 prize in a book contest for men and women who 'have served in the Armed Forces of the United Nations'.[69]

Music, both secular and religious, was composed for the United Nations. The most famous composition was Dimitri Shostakovich's 'United Nations March' which was used as the finale of the 1943 Gene Kelly movie *As Thousands Cheer*.

The United Nations was also a focus of religious life during the war. In the United States, prayers were said across the country on D-Day for the United Nations.[70] At the end of the war in Europe, the Church of England printed a glossy brochure of 'THE FORM & ORDER OF THE SERVICE OF THANKSGIVING FOR THE VICTORY IN EUROPE OF THE ARMS OF THE UNITED NATIONS' which was used throughout the Anglican church.[71] In parallel, the Liberal Jewish Synagogue in London printed the 'SERVICE OF THANKSGIVING for the FINAL VICTORY of the UNITED NATIONS in the WORLD WAR OF 1939–1945 and for the ENSUING PEACE'. The Rabbi's words include the remark, 'As we prayed to him for help when we were engaged in the struggle, so we thank him now for the triumph of the United Nations which has delivered humanity from a grave danger and restored it to the possession of peace'.[72]

The United Nations at Simpson's

SERVICES CLUB

AS SEEN BY

Anton

THE FAMOUS PUNCH ARTIST

Piccadilly Circus has been called the hub of the universe. Half a minute away from it there is a hub of the United Nations — Simpson's Services Club. Here 'United-ness' grows in comradeship. There are baths, telephones, good bar, theatre service, barber-shop—all under one roof! Above all, a warm welcome to all officers, men and women of the United Nations.

Liberal Jewish Synagogue
London

SERVICE
OF
THANKSGIVING

For the

FINAL VICTORY
of the

UNITED NATIONS
in the

WORLD WAR OF 1939 — 1945
and for the

ENSUING PEACE

August 19*th,* 1945

11 London Liberal Jewish Synagogue service for the victory of the United Nations in the World War and the ensuing peace.

In 1943, the University of London created a United Nations University Centre based at the London School of Hygiene.[73] It was run by an educationalist, A. Clow Ford, and organized lectures on the individual countries and the post-war plans.[74]

In the twenty-first century, we are familiar with non-governmental organizations (NGOs) in the United Nations system, but they were at work during the war. For example, at the end of 1942, the Keswick United Nations Committee, in England's Lake District, raised £185 in aid for China.[75] In 1943, Eleanor Roosevelt, the President's wife, began the American Association for the United Nations.[76] In 1944, a coalition was formed in the USA to work on the proposals for a United Nations organization that had come from the Dumbarton Oaks conference that will be discussed in chapter 8. These NGO coalitions involved both secular and religious groups[77] and evolved into the current United Nations Association.[78] Some had origins in organizations supporting the now defunct League of Nations.

International relations organizations and commentators were much concerned with how the United Nations would win the peace.[79] Chatham House, the London think-tank, published a report of a conference held in December 1942 on the wartime and post-war cooperation of the United Nations in the Pacific and the Far East.[80] Chatham House was linked with the US Council on Foreign Relations as both organizations were engaged in intensive work on ideas for the post-war system. The Twentieth Century Fund published *Postwar Plans of the United Nations* in 1943.[81] It surveyed the national plans of the individual states and discussed how far they were in line with the established war aims of the United Nations alliance and how they might be brought into better harmony. Other books, such as Linton Wells's *Salute to Valor: Heroes of the United Nations*, were designed to support the war effort.[82]

The United Nations featured in cultural life as well. In the United States there was a United Nations jigsaw puzzle[83] and, at the Chicago Art Institute, an exhibition of Art of the United Nations.[84] In Britain, Irene Veal's *Recipes of the United Nations* were published in 1944.[85] And that September, 'Mr Cuthbert's Garden Talk' in *The Times* observed that '... the smashing victories of the United Nations ... seems to be a signal to some of my Gardening Friends to start thinking about a special show of garden flowers next Spring'.[86]

All these civil society activities took place in the context of the war and war reporting. Within weeks of the first global United Nations Day and satisfaction of victory over the Japanese Navy, fresh disasters struck. The Germans and Italians once again defeated the British in Africa, capturing 33,000 Imperial and Commonwealth troops in a single day at Tobruk in Libya. US Army intelligence reported on 30 June 1942 that Rommel would be at the Suez Canal by the end of July, with the whole Middle East before him and the prospect of linking up with German troops in Russia heading south through the Caucasus oilfields and into those in Iraq.

General Marshall wrote to Hopkins on 2 July 1942,

> In the event of a disaster in the Middle East it is believed to be important to the future conduct of the war that the United Nations present a solid front. To this end it is suggested that the President guide public comment so as to indicate that the United Nations stand together in adversity as they ultimately will in victory.[87]

In fact Rommel was stopped by British and New Zealand forces about 60 miles west of the naval base of Alexandria, where officials had started burning files in anticipation of Rommel's arrival. But by the standards of the Russian front it was a mere skirmish. In France, that August, the British tested their ability to launch D-Day. It turned into a disaster. Commanded by Lord Mountbatten, a relative of the present Queen of England, Canadian and British infantry led an attack from the sea, including 60 US Rangers. They assaulted the French seaport of Dieppe on the English Channel. The force suffered 60 per cent casualties and the British Spitfires, once masters of the air war, were outclassed by new Luftwaffe fighters. Without more and improved weapons reaching the fighting fronts, the war could not be won and might still be lost. The political and military organization of the supply of weapons amongst the United Nations is the subject of the following chapter.

CHAPTER 3

Weapons for the Allies: Motown goes to Stalingrad

Ideas for global cooperation helped the United Nations win battles all over the world during World War II. Inspired by these ideas, Americans spent billions of dollars on weapons for their Allies. At home and abroad, these ideas also boosted morale with the hope of a better world to come. Supplies were organized under the Lend-Lease programme, whose origins are discussed in Chapter 1. Lend-Lease was a US taxpayer-funded supply of weapons, raw materials and food to America's Allies without any cash payment or loan. Recipients supplied the US and each other with what they themselves could contribute to the collective effort. Lend-Lease supplies began as a trickle in 1941, but by 1944 a tidal wave of war material overwhelmed the Axis from the Pacific to Normandy. To take one example, 300,000 trucks were sent to the Red Army; the robust Studebaker 6X6, produced in Detroit (Motor or Motown to Americans), was a particular favourite.

This chapter explores the political and military history of Lend-Lease, concentrating on the critical years of 1941 and 1942. The political history illustrates how Roosevelt convinced Americans and Congress to pay for Lend-Lease. The military history demonstrates the impact of Lend-Lease on the war. This is explored in some detail in the case of Stalingrad because of the importance of this battle and the debate amongst historians as to whether Roosevelt's continued supplies of weapons to Stalin made the Soviet Union unnecessarily strong at the end of the war. The political and military interaction described here sets the scene for the high-level diplomacy between Roosevelt, Churchill and Stalin during 1943 and the post-war reconstruction projects that are discussed in the chapters which follow.

In the USA, the politics of Lend-Lease were another phase in Roosevelt's struggle with isolationist conservatives. Roosevelt wrote to Congress in June 1942,

> The concept of the United Nations will not perish on the battlefields of this terrible war. It will live to lay the basis of the enduring world understanding on which mankind depends to preserve its peace and freedom.

> The United Nations have thus declared that they are more than a tem-
> porary military combination, and that they will wage the war together for a
> common victory and a common programme of peace aims.[1]

At this very early stage of America's war, Roosevelt could not have
been plainer in spelling out to Congress and the public his view of the
integration of Lend-Lease, the United Nations and the post-war world.

> The programme of Lend-Lease agreements is also emerging as a factor in the
> combined effort of the United Nations to weave a pattern for peace.

The Roosevelt Administration persuaded Congress to spend a large
part of the US Gross National Product on the Lend-Lease project. The total spent was around $50 billion in 1940s dollars, some 7 per cent of total
national production, civilian and military.[2] In early twenty-first century
terms, Lend-Lease would cost $1 trillion a year on top of the cost of Amer-
ica's own military forces.

Without Lend-Lease, the war would have been longer, might have
resulted in a compromise peace with Germany and more Americans would
have had to fight and die. But the programme remained controversial and
when it was terminated at the end of the war, President Truman did so in a
manner so abrupt as to create tensions with Britain and the Soviet Union.

Roosevelt argued successfully that the war was for a good cause and
that the Allies would help protect the USA from Hitler. But he did not
use the traditional arguments used by national leaders taking their people
to war. He did not argue that Lend-Lease would boost US power in the
world or create a balance of power in Europe, let alone that it would build
an American Empire. Such cynical ideas had little resonance with an American public tired of Europeans' squabbles, disapproving of their empires
and mindful of George Washington's advice that Americans should avoid
foreign entanglements.

The Lend-Lease Act was carried by the twin sentiments of fear of German aggression and support for international democratic ideas articulated
by Roosevelt in the Four Freedoms discussed in the preceding chapters.
The initial budget was $7 billion. By December 1941, $5.5 billion of orders
for weapons had been placed – most of which were delivered in 1943.
These funds were used partly to build weapons factories which, once in
production, also (and principally) supplied America's own forces.

The head of the Lend-Lease programme was Edward Stettinius. In
his mid-40s, he had already run the US Steel Corporation and brought
this knowledge and his status as an industrial leader to the daily task of
phoning factory managers and rail and port operators to urge greater speed
and quantity of supply. He had the energetic, troubleshooting help of Harry
Hopkins in the White House, who implemented Roosevelt's directives on
where the scarce weapons should be sent. In his 1943 book on Lend Lease,

LEND-LEASE AND TOTAL WAR COSTS

TOTAL WAR COSTS

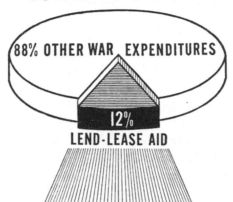

88% OTHER WAR EXPENDITURES

12%
LEND-LEASE AID

TOTAL LEND-LEASE AID $12,900,000,000
(TO JUNE 30, 1943)

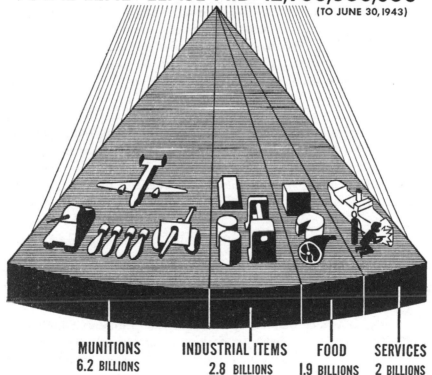

MUNITIONS	INDUSTRIAL ITEMS	FOOD	SERVICES
6.2 BILLIONS	2.8 BILLIONS	1.9 BILLIONS	2 BILLIONS

12 Lend-Lease and total US war costs.

which provides some of the illustrations for this book, Stettinius makes
the point that even in food production the Lend-Lease programme had
an impact in preparing American industry for global war.[3] Stettinius also
points out the British contribution to the anti-aircraft defence of California
in early 1942 as part of reciprocal Lend-Lease.

He noted, '[T]hese [Lend-Lease] agreements, and the operations carried out under them, have formed a hard core of United Nations collaboration in the war and may well provide the basis for an enduring peace'.[4] R.
M. Leighton, a US Army historian of the war, is clear that the early build-
up of US bombers in England was achieved only by extensive reliance on
British sources of supply.[5]

In June 1942, Roosevelt sought an expansion of Lend-Lease. He justified it partly by explaining that it would prepare the world for novel
international regulation of economic affairs. He argued that rather than
seek direct recompense for US military supplies from nations sacrificing a
great deal in the war, there should be a general effort for a better world: 'We
look forward to a period of security and liberty, in which men may freely
pursue lives of their choice, and governments will achieve policies leading to full and useful production and employment'. This would require a
great increase in global trade, 'founded on stable exchange relationships
and liberal principles of commerce. The Lend-Lease settlement will rest
on a specific and detailed programme for achieving these ends', based on
Article VII of the Lend-Lease agreements.[6]

Behind the scenes, the USA extracted economic concessions from the
British but never attempted to do so from the Soviets, not least because
of the huge numbers of Soviet citizens who were dying in battle. Generally, repayment was conceived mostly in terms of a new international economic system. Roosevelt even told the US Congress to expect to consider
legislation from the Administration on a range of United Nations-based
polices:

> Co-operative action among the United Nations is contemplated to fulfil this
> program of economic progress, in many spheres where action is needed. It
> is hoped that plans will soon develop for a series of agreements and recom-
> mendations for legislation, in the fields of commercial policy, of money and
> finance, international investment and reconstruction.[7]

Forty nations created a reciprocal network of military supply by the
end of the war. The vast majority of supplies came from the USA, although
the Canadian contribution was also considerable. Overall two-thirds of US
supplies went to the British and one-third to the Soviets. The British managed the supplies to Imperial, Commonwealth and other allied forces. The
USA received contributions from Britain and other parts of the Empire and
Commonwealth in return. This created, with great help from the publicity
machine, the beginning of multinational and sharing culture. Although the

TABLE 2 The dollar value of military production of the major powers in World War II. Figures are $ billions (1944 US munitions prices), from Hall, 1955.

Country	Date: 1935–39	1940	1941	1942	1943	1944
USA	1.5	1.5	4.5	20	38	42
Canada	0	0	.5	1	1.5	1.5
UK	2.5	3.5	6.5	9	11	11
USSR	8	5	8.5	11.5	14	16
Germany	12	6	6	8.5	13.5	17
Japan	2	1	2	3	4.5	6

contributions of other nations were small, they were significant for their smaller economies.

The industrial muscle power of the war is summarized in the following statistics on weapons production for each of the major states involved, compiled for the official British history of World War II (Table 2).[8] They highlight the importance of US production.

In 1944, the USA produced almost twice as much weaponry as Germany and Japan combined, four times the British and two and a half times the Soviet Union's production.

There are other numbers here which are the most fortunate statistics of the war and indicate that Hitler's enemies had good reason to fear that he would test the military and political framework being established within the United Nations framework even more severely than in fact he did. They show that Germany did not increase weapons production when it could have in 1940 and 1941, allowing the United Nations to catch up and overwhelm it. While Britain doubled production between 1940 and 1941, German production did not increase significantly. Even in 1942, Germany had increased its production by less than 50 per cent compared to 1940, by which time it had been overtaken by each of the Big Three. And yet Germany did manage a great increase by 1944.[9]

The Fuehrer failed to match his military rhetoric with full industrial and national mobilization. He started the war with an accumulation of weapons superior to his enemies and seemed content with the level of production that had created this stockpile. Only under the direction of Albert Speer was there a major increase in output, by which time it was too late. The arrogant complacency of the Nazis is breathtaking: even after declaring war on the USA and having been stymied by freezing conditions in the first Russian winter, Hitler did not ensure coordinated full mobilization. German women were never brought fully into war service as they were in Britain and Russia. But United Nations planners had to assume that Germany would increase weapons production as they were doing in their own countries. A consideration of the impact of greater Nazi strength

gives a better appreciation of why those fighting them felt quite so threatened. With hindsight we know Hitler failed to make as many weapons
as he could have; at the time, his enemies had no reason to expect this
outcome.

Imagine for a moment what the Nazis could have achieved with twice
as many weapons in 1941 and 1942. Hitler came close to winning the U-boat
war, the assault on Russia and the African campaign. With extra armaments
they could all have been won. Then, Roosevelt's fear that the USA could
come under attack itself would have been realized. The jet fighters, V2
long-range missiles and bombers that were either built too late or not at all
might all have become realities. The Nazis might even have been the first
to make the atom bomb. Even as things were, the Luftwaffe did actually
prepare a single long-range bomber to carry a single atom bomb to America
were one ever built, according to Jerry Kuehl, Associate Producer of the
iconic TV series *The World at War*.[10]

Once committed to the war, American industry quadrupled production from 1941 to 1942 and doubled it again the following year. Industrial-
ists were spurred on by profits on government contracts. Initially, half the
weapons produced went to Lend-Lease programmes. The military impact
of these supplies and the political climate that made them possible have
not been given the prominence in historical accounts of the war that they
warrant. As the Soviet Union began to turn the tide of war, there would,
under the idea of letting the Russians and Germans bleed each other to
death, have been reason to cut back the supplies in order to prevent Soviet
victory. In less brutal terms, the USA could have forced Britain to make further economic concessions in return for continuing supplies. But Roosevelt
wished to avoid the mistakes made in World War I over arms sales to the
Allies.

By 1940, both Britain and France had no cash left with which to buy
weapons and no means of taking out private loans on the market to meet
their needs. Lend-Lease was a way to supply the Allies without asking for
money that no one could pay, but without making an outright donation.

Some Americans thought their European allies had cheated them after
World War I. None of the Allies from 1918, except for Finland, had repaid
the loans the USA had made them to buy American armaments. Those who
opposed America resisting Hitler saw the past failure to pay as a good reason to insist on cash-only provision of armaments to Britain and France
after they went to war in September 1939. On the other hand, interven-
tionists needed a means of sending weapons without either loans or cash.
This was Roosevelt's Lend-Lease idea, couched in terms of shared democratic values with the British. But while he, and many Americans, liked
British democratic traditions, he distrusted and disliked Britain's imperial
behaviour.

The negotiations on Lend-Lease included a clause – Article VII – aimed at Britain's wealth. Chapter 6 discusses the wartime development of world economic policy. That discussion encompasses the struggle between Washington and London over the future of Britain's imperial economy. For now, though, we can note that, in private, Churchill and his colleagues, meeting in the Cabinet bunker in central London, did not think that Lend-Lease was quite such an act of charity as they proclaimed in public.

Hitler's invasion of Russia produced further strains on American military production as Roosevelt sought to add American supplies to those sent by Churchill. These demands also strained to breaking point the political idea that the war was for idealistic ends. Anti-interventionists, led by former President Herbert Hoover, were categorical that no military assistance should be given to Stalin.

The US public, though, were prepared to suppress their anti-communist sentiment in order to prevent a Nazi victory. In July 1941, Americans preferred a Russian victory to a German one by 72 per cent to 4 per cent in George Gallup's opinion because if Russia were to win it was unlikely to attack the US, while if Germany were to prevail it probably would.[11] Public support for an immediate entry into the war dropped slightly from 21 to 20 per cent at this time. After three months debate, the Lend-Lease Act was passed.

There were hard choices for policymakers after the USA went to war. Where should American weapons be sent as they came off the production line? The U-boats had to be beaten or no weapons or troops could be shipped safely to Europe – and that meant more ships and planes to sink these submarines. How many weapons should be sent to the British, fighting General Rommel in Africa? And should they go with American soldiers to England to launch D-Day at once, as Stalin demanded, or to Russia to help in fighting the German Army?

The British had already chosen to ship tanks and planes to Russia when they could have been kept to defend the country from invasion, or drive the Axis from Africa. The British weapons that got to Russia helped tip the scales against the Nazis as they tried to get into Moscow – something Hitler helped with too. His indecision in the autumn of 1941 over whether to capture the oil of the Caucasus or the capital city of Moscow sent his elite Panzer units racing up and down the Russian countryside until neither were achieved.

Roosevelt had had to personally and repeatedly intervene in order to get Lend-Lease supplies to Britain and Russia quickly. The US Army and Navy along with much of the Congress wanted to hang onto American weapons for American forces, even though they were not yet at war. However, Roosevelt prioritized the Soviet Union and Britain, whose forces were in the thick of the fighting. The industrialist turned diplomat Averell

TABLE 3 British dependence on US Lend-Lease by type of supply.* Percentage of each type of weapon or material used by British forces and industry supplied by the USA under the Lend-Lease programme.

Type of weapon or material used by Britain	Per cent given by USA
Tanks	50
Synthetic rubber	100
10-ton trucks	100
Transport aircraft	100
Convoy escorts	68
Small aircraft carriers	85
Fighter-bombers	68
Steel	30

*Memorandum from the British Mission in Washington to the US Government. October 1942, cited in Hall, 1955: *North American Supply*, p. 391.

Harriman, who was sent to London to speed up the process, and Harry Hopkins, who had built up national industrial expertise through leadership of New Deal programmes, became the driving force within the USA.

Tanks for the battles in Egypt and food for Britain were the most significant Lend-Lease shipments in 1941. In mid-1941, around 1,000 US medium and light tanks arrived in Egypt, helping keep the Germans and Italians away from the Suez Canal and Middle East oilfields. The first convoy of ships carrying food for Britain docked in the spring of 1941.[12] At this time, civilians were allowed to purchase food only in strictly rationed amounts: milk was rationed at two pints a week in winter, all powdered Lend-Lease supplies. Stettinius recorded that 'in Britain, eggs today are a great luxury. During the first part of 1942, the average person got just three eggs a month', and was then reduced to two. Lend-Lease dried eggs arrived that summer and were sold in 5-ounce packets and were used in baking 'or even turned into passable scrambled eggs or an omelet'. Two hundred million pounds weight was sent by mid-1943.[13] In all, 10 per cent of British food needs during the war were met through Lend-Lease, and Britain was able to divert some farm labour into other work.

All the tyres, big trucks and transport planes, two-thirds of key types of Royal Navy ships and RAF planes came across the Atlantic. Machine tools for weapons production was another area of British dependence. Nevertheless, the UK supplied 70 per cent of munitions used by the British Imperial and Commonwealth forces and around 9 per cent came from Canada.

The contribution of Lend-Lease to the battles with Japan should not be overlooked – we will look briefly at this before turning to the war in Russia.

Anglo-American strategy called for containing the Japanese while concentrating on Germany, but it soon became a question of preventing defeat by the Japanese in much of Asia and the Pacific. Lend-Lease was a two-way street in the Pacific war of 1942 and 1943. The total cost of Lend-Lease to Australia and New Zealand to support the US military in the Pacific was a quarter of a billion dollars; these countries in return received about twice as much from the USA. The United Nations provided the political basis for these exchanges. This mutual support was clearly in everyone's interest, but in World War I and earlier conflicts this easy sharing between nations had not taken place. Now, the United Nations alliance smoothed the process.

By February 1942, the Japanese Navy had reached the Indian sub-continent, cutting the sea lanes along the eastern Indian seaboard. India thus became a front-line nation. The result was that the ports of Bombay, Karachi and Cochin became jammed with shipping and supplies. The USA sent equipment such as cranes, as well as all forms of munitions and machine tools for Indian factories, which then supplied US forces. Indian production was important enough for the creation of a multinational munitions assignment committee that determined where the weapons produced would go.[14] Stettinius held up as an example of international cooperation a United Nations pilot training school at Lahore, equipped with American and British hardware and Chinese instructors.

Along with supplies to the British, those to the Soviet Union had great importance in the outcome of the war. Roosevelt issued an order prioritizing supplies to Russia over those to Britain and America's own armed forces. He justified this mainly in terms of achieving more 'dead Germans and smashed tanks'.[15] Supplies to the Soviet Union had characteristics that differentiated them from those to Britain. The Red Army was doing almost all the fighting against the German Army. The supply routes to Russia were difficult and at times impossible and the supplies were politically controversial, especially in the USA during and after the war.

A key case to examine is the battle of Stalingrad and the parallel effort to reach the Caucasus. For Hitler, victory meant destroying this symbol of Stalinism and being able to take the oilfields of the Caucasus. His goal was to push the Soviet forces back into Asia, leaving Moscow isolated. With only Romanian oilfields to call on in Europe, oil supplies to fuel his tanks and warplanes was a decisive issue for him.

But Admiral Karl Doenitz, commander of the German Navy and an ardent Nazi to the extent that he briefly became Fuehrer after Hitler's suicide in 1945, warned his hero in April 1942 that,

> In their effort to support Soviet Russia, Great Britain and the United States will make every effort during the coming weeks and months to increase shipment of equipment, materiel, and troops to Russia as much as possible. In particular, the supplies reaching Russia on the Basra-Iran route will go to the Russian

Caucasus and southern fronts. This is extremely disadvantageous to our land offensive.[16]

The post-war discovery of Doenitz's warning supports Roosevelt's decision to try all he could to keep the Soviet Union fighting. But even in 1943, Stettinius was quite frank about how little the Roosevelt Administration knew about the impact of US supplies on Russia:

> The role of Lend-Lease weapons in the Red Army's battles against Germany in the summer of 1942 is difficult to assess. In terms of making up critical deficits in Russia's stocks of war supplies, such as trucks and field telephone equipment, Lend-Lease played an important part. But in the overall picture, the volume of fighting equipment that we sent could not have bulked large. We know that American tanks were put to good use in the defense of Stalingrad. On the whole, however, we frankly have little detailed knowledge of the use to which the Russians put our weapons in that year. In 1942 we and the Russians were just beginning to learn to work together as allies. It would be foolish to pretend that our relations with Russia were at the beginning as frank and as intimate as our relations with Britain and China ... pooling of information from the start was hardly to be expected in the face of our lack of mutual confidence in the years before.[17]

Anthony Beevor is clear that Lend-Lease was a significant factor at Stalingrad.[18] A closer look at the impact of Western equipment on the war in the Soviet Union shows just how important this contribution was. The American reporter Henry Shapiro, who visited the battle area, estimated that at Stalingrad, 'a fairly high proportion of the food was American – especially lard, sugar and spam'.[19] The ham and dried eggs were known amongst the troops as 'second front' and 'Roosevelt's balls', the terms contradict the idea that Stalin kept the Russian people ignorant of the origin of these vital supplies.

It is possible to estimate in numbers the number of Western weapons sent to the Soviet Union by the time of the battle of Stalingrad. But their impact on the outcome of the battle cannot be calculated with certainty. In summary, by mid-1942 the USA had shipped 2,000 tanks and 1,300 planes to Russia, while the British had sent 2,400 tanks and 1,800 planes.[20]

In 1942, there were few and very difficult ways to get Western weapons to the Russian front: by sea directly into the Arctic ports of Murmansk and Archangel; by mountain railway and dirt road over the Caucasus mountains from sea ports on the Persian Gulf and by rail or plane across Siberia from the Pacific coast. The route for air deliveries of planes from California north across Canada, Alaska and Siberia was opened in October 1942, but only a few-score planes made the trip that winter.

The Arctic convoys of merchant ships were under fierce attack from German planes, warships and submarines. The Germans sank almost one in three – 18 out of 62 – ships that sailed from the USA for Murmansk in March 1942.[21] Then, in May 1942, the convoy whose code name was

PQ-16 lost 25,000 tons of cargo and seven of 35 ships. The tragic PQ-17 convoy lost 23 out of 34 merchantmen carrying 3,350 vehicles, 430 tanks, 21 bomber aircraft and 100,000 tons of cargo; just 1,896 vehicles, 64 tanks and 87 planes got through from this convoy.[22] In the constant sunlight of the Arctic summer the ships were sitting ducks. In order not to waste men, ships and supplies, Churchill and Roosevelt stopped the convoys in mid-July until a little darkness in the coming winter gave some protection.

With the Arctic route shut and the Siberian route not capable of taking many supplies, this left only the route highlighted by Doenitz: from the Persian Gulf through Iran and the Caucasus. The Anglo-Soviet occupation of Iran in 1941 had made this possible by ousting the pro-German regime. The US official history describes the rise of German influence:

> On they [the Germans] came advising in education, lending technical skill, building roads, and parts of the railway, adorning a new station at Tehran with the swastika (symbol of Aryan brotherhood)... by the time the British and Russians entered Iran in 1941 some 2,000 Germans had to be run to ground.[23]

In the autumn of 1942, a key question in the minds of all concerned with Iranian-routed supplies was, would enough get through to make a difference to Soviet resistance or would the Nazis get the oil and cut the supplies?

On the Persian Gulf, US Brigadier General Wheeler organized the re-building of the port of Khoramshahr with new dredged channels, wharves, piers, jetties and cranes. On 23 February 1942, the first convoy of 50 vehi-cles set out from Bushir; the whole journey to Russia could take up to a month. 'Subsequently, 120 trucks and light Willis motor vehicles [jeeps] were despatched daily'.[24] Altogether, 180,000 US trucks were assembled here for the Soviet Union during the entire war. In 1942 though, 32,500 vehicles were sent, 17,000 via the Arctic route, 10,000 on the Iran route and 5,000 through Siberia.[25] Throughout the war the Soviets produced 205,000 motor vehicles; Lend-Lease supplied more than 400,000.[26] The supplies from the Gulf went straight to the front, sometimes to be caught by the Germans before they could be used.[27]

In the air war, British and American warplanes had a significant part to play: 'Roar of engines, chaos. Cobras, Yaks, Hurricanes. A large Douglas [DC-3 Dakota] appears, flying effortlessly and smoothly...', noted Vasily Grossman, the heroic Soviet war correspondent, in his diary at an airstrip near Stalingrad. (The Yak was a Soviet built plane; the Hurricane, British; and the Douglas and Cobras, American.)[28]

Two hundred and eleven of 1,646 fighters, or every ninth fighter plane in the Red Air Force, was of either American or British manufacturer on 19 November 1942, the day the Red Army counterattacked and began to surround the German Army in Stalingrad.[29] The front-line fighter ace F. A. Zhelvakov, who fought in 1942 on the Voronezh Front, said that at that

VI The Caucasus.

time the US-made Bell Aerocobra fighter was the only plane in the Red Air Force that was a match for the Luftwaffe. In addition, over 700 US light bombers were flown from the Persian Gulf to be used by the Red Air Force to attack German forces.[30]

A remarkable perspective of a Soviet fighter pilot working in America on Lend-Lease supplies has been written by Igor Lebedev, along with his own assessment of the archival information made available after the end of the Soviet Union. Posted to Washington with his wife after combat at Stalingrad, he worked at air bases and factories all over the USA. At these bases, the Red Flag flew alongside the Stars and Stripes. He took the opportunity to make the classic American road trips to Key West and across the country. His speeding got him into the papers, and in general he seems to have had a high old time. Lebedev's researches after the end of the Cold War, in the 1990s, concluded that at the beginning of the summer-autumn campaign of 1942, 14 per cent of Soviet fighters were British or American.[31]

Supplies to the Soviet Union had considerable public support in the USA, and some weapons were paid for by donations from the American public. In New York a local society akin to the *Rotary*, the *Knights of Pythias Fraternal Lodge*, raised funds to buy the first P-47 Thunderbolt fighter plane for the Red Air Force, and this was delivered in late 1943.[32]

By the end of the war, total US supplies to the Soviet Union included: 14,000 aircraft, 363,000 trucks, 100,000 jeeps and motorbikes, 6 million pairs of boots, 35,000 radio transmitters, 380,000 field telephones, 2,000 locomotives, 11,000 railroad cars and 4 million tons of food (mostly wheat), as well as large quantities of machine tools and raw steel for industrial production.[33] These greatly improved the mobility and electronic communications of combat troops and their supply systems.

Some American Cold War warriors liked to argue that the Soviets themselves had nothing but soldiers and were largely reliant on US weapons.[34] 'Lend-Lease to Stalin' became the centrepiece of arguments by right wing Americans that Roosevelt appeased Stalin during the war and could have forced concessions in return for aid.

But Soviet industrial capacity, allied to the fighting skill and tenacity of its people, was the most important part in the defeat of Hitler's armies: 'The Soviets produced 88,000 tanks from June 1941 to December 1945, as against 23,500 by Germany from 1939 to 1945'.[35] Nevertheless, from 1943, American supplies of food trucks and communications equipment kept the Red Army eating, talking and rolling. Redirected to American and British forces, these supplies would at a minimum have required these countries' soldiers to do battle and take casualties on a far larger scale.

Without those supplies and this tangible form of the United Nations alliance, the temptation for Stalin to make a compromise with Hitler, or a successor, if it had been on offer, would have been greater. Hitler would have been more likely to have conquered Russia were it not for the weapons that the USA and the UK sent to Russia by the end of 1942.

In a major work on Lend-Lease, Hubert van Tuyll rebutted the 'appeasement' argument thus:

> Any major shift of military resources by Germany would have had devastating results for the United Nations forces. It is for this reason that the argument occasionally made that Allied aid somehow contributed to the Soviet conquest of Eastern Europe fails. Lend-Lease did help the Soviet forces advance, however, the Germans might have been able to foil the Anglo-American liberation of Western Europe.[36]

From 1943 onwards, Lend-Lease enabled victory after victory and created a momentum that helped keep the Allies together until the final defeat of the Axis. In the West, D-Day itself was a close-run battle, as was the Battle of the Bulge – more Germans on the beaches of Normandy or at Bastogne, released by less pressure in the east, might have turned the tide.

There are two more points concerning this aid to Russia. They concern the Holocaust and concessions made by Stalin. Regarding the Holocaust, a slower advance of the Red Army would have kept the extermination camps open longer and left even fewer Jews and other victims of the Nazis alive at the end of war. This fact escapes those who criticize Roosevelt for his 'appeasement' of Stalin and sometimes also for doing too little too late to stop the Holocaust.

The issue of Roosevelt receiving little from Stalin in return for Lend-Lease is discussed in Chapter 8, but here we can note two points. First, over 18 million Soviet citizens died in the war, while US dead amounted to around 300,000 – a 'concession' or contribution enough from the Soviet perspective. And second, Stalin did, as we will see in the subsequent chapters, make a succession of political decisions to move closer to the West, and in addition to restoring religion, he closed the organization for preparing worldwide communist revolution – the Comintern – and joined the new capitalist global economic system at Bretton Woods.

The Lend-Lease programme was always designed to end soon after the war, but the abruptness of its termination by President Truman created suspicions among both the British and Soviets. These are discussed in Chapter 7 in the context of the end of the war in Europe and the negotiations at San Francisco on the UN Charter.

At the beginning of 1943, victory was still far off and Lend-Lease remained a driving force of the political momentum that helped keep the United Nations together. In the USA, Republican success in the mid-term elections in November 1942 alarmed Roosevelt and Hull. Arthur Schlesinger describes how the isolationist conservatives beat off a 'concerted challenge' from Roosevelt in the election. Republican success was 'creating fears for Hull and FDR of a repeat of the 1918–1921 fiasco', when

America created then backed out of the League of Nations.[37] In London, *The Economist* noted in early January 1943, as Congress reassembled, that the Republicans were gearing up to attack Lend-Lease. Their cheerleaders in the press were newspaper columnists Arthur Crock and Drew Pearson.[38]

The domestic pressure in the USA against Roosevelt's strategy added to the international pressures hindering the ability of the Allies to take advantage of the victory at Stalingrad and defeat Hitler. The inter-Allied disputes and initiatives that played out during 1943 are the subject of the next chapter.

CHAPTER **4**

Keeping the Allies together: Casablanca and Tehran

Throughout 1943, the practical development of the United Nations continued to help build support for the war at home, keep the Allies together and prepare a stable peace. The international ideas incorporated into the United Nations had their most concrete impact on the war through providing the political basis for Lend-Lease. Then, as the war progressed and prospects for victory improved, the ideas began to take on a life of their own as international organizations were created that helped bind the Allies together and prepare them to manage the peace together.

At the beginning of the year, the war was far from being won and there were strains between the Americans, British and Russians both over how to fight the war and over the prospects for peace. That these were overcome took huge political as well as military effort. At the start of the year the Germans suffered their first major defeat of the war at Stalingrad and by the end of the year the Red Army had the Germans on the defensive everywhere. In the Atlantic the U-boats were still winning in March, but convoys were sailing safely by year's end. In March the Anglo-American-led forces were still fighting in Africa; by October they were in Italy with Italians at their side. In the Pacific and South East Asia, the Japanese were slowly driven back towards their homeland.

Nevertheless, by the end of 1943, D-Day was still in the future, and the massacre of Jews and others continued under Nazi occupation. Painful military progress was mirrored at the political level. In the USA, Congress split on party lines on Roosevelt's plan to continue Lend-Lease. The delay to D-Day caused conflict between the Allies. And the Big Three did not meet until November in the Iranian capital, Tehran.

The question of what sort of peace would be made at the end of the war was of great concern politically, though naturally enough those engaged directly in the fighting had little time for anything else.

The first summit meeting of the year came in January. On the 23rd, American moviegoers went to see the opening of *Casablanca* with Humphrey Bogart and Ingrid Bergman. They got home to learn from the radio that the same city was in the news,[1] for this was the Casablanca summit between Churchill and Roosevelt. In Paris, Texas, the newspaper headline on the summit was 'Objective: Surrender: UNCONDITIONAL SURRENDER of "the Axis"'. The article explained, 'There you have the objective of Allied war planning. Already the Atlantic Charter has furnished the outline of Allied post-war planning. Now the United Nations are ready to get down to business "for sure"'.[2] That is to say that removing the prospect of negotiating with the enemy meant that the ideals of the United Nations were more likely to be developed seriously.

The core meaning of the statement arising out of the Casablanca summit was to refuse any negotiated peace. The intention of Roosevelt in particular was to stave off suspicions that he might compromise with Germany. These had intensified following US agreement with the Vichy French military leaders in North Africa to facilitate the Anglo-American landings there after the French had fought back against the landings, with some success. The Unconditional Surrender announcement answered the question, 'How will you defeat Germany?' 'Totally', was a clear answer, but not exactly a strategy.

The search for a coherent strategy and discussions on the post-war world were key features of the political interaction between and within the USA, USSR and UK in 1943. In the USA, the Republicans had done well in the Congressional elections of November 1942. They added 47 seats in the House of Representatives and nine in the Senate, leaving a small Democratic majority in the House and a majority in the Senate potentially open to filibuster. Roosevelt feared that their conservative isolationist outlook could wreck the fragile alliance of United Nations before peace could be stabilized at the end of the war.

Political commentary in Allied nations mirrored these concerns and was quite pessimistic about the war in early 1943. This was due in part to the expectation that D-Day should have happened in 1942. Moreover, success at Stalingrad and in Egypt had been snatched from the jaws of defeat. In London in January 1943, *The Observer* newspaper repeated a widely held criticism of the conduct of the war, complaining of the lack of coordination and inclusion of Russia in the Anglo-American Combined Chiefs of Staff Committees:

> They do not exist as organs of the United Nations as such. But this is a United Nations war. To conduct it as a British-American war, with a separate Russian war running parallel to it, will certainly postpone victory and may jeopardise peace... The whole second front controversy is nothing but a symptom of a structural gap in the affairs of the United Nations.[3]

The Second Front argument was about when the British and Americans would launch D-Day landings in France. The First Front was in Russia where millions were fighting and dying. Looking ahead, *The*

13 A hopeful US newspaper headline of January 1943.

Observer noted that, 'Informed persons said the United States was interested in making the Big Four the working basis for the creation later of a fully fledged United Nations Council as a successor to the League of Nations'.

Such imagined future cooperation could not be a substitute for its absence in reality. In any case, pointing out the problems did not solve them. The truth was that, despite Lend-Lease, the Anglo-Americans and the Russians were fighting largely separate wars. Geography and political differences created the separation. The danger was that their differences would prolong the war, and risk the Germans being able to reach a peace agreement with either Russia or the Anglo-Americans.

These issues provided the background for the meeting of Churchill and Roosevelt at Casablanca. The reality of continued German power was brought home when, a few days after the Casablanca summit, Rommel counterattacked inexperienced US forces in Tunisia, sending thousands, innocent from their peacetime world, running for their lives. The Americans learned quickly and pushed back with General George C. Patton demonstrating his legendary aggressive spirit. But the experience emphasized German tenacity. As a result, the Allies were unable to get their armies into southern Italy until September 1943.

The American and British landings in North West Africa produced hard political lessons to match those learned in battle. The high principles of the United Nations and the Atlantic Charter were cast aside. General Dwight D. Eisenhower led the African invasion. To stop the French from fighting he permitted a deal with the local Vichy French leader, Admiral Francois Darlan, after which the French troops stopped fighting and co-operated with the Anglo-American invaders, but not before many were killed on both sides.

The international response to the deal was outrage, especially in the USA. People 'felt betrayed and baffled', wrote Wendell Willkie in his best-selling book *One World*. He linked it to Churchill's refusal to accept that the Atlantic Charter would apply to the British Empire and Soviet claims in Eastern Europe. If Churchill and Roosevelt would bargain with Darlan, where would the leaders of the United Nations draw the line? Willkie feared the damage to international ideas would cause a revival of isolationist, go-it-alone politics in the USA.[4]

The arrangement with Darlan (who was assassinated on Christmas Eve 1942) arose out of the fragmentation of French politics after the fall of France, and the very different approaches taken by Roosevelt and Churchill to this. Each had their favourites amongst the military leaders of France and its empire. Roosevelt continued to have diplomatic relations with the pro-Hitler regime that ran France from the hill-town of Vichy. It was not until after the liberation of Paris in August 1944 that the USA finally broke off relations with this regime. Churchill, meanwhile, backed General de Gaulle and the 'National Committee' he led from offices in London, although de Gaulle showed great independence from his mentor.

The whole episode showed the Western Allies in disarray and only aggravated suspicions that if they would cut a deal with French collaborators

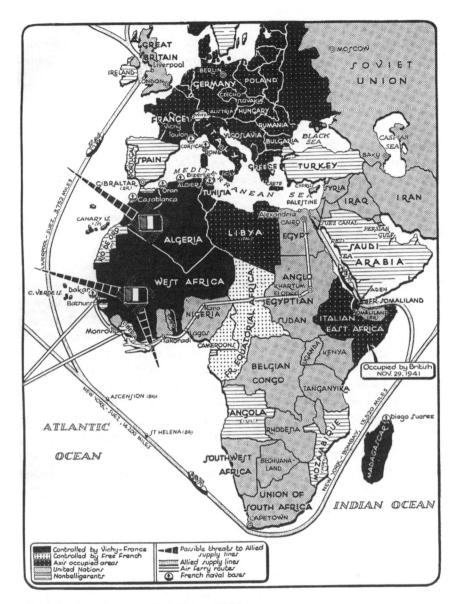

VII Vichy-French-controlled Africa, 1942.

with Hitler they might soon do the same with some German leader such as the Luftwaffe chief, Herman Goering.[5]

To restore confidence in the United Nations' ideals after this embarrassment, Roosevelt announced a policy of 'unconditional surrender' on behalf of the two countries. The previous year's United Nations Declaration had committed its signatories not to make separate peace deals; this went further and said that there were to be no deals at all. There is a debate about whether the policy of unconditional surrender was the right one. Critics argue that the policy made the Germans fight harder since they had nothing to lose. It did not, however, stop assassination plots against Hitler.

What should be asked of those who favoured a compromise peace with Germany is, 'What type of compromise might have been on offer?' Perhaps a compromise peace would have involved a resumption of the Nazi-Soviet pact, effectively calling a draw in the East and leaving Hitler to run Western and Central Europe. Such fears and allegations certainly reached Roosevelt and were taken quite seriously in his Administration and by the public.[6]

The other form of separate peace could have been the creation of an anti-communist alliance of Germany with the West. It was discussed at the time and since then, and was the option that many in Germany favoured. As Alan Bullock, the historian of Nazism, points out, a significant part of the Nazi Party leadership and the army command favoured downplaying racial politics and building anti-Russian and anti-Communist armies of auxiliaries from the populations of Poland, Ukraine and the Crimea.[7]

A section of the German military regarded Hitler's insistence on en-slaving the Slav peoples of the East (if not the destruction of the Jews) as counter-productive. They favoured Germany liberating and arming the peoples of Eastern Europe, including the Russians, against the communist regime. Many of the people in the Soviet Union had initially welcomed the Nazis as liberators only to find the repression they then suffered was far more intense than that from the Communist Party. This Nazi policy was changed partly as Germany's situation became desperate, with the development of a puppet Russian liberation army; SS units even included a Moslem unit from the Balkans.

Any attempt by the Western Allies to make a negotiated peace with Germany would have had to deal with these political forces. Such a deal with the Germans would also have been likely to have left intact the heart of the German military state which was the professional staff of the army. It was this permanent staff, with a two-hundred-year history, which much of the world saw as the perpetual government of Germany. Breaking this power once and for all was the key objective of American and British policy in seeking to liberate Europe. A compromise with it would have enabled this staff to once again blame the politicians for its own failures on the battlefield. In 1918, they had blamed the politicians and could again, given the chance, blame another political leader, this time what they saw as a jumped-up Austrian corporal, Adolf Hitler.

Unconditional surrender by itself was a doctrine that could be inter-preted as the annihilation of the German people in the manner that Hitler was behaving in the East. But Roosevelt, Churchill and Stalin usually took

14 Franklin D. Roosevelt and Winston Churchill at Casablanca, January 1943.

some care in their main public statements to emphasize that their fight was with the Nazis and not with the German people. And unconditional surrender was put forward in the context of the brighter, prosperous world outlined in the Atlantic Charter and in which Germans and Italians could play a part. This was an altogether more positive prospect – for the enemy, for the Allies, for neutrals and for public opinion.

The fear amongst the Allies that Germany would again, after a generation of recuperation, attempt to launch an aggressive war, deeply concerned all its enemies and provided a motive to maintain the United Nations alliance after the war. The detailed options for managing Germany after the war were given close attention by Churchill, Roosevelt and Stalin. Their mutual need to manage Germany, and to a lesser degree Japan, is important as a driver of their longer-term security cooperation.

But the implementation of the Atlantic Charter and the UN ideals had yet to happen. *The Economist*, in an editorial of February 1943 entitled 'Towards a Full Alliance', set out the political challenge:

> With the Russian victories, a new phase has opened in the war. For the first time, the end of the struggle is, if distantly, in sight. After three years of hard and apparently endless fighting, men can begin to throw their minds forward to the day when peace will come. Peace – yes, but what kind of peace? To fight on to victory was an ideal great enough and simple enough to hold together half mankind in the coalition of the United Nations. But now that peace is looming up behind victory, where are the new ideals and principles? It is in

this half world of doubt and questioning that Goebbels is waging his new war of words.[8]

In secret, Roosevelt had begun a discussion with both Stalin and Churchill on the shape of the post-war world from the Atlantic Charter meeting onwards. His emphasis was on the four major powers managing the world. He styled America, Britain, China and Russia as the 'Four Policemen' imbedded in a wider United Nations Council. These early ideas became established in the Security Council and General Assembly of the United Nations organization created at San Francisco in 1945 and discussed in detail in Chapter 7.

At the time, these ideas received a mixed response from Britain and the Soviet Union. In his meeting with Roosevelt in May 1942, Molotov was delighted at the influence the American leader was prepared to give to the Soviet Union in post-war councils. The British continued to press for a greater role for Canada and Australia.

Eden wrote to the British Cabinet about the 'The Four Power Plan' in November 1942, following discussions with US officials. He explained, 'I have been driven to the conclusion, therefore, that we should regard the conception of the Four Powers, working within the framework of the United Nations, as the present basis of our foreign policy'.[9] He went on to argue that the UK must join with the Americans in arguing for this in public as the basis of the future world organization. Doing so would be welcomed by Allies great and small, he argued.

The Chinese and other nations wanted to go further, arguing for the immediate creation of a United Nations Council. 'Organization of two United Nations councils – one to prosecute the war and the other to study ways of making effective the Atlantic Charter and the Four Freedoms' was urged by Walter Nash, the New Zealand Ambassador to Washington, in a February 1943 speech to the annual meeting of the American Political Science Association.[10] His remarks were typical of those of smaller nations.

Congressional support for a renewal of Lend-Lease was needed in early 1943 and provided a test of the strength of public disquiet with the Roosevelt Administration's policy following Republican successes in the elections the previous November. The State Department engaged in a comprehensive series of discussions with Congress on the post-war world. Early in the year, though, 'spin' from congressional staff convinced at least some of the Washington Press Corps that the Administration's whole discussion on the post-war world had a more cynical and short-term approach.

As soon as the new Congress convened in January 1943, Hull arranged that every Saturday morning his special assistant Leo Pasvolsky and 'other Hull aides convene with solons [i.e. distinguished senior members] of senate and house and with officials from commerce, agriculture and labor' to discuss the 'world revolution' brought about by the war and ideas for the post-war world. 'Lawmakers invited to these confabs have been sworn to secrecy concerning the conversations. Those who would normally speak about executive [secret] sessions' agenda refuse... But their general reaction is that these conferences are really designed to insure re-enactment of Lend-Lease and reciprocal trade agreement legislation. Both grants expire in June, and there has been some talk that the measures might not be renewed'.[11]

Similar reports stated that Roosevelt was briefing on the same subject. 'Congressmen who have been trotting in and out of the White House lately have talked vaguely of a post-war planning, and there is a report that among the topmost politicians that Mr R has a definite formula prepared and ready'.[12] One result was the Senate resolution called in shorthand B2H2 which called for an immediate United Nations Organization for war and peace issues and provided the basis for debate in the Senate throughout the year. This is raised in Chapter 8 as part of the discussion of the creation of the UN Charter.

In March 1943, on the eve of key votes on Lend-Lease in Congress, the US Ambassador in Moscow, Admiral William H. Standley, publicly accused the Soviet Union of failing to tell its people of the US aid they were receiving. Admiral Standley's remark to the US press corps in Moscow on 8 March that 'the Russian authorities seem to want to cover up the fact that they are receiving outside help. Apparently they want their people to believe that the Red Army is fighting this war alone' was front-page news across America. His actions supported the conservative anti-communists in the Congressional debates. Coming a month after the surrender of the Nazi army at Stalingrad amid appalling Soviet casualties, his intervention indicates the continuing strength of anti-communism in the USA. Stalin had indeed pointed out the obvious fact that the Red Army was taking the burden of fighting the Germans. Stettinius also pointed this out in his statements on Lend-Lease.[13] On 11 March, Roosevelt set out his argument to Congress for more Lend-Lease. He included the claim that 'this mutual aid has become more than a joint weapon of war. In the smoke of battle, Lend-Lease is helping to forge the unity that will be required to make a just and lasting peace'.[14]

US public information pamphlets kept up the message. In one such title, 'All for one, One for all: the Story of Lend-Lease', the idea was repeated: 'And when peace comes, the Lend-Lease idea – the idea of "all for one and one for all" – can help lay the foundation for that better world toward which the United Nations are marching together'.[15]

In Congress, the Republicans tried to impose political conditions and repayment terms in an amendment to the legislation, so jeopardizing the entire Lend-Lease programme at a time when the Anglo-American armies were still stuck fighting in Africa.[16] Only after their wrecking amendments were defeated narrowly on party lines did the Republicans decide to vote for the renewal and extension of Lend-Lease. *The Economist* reported this combined Senate debate on a comprehensive set of United Nations organizations in conjunction with the skill of Stettinius in getting Lend-Lease renewal through without amendments.[17]

The political mobilization around the Lend-Lease debates opened a new phase in domestic and international political activity. In early March 1943, the British Foreign Secretary Anthony Eden came to Washington. Sherwood recalled,

> During Eden's visit there was a very considerable amount of spade work done on the organization of the United Nations. From this work there resulted the UNRRA organization and the conferences at Moscow, Tehran, Bretton Woods, Dumbarton Oaks, Yalta and finally San Francisco.[18]

Some of these were meetings of the Big Three but others were of all the United Nations, which by now involved over 30 countries so that the practice of multinational organization and diplomacy was rapidly developing.

In the spring of 1943, in parallel with the Congressional debate on renewing Lend-Lease, the Roosevelt Administration made public a series of proposals for the post-war world. Within a few weeks of each other, there were announcements of preliminary plans for international economics, post-war aid and relief, war crimes trials and the prevention of starvation. The domestic propaganda effort included United Nations postage stamps and the creation of a United Nations flag. Lacking for many was any immediate overall United Nations organization, or concrete plans for the world security body.

The remainder of this chapter focuses on two of Roosevelt's efforts to create structures for the post-war world and on the inter-Allied diplomacy that culminated in the Yalta meeting of Churchill, Roosevelt and Stalin.

The UN Food and Agriculture Commission was created in 1943 and still exists in the twenty-first century as the UN Food and Agriculture Organization (FAO). But Roosevelt failed to get British agreement on a United Nations Declaration on National Independence that would have dismantled the British Empire. The negotiations between the three major powers hit a crisis in the middle of the year over delays to D-Day and culminated that year in a meeting of Foreign Ministers in Moscow in September and of the three leaders in Tehran in November. Subsequent chapters examine the other initiatives.

The net result of this wartime effort for peace was that, as Arthur Schlesinger argued, a series of US-led international conferences had created global political structures that endure into the twenty-first century. These encompassed international organization, finance and trade and development, food and agriculture, civil aviation, and relief and reconstruction.[19]

'He has it all worked out in his mind', noted Roosevelt's daily companion, Daisy Suckley, at the beginning of April 1943. She had been with the President at Hyde Park in the long conversations with Eden.

> The P. was relaxed & peaceful, & talked mostly about his hopes for future peace. He has it all worked out in his mind already. [He] told the story of providing advice to Morocco for its benefit while at Casablanca. If F's plans work out, he would like to be chairman of the peace organization, whatever his title would be. He wants to do it *'simply'*, not at Geneva in a huge building, etc.[20]

The reference to Morocco is corroborated by Sherwood and Elliott Roosevelt's accounts of the Casablanca meeting. They reported that the Sultan of Morocco had said it was unprecedented to hear that ideas for developing his nation's oil wealth were to be for its benefit. Roosevelt sought to go further even than Schlesinger's list with independence for India and the rest of the European colonies, only to be blocked by Churchill. In addition, the Polish, Czech and other governments in exile led the way in the creation of the United Nations War Crimes Commission in 1943.

If the seeds of twentieth and twenty-first century world organizations are to be found in the Four Freedoms, Atlantic Charter and Declaration by United Nations, then they began to sprout green shoots in 1943. The breadth of the issues that were treated by governments as essential to national and international security is a lesson in need of re-learning in the twenty-first century.

Hot Springs, Virginia was the scene of the first United Nations Conference, with more than 30 nations participating. Why start with food? Were there not more pressing issues? Certainly, Dean Acheson, the US State Department official charged with overseeing the conference, found it curious. He could find none of the usual lobby groups pressing for it.[21] However, the British Ambassador, Lord Halifax, sent a message to London that provides an explanation and a confirmation of the visionary purpose described by Sherwood and Schlesinger. He used the shortened, telegraphic style of writing used when every word had to be coded and decoded manually:

> As you know [the] President had wished first United Nations Conference to be held in the United States and to be on a subject which should be humanitarian rather than political with object of accustoming American public opinion to United Nations Conferences and presumably of preparing way for further conferences on more difficult subjects if first conference was a success State Department considers that its success is a good augury.[22]

This clarity of intent is only somewhat apparent in the recollection of US State Department officials Cordell Hull and Dean Acheson. Hull, who occupied the post of Secretary of State, was rarely confided in by Roosevelt. His assessment was that Roosevelt simply wanted four policemen, with regional organizations – everyone disarmed except for the Big Four.[23] Hull thought that on economic issues, Roosevelt,

> [F]avoured the creation of entirely separate functional agencies. It was on this basis that at his insistence, a plan was developed early in 1943 for the convocation of the Hot Springs, Virginia, conference on food and agriculture, and for the holding of a similar conference on other economic matters with a view to creating a series of uncoordinated specialized agencies. I differed with the President in that I thought it was also necessary to have some sort of over-all agency of coordination in the whole field of economic and social co-operation, such as the United Nations Economic and Social Council which later came into being.[24]

Hopkins noted that the British were trying to get Australia and Canada onto the Executive Committee of the agriculture organization alongside the USA, China and the Soviet Union. The British, though, had to accept the formula of a general assembly of all members and a small decision making group of the most powerful. This compromise between power and consensus amongst states, which began in these debates, was recreated in the subsequent wartime UN organizations, so that by the time the Charter came to be considered at San Francisco, most nations were accustomed to, if not entirely happy with, this formula.

One reason why the history of the first United Nations Conference has been obscured is that there are misleading accounts in influential memoirs of the period. Dean Acheson's were influential in shaping the understanding of post-war generations as he became one of the most eminent US political figures of the Cold War, serving as Secretary of State to President Truman. But people seeking an understanding of Roosevelt's policy on this occasion are not helped and are positively misled by his account of the Food Conference. Notwithstanding the fact that he gave the opening address to the conference and managed the Aid Conference that created UNRRA, he never explains the United Nations context of the project. But at the time, Roosevelt made plain to delegates to the Food Conference why he considered it important and emphasized the fundamental link between poverty and war:

> We know that in the world for which we are fighting and working the four freedoms must be won for all men. We know, too, that each freedom is dependent upon the others; that freedom from fear [war], for example, cannot be secured without freedom from want. If we are to succeed, each Nation individually, and all Nations collectively, must undertake these responsibilities:
>   They must take all necessary steps to develop world food production so that it will be adequate to meet the essential nutritional needs of the world population. And they must see to it that no hindrances, whether of international trade, of transportation, or of internal distribution, be allowed to prevent any

Nation or group of citizens within a Nation from obtaining the food necessary for health. Society must meet in full its obligation to make available to all its members at least the minimum adequate nutrition.[25]

In his statement at the end of the conference, transmitted by radio and shown in cinema newsreels, Roosevelt said in solemn, sermon-like language,

> It gives me great pleasure to welcome to the White House you who have served so splendidly at the epoch-making United Nations Conference on Food and Agriculture.
>   I use that word 'epoch-making' advisedly. The Conference could not have failed to be significant, because it was the first United Nations Conference; but it has succeeded even beyond our hopes. It is truly epoch-making because, in reaching unanimity upon complex and difficult problems, you have demonstrated beyond question that the United Nations really are united – not only for the prosecution of the war, but for the solution of the many and difficult problems of peace. This Conference has been a living demonstration of the methods by which the conversations of Nations of like mind, contemplated by Article VII of the Mutual Aid Agreement, can and will give practical application to the principles of the Atlantic Charter.[26]

His rhetoric soared rather higher than the achievements of the meeting. It had no executive function, although it did create an interim UN Commission on Food and Agriculture that sat in a rented house in Washington, DC to await the creation of the post-war UN. Amongst United Nations member states the meeting was also recognized formally and is included in the set of State Department papers provided to Congress. In Britain, its agreement was published as a formal government 'command' paper.[27] It was mainly concerned with developing best practice at national level to address the global food shortage after the end of the war.[28] The UN, created by the Charter in 1945, recognized the interim Food and Agriculture Organization as a permanent specialized agency, providing a clear institutional connection between wartime and post-war United Nations.

In 2008, the Food and Agriculture Organization initiated a global conference in Rome in response to the worldwide fear of famine. It has not been the most prominent international organization of the UN system, compared to efforts on children, humanitarian aid and peacekeeping for example, but its existence is living proof of the United Nations created during and not just after World War II.

The creation of a United Nations food agency in 1943 demonstrates that internationalist humanitarian multilateral policies were supported widely at the height of a brutal global war. They were supported because the scarcity of food was accepted to be a cause of military conflict and because recognizing and acting on that fact was seen as useful to generate the political will to win. Starting with the food issue, the political focus on economic, social and humanitarian issues during World War II provides a broad and far-reaching approach to global security and global governance. The 1940s agenda assumed that the negative consequences of war were unmanageable and unacceptable, as the two world wars had shown, and that only by humanizing security rather than by securitizing/adding a military dimension to humanitarian activity could global governance deliver what was required.

The issue of the European imperial colonies was one where many in the USA considered that injustice would create further conflict. But these debates were as contentious as the food and agriculture problem was consensual; not least because of the connection between the lack of civil rights in Mumbai, India, with what was going on in the southern states of the USA and the US armed forces practice of putting African-Americans into segregated units.

At the heart of colonial policy lay the idea of the supremacy of European culture and of the European race. This idea also underpinned the oppression of African-Americans, who were then called 'Negroes' or 'Colored People' by whites in the United States. Thus, there was a close connection between liberation of colonized peoples overseas and what was happening within the United States.

As Mahir Bose had pointed out, the repression of colonial peoples has merited little attention from historians and commentators of the war. Bose points to George Orwell as an exception at the time.[29] Orwell wrote an article, *Not Counting Niggers,* in 1939 in which he lambasts the idea of the British and French Empires as democracies when they were little more than a mechanism for exploiting cheap coloured labour subject to starvation wages of a penny an hour. He questioned fighting Hitler just to sustain such a system. Orwell was echoing an earlier account of the imposition of poverty on India by the British, written at the onset of British rule by Edmund Burke, the philosopher-politician of the late eighteenth century.[30]

Roosevelt's insistence that the principles of the Atlantic Charter applied globally was politically explosive in America as well as in the British, Dutch and French camps. Sumner Welles and the Vice President, Henry Wallace, emphasized this point in US domestic politics, where African-Americans pursued a civil rights campaign under the 'Double V' slogan – that is, victory abroad and at civil rights at home. Wendell Willkie, in a speech to the National Association for the Advancement of Colored People in July 1942, stated that America could no longer tolerate this 'mocking paradox'.[31] The interaction of these issues should not be overlooked. Pursuing anti-colonial policies abroad could only encourage the civil rights movement in the USA. Roosevelt has been much criticized for not going further against racial discrimination inside America. And yet defence contracts were, at least in the North, given on the theoretical condition that there not be racial discrimination in employment. But even in the North, discrimination was rife in the war factories. In Detroit this produced ri-ots in 1943, with running gun battles between civil-rights advocates and police.

Recent scholarship sees the operation of Federal Courts at this time as assisting in the development of civil rights.[32] Legislation penalizing police and county officials who failed to prevent lynchings of blacks had a bare majority of support amongst white Americans in opinion polling.[33]

Thus, one of the consequences of the shift to the right in US foreign policy after Roosevelt was to make domestic repression easier when any progressive action could be attacked as 'communism'.

These arguments leave a poisonous residue in the present century. As late as 2002, CNN reported an uproar over remarks made by the then leader of the US Senate, Trent Lott of Mississippi, at a party for a political leader from the 1940s who still held a Senate seat.:

> 'I want to say this about my state: When Strom Thurmond ran for president [in 1948], we voted for him. We're proud of it. And if the rest of the country had followed our lead, we wouldn't have had all these problems over all these years, either', Lott said at last week's party. .... [Thurmond] carried Alabama, Louisiana, Mississippi and his home state of South Carolina, of which he was governor at the time. During the campaign, he said, 'All the laws of Washington and all the bayonets of the Army cannot force the Negro into our homes, our schools, our churches'. Thurmond's party ran under a platform that declared in part, 'We stand for the segregation of the races and the racial integrity of each race'.[34]

Roosevelt's anti-colonial policy did not outlast him and it is not prop-erly acknowledged. The main achievements were the promotion of an Asian nation, China, to great power status and the inclusion of India as a separate country in the Declaration of January 1942 and in the wartime UN conferences. The main lost opportunity was the demise of Roosevelt's attempt to require that a timetable be established to phase out the British, Dutch and French colonies. In the Atlantic Charter the British and Amer-icans also renounced 'extra-territorial' claims in China, which pleased al-most all politically aware people in Asia as it was this 'extra-territoriality' that had been at the heart of colonial domination of China.[35]

Roosevelt also determined that China should be regarded as one of the four great powers, not least because of the need for China to help prevent any revival of Japanese power. Nevertheless, this was a radical racial shift at the time. Back at the time of the creation of the League of Nations, the white nations had refused to include language on racial equality, humiliating delegates from Japan and elsewhere. Now, in the 1940s as Eden put it,

> In American eyes, China ranks, with us and the Russians, as a Great Power. This may seem to us to be a completely unreal conception, but I am reasonably convinced that the United States will be unwilling to enter into any world organization involving specific commitments outside the American continent,

unless China, too, is a member of that organization on terms of at any rate theoretical equality with the Great Powers.[36]

Roosevelt's attempts to get a timetable for the liberation of the peoples of the British Empire agreed by Churchill throughout 1943, was set out in a draft: 'A declaration by the United Nations on National Independence'. Roosevelt's radical internationalism included a determined effort to end the colonial practices of the British, Dutch and French Empires. The proposals in this paper are more explicit and far-reaching than the evidence usually discussed about Roosevelt's anti-imperial policies. Historians have discussed how this approach by America was implemented through hard-bargaining on post-war economic policy and in the face of Churchill's public disavowal of the application of the Atlantic Charter's principle that people could choose their own government, to the British Empire.

The attempted dissolution of empires was set out in a five-page policy document whose very reasonableness of tone did nothing to assuage Churchill. In a note to Eden and Deputy Prime Minister Clement Attlee only, sent from his meeting with Roosevelt in September 1943, Churchill described how Roosevelt had asked him for his observations on the declaration which he had first given the British back in March: 'I expressed no opinion on this and indeed only read it after leaving the President... We have criticised severely the vague American aspiration which cost them nothing to make and exposed our whole Empire to great embarrassment'.[37]

Far from being as Churchill describes, 'a vague aspiration', the document required the creation of timetables for the dissolution of the British and other European Empires. In wartime, Roosevelt was reluctant to press the issue as the British were military allies. However, his persistence in pushing the paper on Churchill indicates he was intent on following it through. The natural point to reintroduce the topic would have been in the negotiations on the UN Charter at San Francisco and as part of the talks on a post-war loan to the British.

Had Roosevelt secured British agreement, the United Nations Declaration on National Independence would have stood alongside the other institutions created by the wartime United Nations and detailed in subsequent chapters. At the heart of the draft is a section setting out that the colonizing powers had both a duty and a purpose to cooperate fully with the local populations to enable them to attain independent national status:

> The duty and the purpose of each nation having political ties with colonial peoples' (was to include in points a-c) political, educational, social and economic advancement and promotion through the local governments and increasing self-government with the clear objective of:
> d. To fix at the earliest practical moments, dates upon which colonial peoples shall be accorded the status of full independence within a system of general security; and

e. To pursue policies under which the natural resources of colonial territories shall be developed, organized and marketed in the interest of the peoples concerned and of the world as a whole.[38]

This policy went far further than the introduction of Trusteeships in the UN for the colonial possessions of the Axis powers after their surrender. A number of such territories, including Syria and Lebanon, had been created as 'Mandates' under the League of Nations when the territories were handed to the British and French Empires as prizes of victory with the façade of international liberal values. The Truman Administration secured the creation of a Trusteeship Council as part of the UN Charter agreed at San Francisco, and it has been one of the least used organizations since then. Such debate as there has been on Roosevelt's anti-colonial policy has focused on the Trusteeship Council and the economic and trade negotiations.

The draft declaration would have created a series of regional commissions with representations of the colonized as well as the colonizers to manage the independence process.

There was some contradiction in Roosevelt's approach since he also wanted to establish a worldwide system of US military bases, especially in the Pacific – a policy that was implemented. Nevertheless, the post-war world would well have been more peaceful and prosperous had this declaration been pursued as Roosevelt intended.

The declaration certainly spelled the end of empire – it was no vague aspiration but a mandate for an international organization that would fix dates. Roosevelt's acceptance of the British veto on publishing his proposals is both a strength and a weakness of his policy. Here he is proposing a United Nations organization for approval by the then 31 nations, but letting none of them other than the British – the critical stakeholder – into the picture. From this distance we cannot know whether Roosevelt would have been more expansive in a post-war environment and have included others in the debate from the beginning, but with his aspiration to lead the new organization it seems quite likely.

The elevation of China and the pursuit of a schedule for decolonization serve to reinforce the anti-imperial origins of the UN and tend to outweigh the idea that it was partly created to bolster imperialism expressed by Mark Mazower on the basis of the influence of the South African leader, Jan Smuts. Taken together, Roosevelt's anti-colonial and global economic policies offered a prospect to the developing world that were soon dashed when Truman, from the conservative south of the USA, took office.

While these debates took place, a discovery and a delay blighted Anglo-American relations with the Soviet Union in the summer of 1943. The Nazis uncovered the mass grave in Katyn forest where Stalin's secret police had executed thousands of Polish officers they had captured in 1939. For once, the Nazi propaganda machine was telling the truth. The horror of the crime was real enough to outweigh the fact that the Polish government before the war had been a military dictatorship with a public policy of breaking up the Soviet Union. This and the fact that Poland had attacked as far as Kiev in the early 1920s may have motivated Stalin but is no excuse for his brutality. However, with bigger issues at stake neither Churchill nor Roosevelt had much interest in supporting the Polish cause.

The issue which caused the greatest rift between Moscow and the West was the Anglo-American decision to delay D-Day for another year. At Casablanca, the Anglo-American military staff had agreed on an invasion of Normandy timed for August of 1943. By May 1943, the British no longer supported the plan, fearing failure, and at the meeting in Washington it was agreed to postpone the attack for a year, until May 1944. Some public political debate caused alarm that Germany might no longer be the top priority: 'Several United States Senators, for instance, go so far in their eagerness to join issue with Japan that they would call a truce with Germany... Mr Curtin [the Australian Prime Minister] has on occasion come close to the same conclusion... Time is not on our side. The Soviet Army and people will not fight on alone for ever'.[39]

Roosevelt sought a meeting alone with Stalin with Churchill's reluctant agreement. This was finally agreed for 15 July, after Roosevelt had sent a personal message seeking a meeting with Stalin via his representative Joseph Davies, the former US Ambassador to Moscow.

It was not until June 1943, after the visit of Davies, that Stalin learned of the decision to delay D-Day by yet another year, first from Churchill and then in a joint statement from the two Western leaders. Stalin's response to the delay was bitter, and as a result of this and renewed crises at the front, the summits with Churchill and Roosevelt were cancelled. Stalin precisely and repeatedly sent back to the two leaders their own words in which they had committed themselves to invading France in 1943. Stalin was explicit that their decision to delay would cost the lives of millions and accused the Western Allies of deliberate bad faith.

Sherwood recounts, 'During this period of tension, Stalin recalled Litvinov from Washington and Maisky from London. There was now an atmosphere alarmingly reminiscent of that which had preceded the Molotov-Ribbentrop Pact of August 1939, and fears of a separate Russian-German Armistice were revived. The Roosevelt-Stalin meeting was postponed indefinitely'.[40] The Molotov-Ribbentrop Pact had followed a breakdown in British and French discussions with Stalin over forming an alliance against Hitler.

Lord Beaverbrook, Britain's armaments minister, reflected the mood of scepticism over US and British seriousness about attacking France when he wrote to US officials that the Western Allies should think of launching

D-Day around 1950 unless they were prepared to face up to the risks and get on with it.[41]

In August, Roosevelt and Churchill met again, this time in Quebec. The Associated Press's Sigrid Arne put bluntly a widespread view that 'they were trying to hold together the fabric of the United Nations'. It was mostly a military meeting, checking on plans for the Pacific, Italy and the invasion of France. At the end of the meeting Churchill engaged in what appeared to be extraordinary public diplomacy with Stalin. He used a radio broadcast to invite the Soviet leader to a meeting with himself and Roosevelt. As Arne explains, 'That broadcast shows that the two Western Allies were still on an uncertain footing with the third'. Normally such meetings are arranged in secret, and yet 'here was Churchill broadcasting to the world that he would like a meeting with Stalin'.[42]

Later in the summer of 1943, further military success against Germany – helped by Lend-Lease – smoothed the way for renewed diplomatic contact between the Anglo-Americans and the Soviet Union. The Red Army defeated what turned out to be Hitler's final major attack in Russia. This, the largest tank battle ever seen, took place around the Russian town of Kursk, assisted by the ever-increasing flow of American food, trucks, telephones and war planes. Anglo-American troops landed in southern Italy that September, having landed in Sicily in July.

For Stalin, the top diplomatic priority in late 1943 was still to get the Anglo-American armies into a major ground war with the Germans in Europe. For Roosevelt, it was to ensure that the Soviet Union would join the war on Japan when Germany was defeated and to ensure Soviet inclusion in a post-war settlement along his American-internationalist lines. In the end, both men got their way in the meetings that followed, and the United Nations concept took further material shape. For Churchill and the British, their waning influence resulting from past battlefield failures and exhausted resources was becoming clearer as the debates continued.

In mid-October, renewed criticism of Lend-Lease led to a Senate investigation by Senator Harry Truman's Committee investigating wasteful military spending. In St Petersburg, Florida, the local paper reported on 15 October 1943 that Senator Butler, a Republican from Nebraska, had attacked Lend-Lease as 'the most colossal dole of all time'.[43]

The Foreign Ministers of the Big Three met in Moscow at the end of October to prepare for the meeting of their leaders. The Chinese were invited to sign onto the documents the three agreed. This was followed by a meeting in Cairo at which Churchill and Roosevelt met Chiang Kai-shek. Then finally in Tehran at the end of November the two leaders met with Stalin.

It is worth highlighting the presence of the US Secretary of State, Cordell Hull, in Moscow for the first time. By now, Hull was in his

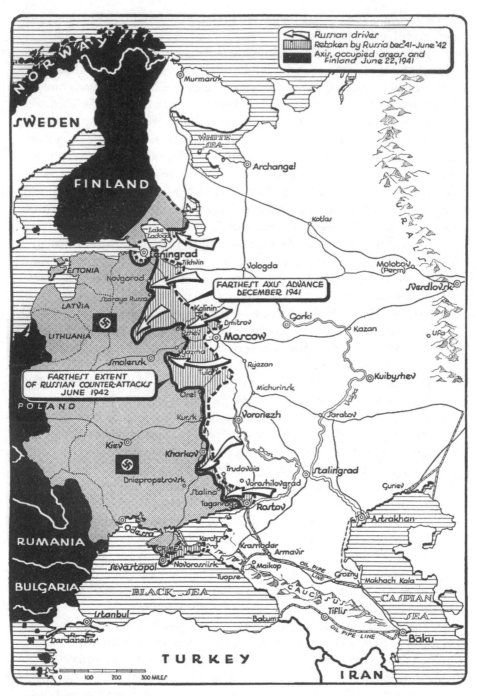

VIII The Russian Front.

seventies and taking his first plane trips in days without the modern comfort of pressurized cabins that feel much like being on the ground. His visit appears to have impressed Stalin with the seriousness of US intent. A great deal has been written of these meetings and much space devoted to the interminable drinking sessions and to Churchill's birthday party in Tehran. Both Churchill and Roosevelt were assisted by their children at the Tehran conference; Churchill by his daughter Sarah and Roosevelt by his son Elliott – both were serving in their countries' air forces. Elliott along with his three brothers was decorated for bravery, in his case for taking aerial photographs of Nazi bases in Italy and France.

The leaders' public statements received great attention around the world while their secret war plans determined both how the war ended and their approach to peace. Sherwood cites a US high-level military assessment that Russia would dominate Europe and that British power was in great decline, thus giving a high priority to the US alliance with Russia. Equally important was to get Russia to fight the Japanese. These priorities guided US policy at Tehran and later at Yalta.[44]

Stalin, who had rebuffed Roosevelt's earlier ideas for a meeting of the two of them alone, began in the late summer to agree to a trilateral meeting including Churchill and to the preparatory meeting of Foreign Ministers in Moscow. In Moscow, four short documents were issued,[45] covering German atrocities, Austria, Italy and 'General Security'. The 'three Allied powers, speaking in the interests of the thirty-three United Nations' determined that Germans who had committed 'atrocities, massacres and executions' would be sent back to the countries where they had acted and would be dealt with by that country, except for the few leaders who would be dealt with by the 'joint decision of the Governments of the Allies'. The declaration on Austria encouraged it and other German satellites to act for their own liberation if they wanted to be treated well by the Allies at the war's end. The statement on Italy, like that on Austria, envisaged a gradual return to democracy.

It was the statement on general security that attracted most attention. This was the first time that the Soviet Union committed to the unconditional surrender policy. And this was also the first time that the USA and the Soviet Union endorsed a general international organization based on the sovereign equality of 'all peace-loving states ... for the maintenance of international peace and security', and 'to bring about a general agreement on the regulation of armaments'. From a Soviet initiative, a three-power group to study the implications of this policy was set up.[46]

The Cairo meeting focused on the Chinese role in the war with Japan. However, the meeting of Chiang Kai-shek with the two Western leaders was a milestone in the recognition of a non-white political leader – though the weakness of Chinese military power and the fact that the Soviet Union

15 The expansion of Lend-Lease, 1941–43.

16 A report of the Moscow foreign minister's meeting in late 1943 highlights the commitment to create what became the UN we know today.

was not at war with Japan meant that the other powers did not think to include China in the Moscow and Tehran meetings.

Churchill, Roosevelt and Stalin finally met together in the Iranian capital Tehran in late November 1943. When the conference was over they all arrived home happy at what they achieved. For Stalin the priority was to get a firm date for D-Day in 1944, and he got it: 1 May. Throughout the conference he and his officials endlessly pursued the question of how D-Day

17 Roosevelt, Churchill and General and Mrs Chiang Kai-shek meet in Cairo in November 1943 prior to the Big Three meeting in Tehran the same month.

was being organized. Afterwards, apparently finally convinced, the Soviet press began to fully praise the Anglo-American war effort.

Critics of Roosevelt's policy towards Russia claim that Stalin always wanted to conquer as much of Europe as possible, enabled by local communist parties. These critics have an analytic blind spot when it comes to the consideration of D-Day. With the Red Army beating the Germans almost single-handed, helped by US supplies, why did Stalin need D-Day? A real communist conspiracy would have had Stalin and his alleged agents abroad urging the West into suicidal missions, such as the infamous Dardanelles expedition of World War I. But the Cold War warriors, including Churchill, never account for Stalin's unrelenting demand that the capitalist armies land in France at the earliest possible moment. Given the Red Army's continued success against the Germans, a further postponement of D-Day into 1945 or 1946 might have seen the Allies being greeted on the beaches of Normandy by a triumphant Red Army; or, disastrously, the opportunity for German armaments production to give the Nazis another chance.

There is a similar thought-gap in much historical discussion surrounding Churchill's approach to fighting in Europe. His much-expressed concern at the prospect of Soviet control of Eastern Europe is linked to his apparent desire to fight in the Balkans so as to get troops into Eastern Europe before the Russians got there. But geography dictated the opposite. The north coast of the Mediterranean Sea is mountainous. Any invaders from the sea would have literally had to fight an uphill battle. The painfully slow progress in Italy was a poor augury of success. It is possible that an alliance with Turkey or with the Yugoslav partisans could have brought the Western Allies across the Alps and into southern Germany, but more likely such an operation would not have gone well, and Turkey could not be persuaded to join the war.

For anti-communist Westerners with the freedom of all Europe at the top of their agenda, it was not the Balkans but the shorter route across the flatlands of northern France and the Low Countries that offered a quicker route into the Third Reich and eastern Europe. But the idea of fighting in France brought back memories of the devastating trench warfare of World War I to the English. As long ago as 1948, Sherwood's analysis got to the point:

> It has often been said that Churchill's advocacy of the 'soft underbelly' approach to Europe demonstrated his farsightedness – that he was motivated by the long-range purpose of keeping the Red Army out of the Balkans... if Anglo-American strength had been concentrated in Southern and South-eastern Europe, what eventually would have stopped the Russians from marching into the Ruhr and Saar and even into Normandy?[47]

At Tehran, the major powers had created better military and political cohesion. Their armies were still far from Germany. Nevertheless, as part of the cooperative process under the United Nations framework, the UN War Crimes Commission and the UN Relief and Rehabilitation Administration, both internationally staffed and funded, were up and running in 1943. They began to turn the political rhetoric of the United Nations about the postwar world into something tangible that the public could relate to – and it is to their creation and operation that the next two chapters are devoted.

CHAPTER 5

Justice for war crimes: Auschwitz and Nuremburg

Rudolf Hoess, commander of Auschwitz, was convicted and sentenced to death in April 1947 by the Polish War Crimes Tribunal in Warsaw for murdering people,

> by [agonizing] asphyxiation in gas-chambers, shooting, hanging, lethal injections of phenol, by medical experiments causing death, systematic starvation, by creating special conditions in the camp which were causing a high rate of mortality, by excessive work of the inmates, and by other methods.[1]

In December 1942, the Big Three had issued a statement on behalf of all the United Nations which explicitly accused Germany of implementing Hitler's oft-stated goal of exterminating the Jews of Europe and using Poland as the principal slaughterhouse. Given this statement, it is hard to understand why there has been discussion since the war as to when the Allied governments knew about the Holocaust.

The Polish tribunal that brought Hoess to justice was one of the national prosecution systems encouraged by the United Nations War Crimes Commission (UNWCC), created in October 1943 by 17 nations at war with the Axis. The UNWCC was the main legal response to Nazi crimes during the war and laid the groundwork in law and evidence for the trials at Nuremberg. The UNWCC provided the first multinational agreement on a range of international crimes prior to the celebrated Nuremberg and Tokyo trials. Moreover, the national tribunals supported by the UNWCC brought thousands of war criminals to justice.

The UNWCC is virtually unknown today. Access to its files at the UN in New York remain blocked by undisclosed nations. Anyone seeking access needs authorization from both their government and the UN. Even then they are not permitted to make any record of what they read.[2] Both the history of Nazi crimes and ideas for effectively bringing criminals to justice remain hidden. This chapter explores what is known of its work and why it may be still suppressed. The discussion by its very nature is something of a bureaucratic detective story.

The trials at Nuremburg and Tokyo have occupied a disproportionate position in modern legal scholarship and are generally considered to be the exclusion of the work of both UNWCC and national tribunals, including those in Belgium, China, France, India, The Netherlands, Norway and Yugoslavia.

The UNWCC established in 1943 consisted of representatives of states and a secretariat. It was based in London and organized into subcommittees, which dealt separately with compiling lists of accused war criminals, deciding whether *prima facie* cases existed and developing and agreeing what constituted crimes. The committees provided advice and support to member states' own national tribunals which carried out trials. In parallel, in November 1943, Britain, the USA and the Soviet Union agreed that the major criminal leaders of Germany would be tried by a tribunal constituted by themselves, and this was the basis of what developed into the Nuremburg International Military Tribunal, with the authority of all the United Nations.

The UNWCC and then the International Military Tribunal (IMT, opened on 18 October 1945 in the Palace of Justice in Nuremberg) developed the concept of international crime to include crimes against peace, against humanity and then genocide. The idea of criminal responsibility for launching an aggressive war was new, as was the creation of the concept of criminal organizations and the development of mixed civil/military courts. Particularly controversial was the idea of trying Germans for crimes against other Germans as well as for citizens of states attacked by Germany.

The development of the UNWCC was the result of pressure from the exiled governments of Europe, and of civil society, notably Jewish and Christian organizations. That they sought and succeeded in achieving the creation of a United Nations organization to deal with war crimes demonstrates the power of the rhetoric of the Four Freedoms, the Atlantic Charter and the Declaration by United Nations in motivating and focusing people into turning these ideas into a reality that outlasted the war. The development of the UNWCC alongside the new organizations for food, aid and economic development provided a mutually reinforcing sense of a comprehensive approach to the post-war period.

National tribunals supported by the UNWCC conducted 3,470 trials and achieved 2,857 convictions in Europe by March 1948. Of these, the US court at Dachau tried 1,500 cases; 28 per cent of those accused were executed, 57 per cent imprisoned and 15 per cent acquitted. In the Far East, about 1,900 people were tried for war crimes, of whom 480 were executed, 1,030 imprisoned and 414 acquitted. Twenty-two Nazi leaders were also tried at the Nuremburg International Military Tribunal before American, British, French and Soviet judges, but it was the national tribunals that performed the largest role in the prosecution of war criminals.

That the UNWCC and these courts existed at all was the result of intense political argument amongst the United Nations that in the end produced agreement that justice rather than mere revenge was essential. Summary executions of Nazi SS men certainly occurred and Churchill, Roosevelt and Stalin all at various times favoured the summary execution of the Nazi leadership as they were found by their advancing armies. Nevertheless, a judicial system was created and implemented and the visionary ideals of the United Nations provided legitimacy to the process.

Anyone supportive of the international trial of modern war criminals owes a debt of gratitude to those who created and worked for the UNWCC in the mid-1940s. The UNWCC developed the basis in international law for the war crimes trials and established a system of evidence collection and legal support for 17 national offices. In particular, the UNWCC developed the then revolutionary argument that the international community had a right to try German leaders for the crimes they had committed against Germans. The initial tasks of the commission were to investigate and record evidence of war crimes and those responsible, and to report to member governments cases in which it appeared that adequate evidence appeared likely to be forthcoming. A third function was the creation of an expert Legal Committee to advise on what might or might not be considered to be international crimes. Its work had the most lasting impact. And the precedents set by the UNWCC also included agreement that environmental destruction constitutes a war crime, which may indicate its relevance to those seeking to develop international criminal law in the twenty-first century.[3] A good starting point for anyone concerned with the details of UNWCC work, is its official history, published in 1948, which provided a significant resource for this chapter.

The exiled governments of Czechoslovakia and Poland were at the forefront of efforts to create the UNWCC. Their officials were powerless to help their suffering populations at home, and this gave them great incentive to attempt to deter further Nazi atrocities by seeking an international process to bring justice and retribution to their perpetrators. This initial effort from small nations was assisted by Christian and Jewish groups, including William Temple, the Archbishop of Canterbury, and eventually supported by the major powers. But the effort to create a process to hold war criminals to account was resisted by the British Foreign Office and the US State Department; both were opposed to establishing a principle of interference in nations' internal affairs. In addition, the experience of the Treaty of Versailles and its aftermath was not encouraging: the Treaty's provisions on war crimes were never implemented. Instead, a German court at Leipzig tried alleged German criminals. Few were tried, fewer sentenced and none were imprisoned. The creation of the UNWCC not only provided much of the groundwork for modern war crimes prosecutions, it also serves as an example that even in wartime, and even more than 70 years ago, coalitions of like-minded governments and public opinion can bring lasting benefit to the world.

Today, the UNWCC is almost forgotten in a history of war crimes trials that seems to start at Nuremberg. For example, in 2009 the UK National Archive entry for 'War Crime Trials' provided a guide to the topic which has no mention of the UNWCC.[4] Arieh Kochavi, a scholar of the Holocaust, argued in 1998 that the existing holocaust literature does not do justice to the work of the UNWCC, its importance as an action of the Western powers in the face of Nazi actions and as the basis of much of the thinking that went into the Nuremburg Charter.[5] In 1947, the British Foreign Office had held the same view in papers not made public for decades. In a document insisting on the rapid closure of the UNWCC, it argued,

'It has proved to be a most valuable centre for the collection and sifting of information relating to war crimes, and the advice which it has given on questions of law and procedure has been of great assistance to Governments represented on the Commission. The Commission has thus played a great part in the work of bringing Nazi war criminals and their associates to justice.' The first national statements on the unprecedented nature of Nazi atrocities came in a Czech and Polish joint declaration in November 1940,[6] followed by a Polish statement on the Nazi attempt to eradicate Polish national identity.[7] In October 1941, there were parallel announcements by Roosevelt and then Churchill promising 'retribution' – Churchill stressed that these crimes were occurring 'above all behind the German fronts in Russia' and that retribution '[for] these crimes must henceforward take its place among the major purposes of the war'.[8] In November 1941 and January 1942, the Soviet Foreign Ministry issued notes on German atrocities to all nations with which it had diplomatic relations.[9] International lawyers began to develop a discussion on 'crimes against international public order' at Cambridge University, the International Commission for Penal Reconstruction and Development, and the London International Assembly.[10] In the USA, similar work was conducted at Harvard by Sheldon Glueck and an historian of the US Supreme Court, Charles Warren.

The Czechs and Poles continually pushed both Churchill and Roosevelt for the creation of a United Nations War Crimes Commission. In January 1942, the British Foreign Secretary Anthony Eden attended a meeting at St James's Palace with the exiled governments, although his officials opposed his going. They did not wish the proceedings to have the status that the presence of the British Foreign Secretary would accord it. Six months later, the British Government endorsed the creation of a 'United Nations Commission on Atrocities' and the 'Suggested Functions for the United Nations Commission for the Investigation of War Crimes'. Its function was to be fact-finding and to produce reports. The British advised, however, that '[T]he suggestion of some sort of international court for the trial of war criminals is to be deprecated. Nor is it necessary or desirable to create a new body of international law, for war crimes are already sufficiently well defined', but thought that the commission might validate the membership of national war crimes tribunals.[11]

Roosevelt did not yet endorse creating an organization but said on 21 August 1942 that,

> The United Nations are going to win this war. When victory has been achieved, it is the purpose of the Government of the United States, as I know it is the purpose of each of the United Nations, to make appropriate use of the information and evidence in respect to these barbaric crimes of the invaders, in Europe and in Asia. It seems only fair that they should have this warning that the time will come when they shall have to stand in courts of law in the very countries which they are now oppressing and answer for their acts.[12]

By September 1942, John Winant, the US Ambassador in London, was seeking an urgent decision from Roosevelt on US support for a war crimes commission. He had personally received 200 petitions from British organizations supporting the proposed war crimes commission and the British Government was also being pressured to make a public statement.[13] In October 1942, Roosevelt finally agreed to issue a statement in coordination with the British, supporting the creation of the commission. The Soviet Union expressed support and called for the immediate trial of Rudolf Hess (no relation to Hoess), apparently envisaging an internationalized version of the show trials conducted by Stalin during the purges of the 1930s. Hess, Hitler's deputy, had parachuted into Scotland in May 1941 with a scheme to broker a British-German peace agreement. The Soviet Union wanted him tried immediately as a war criminal and suspected he might be used by Churchill in some negotiation with Germany.

Eventually, on 17 December 1942, these negotiations produced a further statement that was issued simultaneously in London, Moscow and Washington on behalf of the United Nations.[14] This was the first multinational condemnation of the fact that Hitler was implementing a programme to exterminate Europe's Jews. It is worth considering in full, not least because it is often ignored in studies that discuss what and when the Allies knew about the Holocaust.[15] In London it took the form of a question and answer on the floor of the House of Commons.

United Nations Declaration
Mr Samuel Silverman, MP (Nelson and Colne)

> Asked the Secretary of State for Foreign Affairs whether he has any statement to make regarding the plan of the German Government to deport all Jews from the occupied countries to Eastern Europe and there put them to death before the end of the year?

Mr Anthony Eden, MP

Yes, Sir, I regret to have to inform the House that reliable reports have recently reached His Majesty's Government regarding the barbarous and inhuman treatment to which Jews are being subjected in German-occupied Europe. They have in particular received a note from the Polish Government, which was also communicated to other United Nations and which has received wide publicity in the Press. His Majesty's Government in the United Kingdom have as a result been in consultation with the United States and Soviet Governments and with the other Allied Governments directly concerned, and I should like to take this opportunity to communicate to the House the text of the following declaration which is being made public to-day at this hour in London, Moscow and Washington:

'The attention of the Governments of Belgium, Czechoslovakia, Greece, Luxembourg, the Netherlands, Norway, Poland, the United States of America, the United Kingdom of Great Britain and Northern Ireland, the Union of Soviet Socialist Republics and Yugoslavia, and of the French National Committee has been drawn to numerous reports from Europe that the German authorities, not content with denying to persons of Jewish race in all the territories over which their barbarous rule has been extended, the most elementary human rights, are now carrying into effect Hitler's oft repeated intention to exterminate the Jewish people in Europe. From all the occupied countries Jews are being transported, in conditions of appalling horror and brutality, to Eastern Europe. In Poland, which has been made the principal Nazi slaughterhouse, the ghettoes established by the German invaders are being systematically emptied of all Jews except a few highly skilled workers required for war industries. None of those taken away are ever heard of again. The able-bodied are slowly worked to death in labour camps. The infirm are left to die of exposure and starvation or are deliberately massacred in mass executions. The number of victims of these bloody cruelties is reckoned in many hundreds of thousands of entirely innocent men, women and children.

The above mentioned Governments and the French National Committee condemn in the strongest possible terms this bestial policy of cold-blooded extermination. They declare that such events can only strengthen the resolve of all freedom loving peoples to overthrow the barbarous Hitlerite tyranny. They re-affirm their solemn resolution to ensure that those responsible for these crimes shall not escape retribution, and to press on with the necessary practical measures to this end'.[16]

It still took almost another year before anything concrete was done to try to bring the perpetrators to justice. When the UNWCC came into being in the autumn of 1943, the declaration on atrocities by the four foreign ministers in Moscow set out the general approach of the major powers to war crimes. Disputes between the Western and Soviet governments over the representation of the Soviet Republics as independent states served to keep the Soviet Union out of the organization. The Soviet Union also criticized the terms of reference of the UNWCC for not going far enough, and especially for not making preparation for committing a war of aggression and crimes against humanity into crimes.[17] The Soviet Union pursued its own war crimes process in Kharkov.

18 Nazi leaders inspecting the Auschwitz extermination and industrial complex, 17–18 July 1942. From left to right, SS officer Rudolf Brandt, Reichsfuhrer-SS Heinrich Himmler, Chief Engineer Max Faust (centre), and Camp Commandant Rudolf Hoess (right) at an inspection of the Monowitz-Buna plant (Auschwitz III) at Auschwitz, Poland.

The statement on the extermination of the Jews and the work to create the commission did not result in major changes of humanitarian policy towards those fleeing extermination. An Anglo-American conference on refugees in the Bahamas in April 1943 achieved nothing substantial, although, in 1944, Roosevelt did establish the US War Refugees Board which enabled the escape of some Jews from Europe.

As a balance to the overall discussion in this chapter of attempts to implement justice, consider this statement by one of Churchill's ministers, Viscount Cranbourne. He explained in March 1943 that the Jews should not really be regarded as a special case and that the British Empire was so full of refugees that it could barely take any more because those fleeing extermination could not be guaranteed an adequate diet. His lack of urgency in the face of the slaughter condemned by Eden is indicative of the indifference and hostility that the members of the UNWCC and the Jews themselves faced from some British officials:

'The noble Lord must not regard this as a Jewish problem. Every nation in Europe is being tortured by the Germans, and the noble Lord will only do the Jews themselves harm by taking that attitude. The present situation in East Africa, from the food point of view, is not a happy one. It is a very difficult one, and I understand, having made careful inquiries, that it is really undesirable to take any more refugees into East Africa at present'. Cranbourne went on to make similar excuses for the rest of the British Empire.[18]

In the presence of such a policy on the living from Churchill's government, the creation of the UNWCC to bring justice for the dead could only ever be a small recompense. But what the commission did achieve, who the energetic people were who gave it life and how their achievement resonates today are what we should now consider.

There were intense debates amongst the commissioners about what exactly constituted war crimes. The representatives of Britain, France, China, Norway, the Netherlands, Greece, India and New Zealand sought 'vindication of law and justice' according to existing ideas of what amounted to a war crime. Meanwhile Australia, Czechoslovakia, Poland, Yugoslavia and Belgium sought to invent new laws – ones familiar to us today – in response to the new circumstances imposed by Hitler's Third Reich.[19]

With the support of some governments, and with an accompanying campaign in the press, a range of new ideas were suggested, many of which were adopted.[20] Within the commission, this effort was led by experts such as the Czech official General Dr Bohuslav Ecer, Jewish organizations, the Poles and the Archbishop of Canterbury who lobbied for the UNWWC to consider crimes against the Jews as a category and crimes carried out by the Nazis against the Jews as war crimes. Ecer led the push in the debates in Commission Committee III to widen the definition of war crimes. The committee developed the notion of aggressive war as a crime and considered assaults by Nazis against Jews to be crimes against humanity; its ideas played a large role in the Nuremberg Charter of 8 August 1945.[21]

Herbert Pell, the US envoy and an old school friend of Roosevelt's, was strongly in support of this, but there was no agreement to specify crimes against Jews as a special category. Nevertheless, the concepts of aggressive war, making organizations such as the SS unlawful, mixed civil/military courts, and crimes committed by Germans against their own nationals from 1933 onwards were all agreed by the end of 1944.[22]

This last category was the most controversial for traditionally minded diplomats. A clear principle of how nations were supposed to behave was that they should not interfere in each other's sovereign internal affairs. Political meddling in other countries has always gone on – and does today – but formally and publicly it was not supposed to happen. This 'Westphalian principle' dates back to the mid-seventeenth century and the religious wars of that period. The Westphalian agreement was supposed to stop Catholics and Protestants fighting wars on behalf of their co-religionists in other countries.

UNITED NATIONS WAR CRIMES COMMISSION

CANADIAN   CHARGES AGAINST   GERMAN   WAR CRIMINALS

CHARGE No. 67/CRO/12 SS/1

Name of accused, his rank and unit, or official position. *(Not to be translated.)*	1. Brigadeführer Kurt MEYER, Commander of the 25th Panzer Grenadier Regiment, 12th SS Panzer Division (Hitler-Jugend) from August 1943 until approximately 10th June 1944 and GOC 12th SS Panzer Division (Hitler Jugend) from the latter date until 7 September 1944. 2. A soldier believed to have been attached to the HQ of the said 25th Panzer Grenadier Regiment on the 8th day of June 1944 and believed to be of the rank of Untercharführer and the actual perpetrator of the crime referred to in Number 1 hereunder.
Date and place of commission of alleged crime.	Period August 1943 to 7th September 1944 at various places in BELGIUM and FRANCE and particularly LE SAP FRANCE and the vicinity of CAEN, NORMANDY also in FRANCE.
Number and description of crime in war crimes list. References to relevant provisions of national law.	(i) MURDER. (xxvii) Giving an order to give no quarter. Breech of Usages of Warfare and Laws of War especially provisions of Geneva Convention 1929. Murder and incitement to murder

SHORT STATEMENT OF FACTS.

The first accused on the 8th day of June 1944 ... ...

CONTINUATION OF 'SHORT STATEMENT OF FACTS'

Village of AUTHIE and a Canadian Chaplain taken prisoner was likewise murdered on the 7th June 1944 in addition to those killed under his direct order at the ABBAYE on the 8th June.

During the period of his command as GOC 12 SS Panzer Division (Hitler-Jugend) 8 cases of the killing of prisoners of War have been reported believed to be chargeable to the members of this division.

... ... understood. 27 Canadian prisoners were murdered at the

19 United Nations War Crimes Commission form for recording war crimes.

Nazi crimes created a strong public desire for intervention, with which Pell agreed. He had had experience as the US Ambassador to Hitler's ally, Hungary, before Pearl Harbor and to neutral Portugal, and had seen something of Nazi behaviour in Poland. Pell argued that the UNWCC legal committee define 'crimes against humanity' to include 'people attacked because of their race or religion'.[23] However, his superiors in the State Department were adamantly opposed to this course of action and his actions in the commission on this policy were in direct contradiction to his instructions.

In May 1944, at its offices in the Royal Courts of Justice in London, the commission produced a groundbreaking paper on broadening the definition of war crimes. The commission had been blocked from agreeing to a policy of charging Germans for crimes against Germans, but the reaction of the commission members was to send out a paper to a wider group of officials back in their national capitals, and especially in Washington, DC, seeking support for broadening the definition of crime. The paper stated:

> The Commission is of the opinion that the question of the punishment of offences committed in enemy territory [i.e. Germany] against enemy nationals [i.e. Germans] or stateless persons on account of their race, religion, or political opinions, requires immediate consideration. Unless other steps have already been taken, or are in contemplation, with a view to such consideration, the Commission would be ready to undertake this task, if the Constituent Governments so desire. The Commission accordingly requests those Governments to state whether they desire it to undertake a study of this question with a view to making recommendations to them upon it.[24]

The reaction from London and Washington was to fire their representatives to the UNWCC for trying to make German actions against other Germans into crime. But though they slammed the door, the horse had bolted – the commission's papers were already in use around Washington.

In the USA, the sacking was done by the extraordinary step of Congress cutting the funds for Pell's salary out of the US budget. The Acting US Secretary of State, Joseph Grew, and legal chief, Green Hackworth, appeared to have initiated the action in conjunction with those members of Congress who favoured delaying the creation of the court until after the surrender of Germany. That idea was 'just damned nonsense' according to Pell, and 'would guarantee the escape of the criminals'.[25]

In Washington, DC for consultations at the State Department and with Roosevelt, Pell was tricked. He checked in with Hackworth before going to see Roosevelt, but Hackworth kept both Pell and Roosevelt in the dark about the Congressional action. Roosevelt supported Pell's view and told him to get back to London immediately and get the UNWCC moving. Pell took the message back to Hackworth, who at that point told him he had been sacked by Congress.

Though Hackworth and Grew succeeded in getting rid of Pell, they failed to prevent the ideas he favoured being incorporated into the Nuremburg Charter. The wider argument in Washington on war crimes in early 1945 centred on whether to simply execute Nazis on the spot as they were found, or whether to have a legal process. Henry Morgenthau, the Treasury Secretary, favoured summary execution. It was Henry Stimson, the Secretary of War, who most strongly favoured trials. He had been Secretary of State in the 1920s and regarded German actions as a violation of the Kellogg-Briand Pact (named after the French and US foreign ministers who led the negotiations). Those states that signed 'solemnly declared in the names of their respective peoples that they condemn recourse to war for the solution of international controversies, and renounce it, as an instrument of national policy in their relations with one another'.[26] Stimson considered that violation of the pact by waging aggressive war constituted a crime in international law.

The UNWCC papers went to Stimson's official in charge of war crimes policy, Lt. Col. Murray C. Bernay. He agreed with the commission's position that an international court should consider the internal crimes of the enemy.[27] But agreeing what was a crime was one thing; agreeing who should try the cases was another.

After complex debate, the commission agreed to recommend to member governments the creation of a permanent United Nations international war crimes court: the 'Convention for the Establishment of a United Nations Joint Court to try crimes against the laws and customs of war', agreed on 26 September 1944. This convention was strongly opposed by both the US State Department and the UK Foreign Office; neither wanted a supranational body of this sort and it was never adopted.

The rejection of the UNWCC proposal for an international criminal court left the use of national courts, such as that which tried the Auschwitz commander in Poland, as the only proposed legal recourse until the closing weeks of the war. As the war in Europe ended, two new facts influenced the establishment of the Nuremberg tribunal. Harry Truman became President on the death of Roosevelt, and Western troops and reporters entered Nazi camps. The shock, media outrage and public revulsion over the camps created a new impulse to ensure that the Nazis were held to account for their crimes against the Germans. Truman personally favoured the creation of a tribunal for the senior officials in the Nazi regime. The Moscow Declaration of October 1943 had stipulated that these senior officials were to be tried by the major powers, supported court appointed by the United Nations as a whole. The President and his advisors had to take the initiative as the Soviets had their own trial system and the Western Allies were looking to Washington to lead.

In this new political climate, the principles proposed by the UNWCC bloomed under the belated glow of official support. The UNWCC proposals, transmitted to the receptive Stimson, as well as to the politically deaf officials at the State Department, were adopted in large part. Truman's choice to lead the USA at the Tribunal, Justice Robert Jackson, also favoured this approach.[28] Without the ideas from the UNWCC at this critical point in a fast-moving process, the Nuremberg principles would have been likely to have lacked ideas such as criminalizing organizations and making the Nazis responsible for crimes against Germans – and in that case, so too would have been international criminal law in the twenty-first century.

In addition to contributing to the ideas that propelled the International Military Tribunal at Nuremberg, the UNWCC made other important contributions to bring war criminals to justice, in particular the identification and pursuit of the accused.

Sir David Maxwell Fife, Britain's main prosecutor at the Nuremberg trials, explained that,

> It should not be thought, however, that the selection of the accused was a random matter. By the beginning of 1943 the British Government had taken steps to initiate the United Nations War Crimes Commission. ... The procedure of the United Nations War Crimes Commission was that the National Office of each country sent in particulars of any war crime of which it received information. The Commission then examined the report to see whether there was a prima facie case. If it so found, the case was then passed to the legal authorities of the country concerned.[29]

The commission relied on reports from the 17 national offices as it did not have investigative or executive power. Some of the national offices, notably Canada's, conducted their investigations under the title of the UNWCC using a standard document for recording war crimes charges. The Research Office of the UNWCC compiled *prima facie* evidence against major and lesser suspects and provided these according to the category of crime to the International Military Tribunal.[30] UNWCC officials also encouraged the Western military in Europe under General Eisenhower to start hunting for war criminals. Eisenhower's headquarters (SHAEF – Supreme Headquarters Allied Expeditionary Force) had set up a system, the Central Register of War Criminal and Security Suspects (CROWCASS), for interrogating German prisoners, but did not on its own initiative start looking for new ones. With UNWCC's encouragement, it took on an investigative function.[31]

President Truman issued an Executive Order requiring that the US Chief Counsel to the IMT, Justice Robert H. Jackson and his staff 'examine the evidence already gathered by the United Nations War Crimes Commission in London and by the various Allied Armies and other agencies'.[32]

Jackson confirmed in June to the President that he had 'arranged cooperation and mutual assistance with the United Nations War Crimes Commission and with Counsel appointed to represent the United Kingdom in
the joint prosecution', and that while the IMT would deal with the major
criminals, 'a second class of offender, the prosecution of which will not
interfere with the major case, consists of those who, under the Moscow
Declaration are to be sent back to the scene of their crimes for trial by local
authorities . . . The UNWCC (in full) is especially concerned with cases of
this kind'.[33] The UN archives still hold the UNWCC files which contain
lists of 36,000 suspected war criminals and the Central Register of War
Criminal and Security Suspects.

After the trials, the commission selected and prepared for publication
(by the British and other governments) the *Law Reports of Trials of War
Criminals* in 15 volumes. Lord Wright provided commentaries to each volume on both the substance of the trials and the evolution of national and
international criminal law and the laws of war. The mere publication of
the trial reports was a vital action in establishing the legal precedents of
the application of international law that are the building blocks of law in
Anglo-American systems. As the Commission's chairman, the Australian
Lord Wright explained,

> The cases reported here, like the other cases reported in this series, have as their
> purpose the illustration of the general principles of that part of international
> law which deals with the law and custom of war. . . . This represents the normal
> course of procedure in the evolution of the Anglo-American common law but
> also of the rules of international law.[34]

These publications provide a rich source of material for international
lawyers concerned with the development of international criminal law.
Additional research is needed into the surviving records of the national
tribunals, as well as the minutes of the proceedings of the various UN-
WCC committees, for Wright's official history is the only known survey
of these materials. Particular attention should be given to the proceedings
of the London conference of the 17 national offices held in March 1945 at
which the commission and national delegations discussed how the central
organization could support national efforts. The UNWCC also published a
weekly bulletin from July 1945 to February 1948 and a 'War Crimes News
Digest' from October 1945 to March 1948. The archives of the UNWCC
should be made public.

In the twenty-first century, the precedents established by the UNWCC
are used in legal analysis, for example, as the first point at which gender-
based crimes became international law, but only in a fragmentary
way.[35]

Until the establishment of the UNWCC, international criminal law
barely existed. The UNWCC provided the base not just for Nuremburg and

the Tokyo trials, but also for the present International Criminal Court (ICC) and the special international criminal tribunals established for Yugoslavia, Rwanda and elsewhere.

The demise of the UNWCC, in 1948, related directly to shifts in US policy away from international organizations in favour of bilateral arrangements. The US Government moved to reduce attention on German war crimes and make secret the lists of suspects during the later 1940s. The British and US priority was to rebuild Western Germany and use former Nazis to pursue Western goals.

One of the most notorious examples of this policy concerns Claus Barbie. Barbie was Gestapo Chief in the French industrial centre of Lyon in 1943 and 1944. He had led German efforts to crush the resistance and ordered the capture of Jean Moulin, head of the resistance. His awards from the German government for his work included a letter from the head of the SS, Heinrich Himmler, praising Barbie's 'special achievements in the field of criminology and untiring efforts in combating a resistance organization'.[36] In 1947, the US Army recruited Barbie as an agent and then ensured his safe passage to Bolivia where he lived for over 30 years. In 1983, he was expelled by the Bolivians and returned to France. As a result of the public scandal which ensued, the US Government produced a detailed and frank account of its earlier protection of Barbie and the British and American policy of using and protecting Nazis. If Barbie provides an individual example, the wholesale absorption of the Nazi intelligence organization run by Colonel Rheinhard Gehlen provides the example of the institutional approach of the US Government. Gehlen, 'the brains' of the Nazi army in the East, was taken on as an agent by the US Army in May 1945, and thousands of Nazis found protection through his organization which had a strong influence on the way American intelligence, and thereby the US Government, saw the Soviet Union.

Christopher Simpson argues that the UNWCC was shut down at the instigation of the State Department's legal chief, Green Hackworth, in order to facilitate the rehabilitation of Nazis into West German society and cooperation with the USA. He contends that Allen Dulles, a leading US intelligence official, used an agent, Ivan Kerno, who was the legal counsel at the UN in New York, to suppress the files the UNWCC had collected.[37] Other nations also used the UNWCC for political purposes. For example, Michael Palumbo argues that a file faked by the Yugoslav communist government on the Austrian Secretary General of the UN, Kurt Waldheim, was at the heart of allegations against Waldheim concerning his wartime activities (Palumbo, The Waldheim Files, 1988).

One especially sad result of the premature closure of UNWCC in 1948 was that it prevented the Ethiopian Government from obtaining the assistance of the international community in pursuing the Italian generals who

20 A pile of human bones and skulls at Majdanek extermination camp, 1944.

had conquered them. Evidence of Italian war crimes in Ethiopia was only submitted to the UNWCC by the Ethiopian Government of Emperor Haile Salassi in November 1948, by which time the commission was closing. The delay in presenting charges was caused by the extreme difficulty the Ethiopian Government had in working in a country where all the educated people had been systematically killed by the Italians.

Amongst the crimes it hoped to prosecute was the use of poison (mustard gas) spread by crop-spraying equipment from Italian warplanes. The correspondence between the Italian generals and Mussolini authorizing the gassing was published with the charges. The leading exponent of this policy was General, later Marshal, Badoglio who later arranged for Italy to change sides in September 1944. Amongst the evidence was a statement from Sidney Brown about the use of poison gas on the Ethiopian Army's positions. Brown was the International Committee of the Red Cross (ICRC) delegate on the spot at the time. He recorded that 'the whole plain of Kworam looks like a vision from Dante's Inferno; from 7 a.m. to 5 p.m. the Italians never cease dropping bombs and spurting poisonous gas'.[38]

Badoglio became one of the first to distance himself from war crimes. John Stanleigh, a German Jewish refugee, fought in the British parachute regiment. In September 1943, he was sent as the translator with a British and US general to negotiate with Badoglio.[39] The talks took place in English and Stanleigh's Italian was unnecessary – but he took advantage of the Allied generals' inability to comprehend Italian to question the marshal.

I was told many years later by John Stanleigh, then a British sergeant, of his attempt to take issue with Badolgio. He was present during the secret armistice negotiations in Italy and, in a side conversation, asked Badoglio whether he was not worried about being held accountable after the war. 'For what?' answered the marshal. 'The gassing in Ethiopia, for example', came back the sergeant. 'Oh that was the Fascists', said Badoglio.[40]

The fact that war crimes are a normal part of our political language and legal debates is usually traced back to the trials of Nazi leaders at Nuremberg and the Japanese at Tokyo. Although the UNWCC did not itself try cases, the scope of its work was broader than today's International Criminal Court (ICC). For example, as African states seek to develop their capacity to conduct trials, they would have benefited from the advisory and legitimating functions performed by the UNWCC. In the twenty-first century, the idea of a worldwide network of war crimes investigations and prosecution offices linked to UN headquarters and investigators going to battlefronts around the world gathering evidence of war crimes may, to some, be a case of world government gone mad, or to others as essential to bringing justice to the aggrieved.

The ICC is prepared to take evidence but it has little investigative ability. Yet almost 70 years ago there was a United Nations war crimes commission with national staff collecting evidence gathered by member states in Europe and in Asia. In America, conservatives oppose UN-organized efforts against war criminals and yet the USA led the effort for prosecutions through a United Nations system in the most dangerous war that the USA has ever been engaged in.

Nevertheless, a key problem remains. Was this just victor's justice? The victorious nations were never going to try their own service personnel before the same courts as faced by the defeated. This alone gives grounds for the accusation of partial or victor's justice. However, on occasion, the victorious powers did try their own service personnel for violations of the laws of war.[41]

The broader accusation is that the mass aerial bombing of civilians in Germany and Japan, including Hiroshima and Nagasaki, constituted war crimes. Robert McNamara came to the view that the bombing of defenceless Japanese cities, in particular by mass raids of B-29 bombers flying at high altitude above the reach of any Japanese air defence, were such crimes.

Most obviously, the debate in the UNWCC on the prosecution of state leaders for crimes against their own people was not led by the major powers but by small nations that had been conquered by the Nazis, by civil society and by principled officials within the American and British Governments. A study of national and United Nations statements during the war also shows that there was clear intent and warning of prosecution during the war, with the hope that this would act as a deterrent to further crimes by the Nazis. These warnings contradict the argument that the Nuremberg principles and trials were retrospective.

An evaluation of the UNWCC is helped by comparison with twenty first century practice. The argument made by the UNWCC for the creation of a permanent International Criminal Court in the 1940s was similar to that which eventually succeeded in creating such a court in 2006, to try cases where it was not possible to try the defendants in the host country.

When, in 1998, 139 states created the ICC, based in The Hague, Netherlands, its principal mandate was to try cases where a state will not try its own citizens accused of war crimes, where people were accused in several countries, or to apprehend people seeking to disappear through legal loopholes.[42]

A further and detailed study of the decisions of the UNWCC on what constituted a war crime and on whether *prima facie* cases existed in thousands of individual case files, as well the 17 national processes, would enrich the twenty-first century debates on war crimes with new precedents. In some cases, the quality of justice was doubtless poor. Nevertheless, the number of acquittals and custodial sentences compared to executions are themselves substantive evidence that the trials at the end of World War II were not merely legalized lynching.

The support by the 17 members of the UNWCC, and not merely the major powers, for the inclusion of the ideas that found their way onto the list of international crimes by the four-power International Military Tribunal at Nuremberg provides a greater degree of legitimacy. This would be enhanced by an awareness amongst international criminal lawyers of the debates within the UNWCC, its associated national conferences and the conference of national offices held by the UNWCC. Similarly, the types of charges and the interpretation of the scope with which the courts treated war crimes should be examined.

All in all, the development of the UNWCC, the associated nations' offices and courts and the Soviet trials all provide a broader and stronger base of organizational practice and legal precedent for the development of international criminal law than is provided by the major trials of the war criminals at Nuremberg and in Tokyo. The arguments about Nuremberg and Tokyo continue today with the development of the International Criminal Court.[43]

While the UNWCC tried to bring justice after the atrocities of war, the main focus of the United Nations was on preventing new wars from occurring. There was a general consensus that a prime cause of war was want. Indeed, from the perspective of the creators of the United Nations system, the primary means of preventing the mass abuse of human rights lay in preventing economic collapse and high unemployment. This was the prime motivation behind the creation of multilateral bodies during the war to co-ordinate global programmes for relief of those liberated from occupation, national reconstruction and the first globally regulated economic system. These are the topics of the next two chapters.

CHAPTER 6

Post-war relief and reconstruction: UNRRA

It was reported in July 1944 that 'in Greece it is estimated that half the child population has died of starvation',[1] This scale of suffering is indicative of the experience of millions of people under occupation even when they were far from the major battlefronts, for there had been only a limited resistance war in Greece after it was overrun by German forces in April 1941. In areas where the battles and bombing were prolonged, the experience was far worse.

As the Axis countries were defeated, the United Nations sent help to the liberated areas of Europe and Asia. The organization of such assistance, along with Lend-Lease, provided the most tangible evidence of effective international collaboration for peace, realizing the rhetoric of the United Nations at war. It saved millions of lives, resuscitated national economies and provided a foundation for today's UN organizations. Engagement between the Soviet Union, China, India and the European and American states indicated to all concerned that the powerful would try to work with each other and at least engage with the weak. Altogether, 44 nations created the United Nations Relief and Rehabilitation Administration (UNRRA) in 1943. By 1946, it had become the largest single exporter in the world, shipping supplies to devastated areas in Asia and Europe. In Greece and many other places, UNRRA fed the starving.[2]

UNRRA remains the most important cooperative international post-war aid and reconstruction effort that has ever existed.[3] Its expenditure of $4 billion was administered by an international staff paid for by national contributions. It was directed in succession by two prominent New York liberal politicians, Herbert Lehman, of the banking family, and Fiorella La Guardia. UNRRA headquarters were at Dupont Circle in Washington, DC, using training facilities at College Park, Maryland.[4]

Plans for the liberation included famine relief and disease control, as well as rebuilding infrastructure, farming and manufacturing industries. At their best, UNRRA's operations from 1945 to 1948 were apparently more comprehensive, better coordinated and less bureaucratic than comparable work by the UN, the USA and Europe in the twenty-first century. One in-dividual's experience is an example of the diversity of the programme: too old to fight, Harold Jacoby, a college professor from Oakland, California, went to work for UNRRA. In 1945, he was in Egypt and Kenya organizing the feeding and repatriation of Greek refugees.[5]

The new organization had to put up with waiting until the needs of the military had been met and with all the conflicting pressures of global poli-tics in the mid-1940s. UNRRA itself was seen by its creators as an example and first stage in a spectrum of global civilian operations. It originated in separate discussions in London and Washington, and although UNRRA was never intended to be permanent, many regarded its end in 1948 as pre-mature. In the view of one of its advocates, UNRRA was killed by President Truman to make room for the Marshall Plan of 1948.[6] UNRRA opponents in the USA considered this not a moment too soon to shut down what they regarded as a profligate example of the 'globalony' New Deal poli-cies of the Roosevelt era. Consequently, the Marshall Plan totally eclipsed UNRRA in the history of the post-war period.

UNRRA's resources included donations from all member states, how-ever small, in the form of commodities such as food and textiles as well as cash. Its bureaucratic costs were low; administrative expenses were 1.18 per cent. In comparison, the US Agency for International Development and associated economic development programmes had, in 2010, a budget of around $17.5 billion with administrative expenses in 2009 of $348 million (around 2 per cent) – nearly double the administrative cost of UNRRA.

The lessons to be learned from UNRRA extend beyond administrative prudence to include the democratic self-management of refugee camps. That refugees should operate their own camps on democratic lines is an idea that is alien to the USA and the UN alike in the twenty-first century; however, in the 1940s it was part of the operating manual for both US military government and UNRRA.

In the 1940s, government planning for the post-war world built on what was done by the US Government and private organizations at the end of World War I. Famine and disease had spread across the war-affected areas at the end of the 1914–8 war. Armies consumed huge quantities of food, kept men from farming and laid waste to productive land in the war zones. The influenza pandemic of 1918 then killed 40 million people, many of whom were too weakened by malnutrition to resist the disease.

America had been at the forefront of food aid during and after the 1914–18 war. Led by Herbert Hoover, aid helped people in German-occupied Belgium until the USA entered the war in 1917. Later, he led famine relief to Russia in the years after the 1917 revolution. When Ger-many again conquered Belgium and then most of Europe in 1940, aid from the still neutral USA did not reach those under Nazi rule. Churchill refused to allow neutral ships through the blockade the British fleet enforced around the shores of Europe. He argued that nothing should be done to ease the burden of Nazi occupation, hoping to foment revolt against the Nazis. On 21 August 1940, during the Battle of Britain, Churchill declared his policy on relief to those under occupation in a Parliamentary speech:

> Let Hitler bear his responsibilities to the full, and let the people of Europe who groan beneath his yoke aid in every way the coming of the day when that yoke will be broken. Meanwhile we can and will arrange in advance for the speedy entry of food into any part of the enslaved area when this part has been wholly cleared of the German forces.[7]

Planning for this speedy entry of food began in London. Sir Frederick Leith-Ross, the government's Chief Economic Advisor, chaired a group of exiled governments in a committee that monitored the suffering on the continent and mapped out the minimum needs of relief once liberation came. This Inter-Allied Committee on Post-War Requirements was created on 24 September 1941, at the same meeting that endorsed the Atlantic Charter.

Churchill's statement on refusing to let supplies into occupied Europe when Britain itself faced the threat of occupation was an act of bravado. But the creation of this committee on post-war requirements was an act of optimism bordering on fantasy, for Hitler was at the peak of his power and liberation seemed a distant dream.

The Soviet Union was the first to suggest a fully international relief organization. Dean Acheson acknowledged that 'in January 1942 the Russians tossed into the London arena the first suggestion of an internationally controlled, manned and operated relief organization'.[8] The US State Department presented the UK with an outline proposal for such an organization in May 1942. Eden's positive response was based on the wider concern to build a post-war international structure:

> It must be obvious that for the success of any post-war relief scheme the contribution of the United States will be all-important. For that reason alone we should be well advised to fall in with the American proposals. But I fancy that there is much more than post-war relief in question. The United States Administration appear to be acting on the thesis that the more international machinery that can be got into operation with their participation before the end of the war, the greater the likelihood of American public opinion being ready to continue international co-operation after the war. It would perhaps be putting it too high at this stage to say that the Administration definitely intend to try and establish under the aegis of the 'United Nations' the embryo of the international organization of the future. American post-war co-operation in the international sphere being so vitally important, I submit that we must play up to any scheme of theirs tending to turn the United Nations into an operative piece of machinery.[9]

As 'machine operator', Roosevelt chose Herbert Lehman, one of America's leading bankers and a former Democrat governor of New York State, meeting with him on 11 November 1942. Coming just after the mid-term elections and the landings in North Africa, Roosevelt nevertheless found the time to focus on post-war requirements. He created a new State Department organization that Lehman was to head, the Office of Foreign Relief and Rehabilitation Operations, which became the Foreign Economic Assistance Office in March 1943.

The Roosevelt Administration's strategy was that these US organizations should form part of an international organization and not operate either by unilateral US actions in areas liberated by US forces or by a series of bilateral arrangements with individual Allies. US power was such that it would have been easy for the USA to make bilateral arrangements with individual states. Instead, the policy was to create a fully international agency which provided a collective forum for developing policy and sharing the burden or provision, while US power ensured that its desires usually prevailed.

Lehman first of all sent help to refugees that had fled to North Africa from Europe. He had a fight on his hands to get the supplies through. Naturally enough the military wanted all shipping to support the fighting, and many ships were still being sunk. The aid that did arrive went to camps run by the British in Palestine, Egypt and Kenya. Distribution was hindered by the hostility between the national and political factions among the refugees. Greeks and Yugoslavs, communists and royalists had to be separated to avoid fighting.

The USA finally convened a conference to create UNRRA for the autumn of 1943. The official New Zealand account records a sceptical response from smaller states, though they were reconciled to what had happened:

> On 10 June [1943] the United States sent to all United Nations governments a draft agreement for UNRRA, with the significant note that it had been approved by the big four and was to be published the following day. It was greeted with something like a chorus of protest by small European powers, who resented its 'great power' quality and criticized in particular the provision that its central committee should represent the big four only. They evidently feared that this manner of doing things might become the habit of the post-war world. Some small changes were made to meet – though they by no means removed – small-power criticism and the United States Government sent out a final draft on 24 September 1943. Even those who still felt uneasiness agreed with reasonable cheerfulness to accept it, specifying, in one case, that this was no precedent.[10]

The Conference was held in Atlantic City, New Jersey. This seaside resort's suffering was limited to a lack of tourists during the war, and its mayor lobbied successfully for the UN conference to help fill the hotels. Dean Acheson chaired the conference, although, contrary to his expectations, it was Lehman and not he who was chosen as UNRRA

Continued Cold Tonight

The Corpus Christi Times

Final Edition

VOLUME 26—NUMBER 110   CORPUS CHRISTI, TEXAS, TUESDAY, NOVEMBER 9, 1943   FOURTEEN PAGES TODAY

Germany Will Fall in 1944, Churchill Says

Russians Push Toward Poland And Rumania

Drive Southwest of Fastov Aimed at Trapping Thousands of Germans Still Fighting Between Dnieper, Black Sea

LONDON, Nov. 8. (AP) — Two Russian armies, commanded by Gen. Nikolai F. Vatutin, conqueror of Kiev, today were pounding westward toward the Polish and Rumanian frontiers on the heels of the shattered remnants of 12 Nazi divisions—about 180,000 men—dislodged from the Ukrainian capital in a four-day battle which ended last Saturday.

One Red Army force was reported surging forward beyond Makarov, 38 miles west of Kiev, to within 55 miles of Zhitomir, key junction on one of the two last north-south railways ...

Opening of Typhus Control Drive Here Temporarily Delayed

Canvass of Stores Will Be Started Tomorrow

A temporary delay has occurred in start of the typhus control program ...

Roosevelt Leads United Nations In Pledging Aid to Axis' Victims

WASHINGTON, Nov. 9 — President Roosevelt climaxed the signing of a United Nations relief agreement today with the declaration that it ...

Employees of City Will Get Holiday On Armistice Day

Courthouse Also Expected To Close Offices Thursday

Eighth Army Advances Five Miles To Nazi 'Winter Line'

In West Germans Mass Troops and Guns In Attempt To Halt American Drive Toward Cassino on Road to Rome

ALLIED HEADQUARTERS, Algiers, Nov. 9. (AP) — Cutting a new swath five miles deep through enemy positions ...

Flames Sweep Again Toward Film Colony

Fire Fighters Lose Battle To Keep Blaze Under Control

LOS ANGELES, Nov. 9 ...

Jap General Killed In Airplane Accident

Temperature Falls to 36 To Establish Record for Second Consecutive Day

Tokyo Says City Internees Living Up To True Jap Spirit

Great, Costly Battles Seen Before Victory

Back of Nazi U-Boat Warfare Broken By Allies; Reich's War Machine Wrecked By Russians, Prime Minister Says

LONDON, Nov. 9. (AP) — Prime Minister Churchill gravely proclaimed the "impending ruin" of Germany today, but with all the force of his leadership and language warned that in his belief the Nazis' defeat could not come before 1944.

CHURCHILL
... warns campaign ...

Forty-eight Youths Take Army and Navy Qualifying Exams

Tests Given at Junior College And Senior High

Theft of Gas Ration Books Increasing

Thieves Looting Pockets of Parked Autos

Mann Says He Is Not Yet Candidate For Any Office

The Weather

Official of Czech Government in Exile, Veteran in Underground Fighting Against Nazis, Visitor Here

Capt. Vaclav Palecek, a 41-year-old Czech who holds the portfolio of Director in the Department of Economics in the Czechoslovakian government in exile in London ...

De Marigny Ends Defense

NASSAU, Nov. 9 — Alfred de Marigny concluded his defense against a charge that he killed his millionaire father-in-law, Sir Harry Oakes ...

British Battleship Warspite Damaged, Berlin Radio Says

LONDON, Nov. 9 — The famous British battleship Warspite was brought into Gibraltar yesterday in a damaged condition ...

Fuehrer Wrecked

On the anniversary ...

Child Drowns

DALLAS, Nov. 9. (AP) — Funeral services ...

director. Acheson had the complex task of managing a conference of officials from 44 states, many with national and personal egos in inverse proportion to their size and resources. *Time* magazine gave insight into two of the conference's controversies: starvation in India and help for Germany. Ever since January 1942, following Roosevelt's anti-colonial policy, India had had its own representation at United Nations meetings, and they challenged their British masters.

> Into Atlantic City's Claridge Hotel stalked trouble for the United Nations' brand-new Relief & Rehabilitation Administration. For days India's official delegate, mild Sir Girja Bajpai, had never dared bring up the bitter question of India's right to petition UNRRA for desperately needed food in time of famine. Sir Girja knew that in Bengal this week there was no celebration of the bumper Aman crop (the December rice crop). There was no celebration, only desolation, and silent villages ravaged mercilessly by hunger and disease. For there was no one left to harvest the Aman crop – the stricken peasants sat on doorsteps mourning their dead families, too tired, too sick to take courage from the ripening paddy fields.
>
> But J. J. Singh, president of the India League of America, moved into Atlantic City, called his own press conference, and forced the question into the open. Let UNRRA rush food to India at once.
>
> Chairman Dean Acheson and British Colonel John J. Llewellin demurred. UNRRA relief, said they, was only for areas liberated from the enemy. Bluntly retorted interloper Singh: 'If relief is for war victims, how can the United Nations refuse aid to famine-stricken India, where war has stopped all rice imports from Burma?' The big nations, embarrassed but adamant, refused to reconsider.
>
> But the big nation delegates could not succeed in shushing down small or poor nations on all questions (each participating Government has an equal vote). When the U.S. and Britain proposed that UNRRA relief be given free to postwar Germany if she was unable to pay, the small nations rose in storm. With a violent and tumultuous 'no' they voted down the proposal. Said they: 'Germany must pay for all the relief it gets'.[11]

Part of the value of the United Nations conferences was, as Roosevelt, Hull and Welles all intended, to build habits of cooperation. Acheson was joined at the UNRRA conference by future diplomatic stars, including Jean Monnet of France, Lester Pearson of Canada and Oliver Franks from Britain.[12]

The first item of business on the table of the flag-bedecked ballroom of the Claridge Hotel was 'Who will pay for the relief?' The basis agreed for the funding was that each member of the United Nations would contribute 1 per cent of one year's national income, as a one-off payment. The Brazilians proposed instead that the percentage should be based on the pre-war trade a state had had with the countries to which assistance would be sent, while the New Zealand Government wanted a sliding scale with countries with higher per capita income paying proportionately more.

The 1 per cent idea was first proposed by Harry White, an American Treasury official also involved in the financial discussions that reached fruition at Bretton Woods. The White Plan had the advantage that everyone was contributing what they could, so that it was not simply a matter of US taxpayers subsidizing the world. The system had an obvious equality, a clear limit and the avoidance of arguments over who was supplying how many tons of what foodstuffs while still accommodating the reality of US wealth. At this time the USA produced over half of the world's economic output. The adoption of this contribution system by the UNRRA Council imposed a non-binding obligation on governments and public opinion to equal what others were doing.

The US contribution was over $2.6 billion of the $3.6 billion global cost of the programme. The balance was provided by other countries, mainly by Britain ($600 million) and Canada ($137 million) with small amounts from 40 other members of the United Nations. Contributions included $24,000 from Panama; the Dominican Republic increased its export tax and transferred the revenue to UNRRA; and Brazil made the fifth-largest contribution, of $40 million dollars, nearly double the requested 1 per cent of national income.[13] At the time, Ireland was neutral and so outside the United Nations, but nevertheless it sent 285 tons of bacon and 8,000 beef cattle.[14]

Non-governmental organizations also made contributions to UNRRA amounting to several million dollars worth of commodities. In the United States, contributing NGOs included national patriotic organizations devoted to helping Czechoslovakia, China, Greece, Hungary and Poland. In addition, 5,000 tons of clothing were collected by Americans in 1944 alone. Americans contributed a further 70,000 tons to United Nations clothing collections by 1947. One well meaning, but senseless, initiative was to collect canned food in the USA and ship it to the needy. Fiorello La Guardia, pointed out that these cans – especially those with vegetables – mostly contained water, but not before 700,000 cans had been shipped out. La Guardia appealed instead for cash and nearly $3 million was donated. These early United Nations appeals paved the way for annual UNICEF appeals made on United Nations Day. Altogether, non-governmental contributions came to over $200 million.

In mid-1945, UNRRA had some 7,500 employees in purchasing offices across Latin America, the Middle East and the Indian subcontinent, and its aid operations extended from China to Denmark. Some of these purchases helped maintain demand for goods that had been destined for Lend-Lease and eased the loss of income to those producing them as the war ended. At that juncture, the liberated European states contributed what they could, with Czechoslovakian contributions of sugar and Polish

22 Hollywood actresses promoting donations of clothes to UNRRA with striptease poker, 1944.

coal going to Austria and Yugoslavia. Helping people to help themselves was the motto and the practice.

Once the delegates in Atlantic City had agreed on the financial issues, they had to decide what types of work could be funded, how to distribute resources, how the organization would work and who would benefit. In addition to direct relief such as food and medicine, the word 'rehabilitation' was used. This was meant as an interim step before full-scale reconstruction. UNRRA's guiding principle of 'helping people to help themselves' meant that flour came with seeds to plant the next year's harvest, medicine with medicine factories. Reconstruction was limited to, for example, fixing an electricity generation plant rather than building a new one. The most famous reconstruction project was in China where UNRRA helped rebuild broken dykes along hundreds of miles of rivers.

Some Allied governments were concerned that UNRRA would constitute a different sort of invasion by the USA and the UK. Hence, there was a requirement pressed by the Norwegians and French as well as the Soviet Union that the host government must authorize UNRRA operations.

Agreement at a conference was one thing; agreement by the US Congress to foot the bill quite another. Lehman tried to convince Congress that the UNRRA project was 'the first great test of the capacity of the present world partnership of the United Nations and associated governments to achieve a peacetime goal'. A strong lobby and public information effort by the Administration and UNRRA itself was needed to secure Congressional approval of an initial $350 million. The complex US budgetary processes meant that a first vote was not followed through by full implementation, so that UNRRA purchases of supplies came to a halt late in 1945, with a further $550 million finally approved in mid-December 1945. In the end, it took a personal appearance before Congress by an exhausted and sick General Eisenhower to get Congressional approval.

In London, Churchill and his Cabinet were also less than enthusiastic, although they ensured that the British financial contribution was made punctually. British officials grumbled that they were being asked to help people who had done little to fight the Nazis, and hoped that the British contribution would help rebuild trade with Europe. Churchill wrote to Eden in August 1944 concerning a directive Eden was issuing to government officials to detach good administrators to help UNRRA: 'I have reluctantly initialled your draft directive. I am very apprehensive of Britain being overburdened after the war, but still I recognise the force of your argument that since we have got into this we had better have as large a share of the personnel controlling it as possible'.[15]

Progress on implementation was slow even when the funds were approved. The military had priority on shipping until after the war ended, and sought to retain it even then. The military authorities were permitted not to allow UNRRA into liberated territories for up to six months after they were free of enemy forces, and they also had authority over UNRRA activities. By August 1945, UNRRA was still only working in five countries, one of them Germany.

By 1946, UNRRA operations had gathered momentum worldwide. From Lehman's headquarters in the 'flat iron' building at Dupont Circle, he organized divisions to help with displaced persons (DPs – survivors of camps and slave labour), health, welfare, food, clothing and textiles, as well as agricultural and industrial rehabilitation and medical and sanitary supplies.

The DPs in Germany were the most obviously needy people. The relief planners estimated that 21 million people in Europe had been driven from their homes by 1943 and many were in various forms of slavery inside Germany. In 2008, by way of comparison, there were around 45 million DPs of whom the UN High Commission for Refugees was assisting some 25 million worldwide,[16] with an annual budget at a record high of $2 billion in 2009.[17]

Of the 21 million uprooted Europeans, about eight million had been taken as slaves, prisoners or forced labourers to Germany and Austria, and a further eight million were homeless in their own countries; more still were fleeing the Red Army. Most survivors found their own way home. However, by the end of 1945, 750,000 displaced persons were being fed and housed mostly in the Western-occupied sectors of Germany. As people returned home, others took their place. Eighteen months later the number had fallen to 640,000, of whom 147,000 were Jews mostly hoping to go to Palestine. The new UN International Refugee Organization took over the task from UNRRA in mid-1947. By then a total of a million people had been helped home, half of them Poles.[18]

A key part of the success of the process which enabled people freed from Nazi control to regain control over their lives was a system of self-government. UNRRA's official history claims that UNRRA had been successful in ensuring that its camps were self-governing, with elected councils, courts and fire services, which would 'not have been possible if UNRRA had pursued a policy of efficient command'.[19] 'Although many leaders had been appointed at the beginning of the operation by UNRRA or military officials, by the summer of 1946 almost all had been elected by the camp residents'.[20]

According to Woodbridge, the official historian of UNRRA, in his chapter on self-government it was 'no exaggeration to say that it was the goal toward which all activities were pointed'. And the concept originated with the US Army, as well as with UNRRA. Eisenhower's headquarters' "Guide to the Care of Displaced Persons in Germany" stated that "displaced persons should be encouraged to organize themselves as much as is administratively possible".[21] According to Woodbridge,

> In each camp there was usually a camp committee elected by the entire population, either at large, by nationality (if in a mixed camp), by area or block within the camp, or by some other means. This committee usually selected the camp chairman or camp leader, although in some cases he was directly elected. This committee supervised all activities and represented the population in all dealings with outside authorities.[22]

The camp committee was responsible for housing, catering, police and fire, and courts depending on the size and longevity of the camp. This was the model, but practice was slow and imperfect. Later, in 1946 and afterwards, the political character of the camps became part of both the emerging Cold War and the attempt by Jews to immigrate to Israel.

The control of disease was a high priority. There was little point in repatriating refugees who might infect their home population or become ill from some new disease on their return or both. Diphtheria, typhus and typhoid are just names to the vast majority of people in the twenty-first century; in the 1940s they were killers – and most unpleasant ones at that.

People can be suffocated by the growth of a membrane in the throat caused by the diphtheria bacteria, transmitted in droplets like colds or flu and carried in clothing and blankets. Three-and-a-half million children were inoculated by UNRRA against this disease in Yugoslavia in 1946, millions more in other countries. Medical scientists assess a death rate of up to 60 per cent for untreated weak and elderly patients infected with Typhus. Typhus is transmitted by lice and other insects amongst people with little or no access to clean water for washing. The cause of death is a combination of respiratory and bowel failure combined with a bleeding rash and fever in excess of 40° C.[23] UNRRA administered huge quantities of DDT to kill the lice, and in Germany alone, three million doses of preventive typhus serum were given to camp survivors. A serious outbreak was averted in Sicily and mainland Italy by the copious use of DDT.

One example of the value of prompt action in saving survivors of the Holocaust is given by Francesca Wilson, who worked with an UNRRA team that arrived in the Dachau area of Bavaria in early May 1945. She described how her team found that the 'Nazis had put the Jews, on purpose, in an infected train. Typhus was spreading rapidly'. The use of DDT eliminated the lice and so stopped the spread of the disease.[24]

UNRRA teams were made up of groups of around eight people with multiple skills. In her memoir, *Aftermath*, Francesca Wilson describes the French doctor, the French and Belgian resistance fighters, the Russian woman and the English nurse who made up her team as it set out from the training school in Normandy to help at the concentration camp at Dachau. Wilson, an Associate of Newnham College, Cambridge, provides an account of the immediate post-war world of Germany and Yugoslavia that is still fresh. Her perceptions are underpinned by her earlier work with refugees and the hungry in Holland, France and Tunisia in World War I and then in Serbia, Austria, Russia and Spain.

Typhoid fever (which despite the similarity of name is unrelated to typhus) can kill one in five of those affected, especially people who are already weak and who receive no treatment. The disease is transmitted via infected water supplies. It was prevalent in Europe during the industrial revolution and killed Prince Albert, Queen Victoria's husband. Clean water and the use of disinfectant is a simple and effective preventive measure. But in the post-war period, it also required the mending of sewage systems destroyed in the fighting. Other epidemics in the liberated territories included venereal disease, cholera and, in China, plague.

As part of the overall response, UNRRA and the national governments distributed penicillin, sulfa drugs and aspirin. Equipment for the then brand-new life-saving drug penicillin – the first of the powerful antibiotics – to be produced at specially constructed factories, was supplied by UNRRA to China, Czechoslovakia, Poland, Ukraine and Yugoslavia by 1947.

Starvation continued and even intensified after the war. In 1945, four years of international planning failed to take sufficient control of the global market to meet the needs of the starving in the liberated areas – despite the largely government-controlled economy of the USA and other Allied states. In the USA, animal fat was used to make soap rather than feed people, and controls on wheat supplies were lifted by Canada, the UK and USA through their Combined Food Board. UNRRA was not permitted to build up food stocks to send in after the Nazis were driven from territory they had occupied. Instead, it had to buy supplies for starving people rather than plan for what could be anticipated.

By January 1946, food shortages in Europe were increasing rather than declining. In India the monsoons had failed. As a result there was a tripling of its food import requirements. In addition the Japanese and Germans could not yet either feed themselves or import food. Further cash from the US taxpayer and renewed efforts to find supplies resulted in food being sent urgently to Europe and China from the USA, Canada and other suppliers throughout 1946 and into 1947.

This broad picture of the global effort to get people home, stop and cure disease and feed the hungry provides the context for a look at UNRRA's regional programmes.

Poland provides an example of what UNRRA achieved in the face of multiple economic and health crises. In Poland, as also in China, Yugoslavia and Greece, aid was hampered by politics, though not by civil war. The Soviet Union did not permit the Poles to allow UNRRA in for months and when it was operating, it did so under twin criticisms: the communist press accused it of being a tool of the USA and Britain, while in those two countries aid to a communist country was already anathema to some conservatives.

UNRRA Poland was led by the dynamic Canadian officer, Brigadier Charles Drury. The situation he faced had a dreadfulness that is hard to describe even now. Around one in six of the people of pre-war Poland had died, and many more were sick and injured. Nearly six million Poles had been killed, about half of them Jews murdered by the Nazis, and on top of this, tens of thousands of Polish army officers had been executed on Stalin's orders.

In addition to the humanitarian catastrophe, the dislocation of Poland had been aggravated by border changes. In 1946, some 20 million people were living within the new frontiers of Poland, most impoverished, some starving. A survivor might originally have lived in eastern Poland; survived the occupation first by the Soviets and then by the Germans; been taken to Germany for slave labour; returned to Poland at the end of the war to find their old home, in the unlikely event it was still standing, now in Russia; and be offered a new one by the Polish authorities in territory in the West from which some two-and-a-half million Germans had been driven westwards at the end of the war. Such an experience was not unusual in 1945.

The supply of food and trucks helped relieve and prevent mass hunger after liberation. The European winter of 1945–46 was terribly harsh and the organizational task of helping Poland immense. At the beginning, all supplies had to be routed from the south by rail from ports in Romania because Poland's own ports on the Baltic were unusable owing to battle damage. Supplies began arriving in Warsaw in June 1945, around the time that the Americans and British officially recognized the Communist-run Provisional Government. The argument over the Yalta agreement to conduct free elections in Poland became for the West a landmark in the developing Cold War. Drury's leadership managed to keep UNRRA's neutrality somewhat intact and separate from the political storm, despite public attacks from the Soviet-controlled government and the conservative press in the United States.

The UNRRA programme in Poland had an important role in restoring agriculture and industry. 'UNRRA's help came as a realisation of all the promises given to Poland in the hardest times of the German occupation. So UNRRA became for Poland not only a source for the most needed supplies, but an expression of the appropriateness and practicality of international agreements, and a symbol of mutual collaboration and protection'.[25]

The Polish Government focused rationed food supplies on industrial workers and others engaged in rebuilding the economy, while the rural farming communities were assumed to be able to feed themselves. Parents had to rely on the free market to feed their children, but money was scarce, food prices high and supplies short. UNRRA supplies and diplomatic approaches to the Polish Government enabled daily milk supplies for urban children and mothers in the summer of 1946. Medical staff and supplies, especially of DDT, prevented thousands of deaths from disease, in particular typhus and typhoid. The Polish Government organized mass dusting with DDT in early 1946 with help and training from UNRRA and Lt. Col. David M. Greeley of the American Typhus Commission. This preventative action in Poland also stopped the spread of disease to Germany with the large movements of people taking place at the time.

In Silesia, which was now part of Poland, typhoid outbreaks were limited because of mass vaccination programmes. In the summer of 1946, specialists from US medical schools lectured on developments in medical services in the war years to the Polish medical community. Cut off from these developments by the war, the surviving Polish medical staff were enthusiastic in working with external assistance.

UNRRA equipment and training restored much of Poland's agriculture and fishing industries. Surviving Polish farmers had just a third of the horses and cows left to work the land as they had had in 1939. 9,000 tractors and accompanying workshops provided the capacity to farm much of the land that lay idle because so many of the horses and cows that

23 UNRRA cattle in Poland.

had been used for ploughing and milk production were dead. The Poles
were able to make 56,000 acres productive – enough land to feed ten
million people, roughly the number living in all the towns and cities.
Seed was delivered and used on over 400,000 acres. Livestock was also
shipped in, branded as 'UNRRA' and proudly displayed in Polish
villages.

Nevertheless, the 200,000 horses and cows sent from the USA and
Canada could not make up for the seven million lost in the six war years.
The delivery of 40 fishing trawlers revitalized the fishing industry, providing scarce protein to a population living almost entirely on carbohydrates.
Thousands of tons of clothing were distributed free through Polish welfare
agencies, while the manufacture of clothing was made possible by a supply
of 70,000 tons of raw textiles, a quarter of it from the Soviet Union.

The UNRRA programmes in Ukraine and Byelorussia (now Belarus)
provide a unique insight into the engagement of the organized international community within the heart of the Soviet Union. The areas involved were amongst the most devastated on Earth. Together, Ukraine
and Byelorussia are larger than California and had a pre-war population
of 40 million, of whom around one in five died. More civilians had died
in and around one small city, Vitebsk, than the total number of Americans
killed in World War II – the city had changed hands between the Nazis and
the Red Army 11 times during the fighting.

The decades prior to the Nazi invasion of June 1941 had been severe enough to make the inhabitants believe things could not get much worse: millions had died in World War I and the Civil War which followed, and as a result of the Polish invasion in 1920 and forced starvation and imposition of collective farming by Stalin in the 1930s. Nonetheless, the introduction of mechanization on the collective farms had produced impressive results and a new-found pride amongst those who had led it. Consequently, the years leading to 1941 had shown considerable economic progress. This was all crushed and swept away by war as the frontline between Soviet and German forces moved back and forth, each side destroying everything they could as they retreated – villages, crops, livestock. The surviving local population was starved and persecuted by the Germans, and many fought and died in the resistance against the occupation.

To help alleviate this situation, Stalin sought UNRRA help in the late summer of 1945. Truman had ended Lend-Lease in Europe after VE Day and there was no follow-on programme. France, but not the major Allies of the USA, benefited from a Lend-Lease loan for the peace. This hurt the British and Russians alike. In the summer of 1945, the negotiations on a US loan to the Soviet Union had broken down. Up to that time Stalin, like the British, appears to have believed that his special relationship with Washington, and Great Power status, meant that he would not need to consider working through an international organization like UNRRA or the World Bank.

After the end of Lend-Lease, the Soviet Union in July 1945 applied for $700 million in aid from UNRRA but was granted $250 million. This was about half that supplied to Poland despite the Soviet Union's greater size and an equivalent level of devastation in its western republics. The negotiations with the Soviet Union on the UNRRA programmes were as bureaucratically difficult as can be imagined from both sides, with Lehman forcing concessions on access to the Soviet republics, and arrangements made for UNRRA and US officials to check that aid was being used properly.

Once agreed, American UNRRA aid to the Soviet Union went by ship to the port of Odessa on the Black Sea. UNRRA reported great resilience in Soviet public health systems, with no serious epidemics. Most of the effort went into food and agriculture. In Odessa, unloading on the dock was supervised by US Government officials. They reported little pilfering at the port and smooth organization on the Soviet side. Around half of the food was provided free to the population and half sold – in common with practice in other countries supported by UNRRA. The supplies went mostly into the towns and cities which were unable to feed themselves. Woodbridge describes how 'children's homes were given first priority in the allocation of food; in fact, the careful attention given by the Governments to the needs of children and mothers was to Mission staffs one of the most impressive features of Soviet life'.[26] Mechanical equipment, including cranes and bulldozers imported through UNRRA, accelerated the removal of rubble in cities such as Minsk.[27] The agricultural sector was assisted with 23,000 tons of seeds and 2,300 tractors, though this met a very small part of the need. In the Ukraine alone, 52,000 of the country's 90,000 tractors had been destroyed by war.

Most of the supplies consisted of food (to the value of $130 million), followed by clothing, textiles and footwear worth $25 million. UNRRA was never informed by the authorities how food was allocated through the ration system, although its observers saw it as quite fair and evenly used within a scale where industrial workers had a nominal right to 3,500 calories per day and dependant adults just 705. Even this was hard to achieve with the food shortages.

In China, gigantic civil-engineering projects were added to the standard UNRRA programmes. As a result, in 1946 and 1947, millions of Chinese farmers were assisted in rebuilding flood-protection systems for their land and developing more modern agricultural practices with UNRRA supplies and technical training. Flood-protection dykes had been built up over centuries by the Chinese to protect fertile land from annual flooding, but these had been neglected or destroyed in the seven years of war since the Japanese attack on the maritime provinces began in 1937. The main reclamation projects were along the Yellow, Huai, Yangtse, Han, Chien Tang and Pearl Rivers and the Grand Canal. In 1938, the Chinese Army had destroyed dykes along the Yellow River to flood their own land and create a massive obstacle to keep the Japanese at bay. The cost was tens of thousands drowned and six million refugees. UNRRA supported the successful rebuilding effort by the people and the nationalist and communist organizations in the areas that each controlled during the continuing civil war. UNRRA supplied almost all of the machinery and much of the timber needed to regulate the rivers. A key part of the process was driving tree-trunks side by side to depths of 40 feet along river banks, providing a frame for stone and concrete fencing. By March 1947, 400 miles of the Yellow River had been regulated in this way.[28]

The flood-protection schemes in China formed part of the same spectrum of activities as were organized in Europe. One feature of UNRRA work in China was the supply and training in the use of tractors. One American UNRRA worker from Oklahoma was Roy S. Tucker. A platoon commander with the US Army in Italy and France, he had joined UNRRA after the war as a tractor driver and instructor and worked for 18 months in Kaifeng, 600 miles north-west of Shanghai. UNRRA imported US-made tractors and put them to work in the bean harvest on land reclaimed from areas that had been flooded since 1938. But by July 1947, as UNRRA was itself closing, the communist victory forced them out of the country.[29]

For all its success in nutrition, health and technical assistance, UNRRA was rife with internal problems and in the end overwhelmed by the international politics of the time. UNRRA salaries had been set too high for Wilson's taste. They were higher than their military equivalents and sometimes double what could be found in Canada, the USA and the UK. A Canadian nurse could earn $1,776 a year in the military and $3,200 in UNRRA. Susan Armstrong-Reid and David Murray give this and numerous other examples in their unique book on UNRRA-Canada, *Armies of Peace*. This is not only one of the few modern studies of UNRRA, but also one that provides a comprehensive insight into the work of the third-largest contributing country.[30] Resentment over salaries amongst the Allied military responsible for UNRRA was reinforced by a sense amongst the military that UNRRA staff were incompetent, though this feeling was reciprocated on occasion.

The largest and most politically damaging charge was corruption and political discrimination by the communists in the distribution of aid. There were numerous charges in the UK and American press and national legislatures. As a result there were a number of commissions of investigation which in the main cleared UNRRA. In Yugoslavia, Wilson's verdict on examining the charge that food 'went to the adherents of the Partisans, while others were left to starve', was that it was unfounded. She found that there was no significant corruption, but that the former middle classes in the new communist era resented the fact that manual labourers were allowed to buy larger rations than clerical workers. She also noted in particular that UNRRA food supplies had kept five million people from starvation in the mountainous parts of the country, where partisan activity had been easier and agriculture poor.[31]

Woodbridge also takes issue with the charges against UNRRA, as you might expect from its official biographer. But one example he makes is telling. The media had charged UNRRA with supplying baseball bats and gloves to the starving of Europe. This had indeed occurred, said Woodbridge, but only as part of pre-packaged goods for US troops being sold off cheaply at the end of the war. The only way to avoid it would have been either not to buy the otherwise useful packages or unpack each one, remove the sporting goods and then repackage them.

More serious political issues lay behind these attacks. For US right-wing politicians, any supplies to communist countries should be opposed, as should UNRRA itself as an international organization in which the Soviet Union was a partner in the management. Grist to their mill came when many East Europeans refused to go back to Poland and the Baltic states. These were complex issues. Some returned home and suffered no ill effects, others doubtless were persecuted – the imprisonment or execution of the families of the Cossacks fighting for the Germans who were turned over to the Red Army (who regarded them as traitors) by the British in Austria is one such example. But alongside the Jews and others innocently and justifiably opposed to communism there were also former allies of the Nazis beginning to fill up the camps, some eager to fight the Russians again.

Ernest Bevin, the British Foreign Secretary, said of the Poles in Italy in early 1946 that,

> ... they are trained to precision and are manoeuvring constantly to be in prime condition to re-conquer Poland or invade the Soviet Union. They terrify the Italians, impoverish the countryside, interfere with local politics when anything like Communism or even Socialism manifests itself, and requisition desperately needed homes, food and other material. In general, the Poles represent a genuine curse to the Italian Government and to Italy.[32]

The Polish-American associations concentrated on a different issue. They accused UNRRA of trying to force people to return to Poland and face communist wrath. The oppressive nature of the communist-dominated regimes of Eastern Europe is well known. What is less understood is the extreme right-wing element amongst those who had ended up under Western control. Maurice Rosen, an UNRRA official in Italy, wrote that,

> It is time we begin to review a little more carefully a policy which lumps together the few thousand dazed and bewildered Jewish survivors of Nazi terror with the Ustachi and Chetniks, the anti-Polish 'Polish' émigrés and the Volksdeutsch, the White Guards and collaborationists of every hue who populate DP camps throughout Germany, Austria and Italy and carry on unmolested, their vicious anti-United Nations and anti-Semitic propaganda.[33]

These issues arose in what, in retrospect, we have come to see as the emerging Cold War. A vitriolic critic of Truman's policies in Germany and towards UNRRA was Ira Hirschmann. Before the war he had been Vice President of both Saks Fifth Avenue and Bloomingdales. Hirschmann's close association with Fiorella La Guardia led to him becoming La Guardia's special envoy in Europe when he became head of UNRRA in 1946. Previously, Hirschmann, who had rare authority to negotiate directly with enemy officials, had helped Jews escape from Europe for the War Refugee Board – which worked with Jewish organizations, diplomats from neutral countries, and resistance groups in Europe to rescue Jews from occupied territories and provide relief to inmates of Nazi concentration camps.

In his 1949 book, *The Embers Still Burn*, Hirschmann attacks the rebuilding of Germany, the neglect of refugees, the encouragement of Nazi-associated anti-communist militia, the invitation to extreme right-wing Europeans to settle in the USA, and what he called the killing of UNRRA.

In September 1947, the US Secretary of State James F. Byrnes, once a senior assistant to Roosevelt, stated, 'We wish to give relief as the United

States, not as a member of an international organization in which a committee composed of other governments determines the allotment of the relief given by us'.[34] In doing so, he rejected a plan that had been proposed by La Guardia for the United Nations Food Plan to be carried out by UNRRA.

A year before, Lehman had already resigned over the lack of support from Truman for UNRRA, and in particular his use of Herbert Hoover, the arch-appeaser, as special reporter, rather than Lehman and the UNRRA professionals.

For Hirschmann, his experience in the summer of 1946 as La Guardia's inspector of UNRRA activities in Europe was the last straw. Two cases stood out: the barracks of Funk Caserne, a camp for Jewish survivors of the holocaust, and the end of attempts to find children stolen by the Nazis to be brought up as Germans. At Funk Caserne, Hirschmann found that the US Army had placed 1,800 holocaust survivors in an unheated Luftwaffe coal store with three toilets between them.[35] In a rage, he charged into the US headquarters only to be told by American officers to forget it, lighten up and go out with them to pick up some German girls in the local nightclubs. He stuck to his task and better housing was found. The issue of the kidnapped children is even more heart-rending. With open files on 350,000 'Aryan' children stolen by the Nazis in the East and given to Nazi families, UNRRA's painstaking and heart-rending social work was continuing at the beginning of 1947. Sometimes it took conversations in their native language or the use of the Orthodox Christian sign of the cross for the children to be found. It was dangerous for them to remember where they came from. Only one war crimes case resulted. Then, in January 1947, the Truman Administration cancelled the programme and handed it over without any resources to the new UN Refugee Organization.

Hirschman also reported an almost universal appetite amongst American and British officers for war with the Soviet Union, and that anti-Semitism and pro-fascist attitudes all too often accompanied anti-communism. But it was Acheson's verdict on UNRRA, not Hirschman's or Lehman's, that carries the greatest weight in history. He wrote that the USA sought closure of UNRRA because of the Republican landslide in the 1946 Congressional elections; the organization's ineffectiveness; its role in black markets; support for communist regimes who used it 'to entrench themselves'; and because the staff obtainable had been weak and the leadership weaker.[36]

UNRRA, though, was never meant to go on for long. The intention was to alleviate the suffering and get economic activity moving. This it achieved to an astonishing degree in the face of the many obstacles. Perhaps the last obstacle is for UNRRA to be seen once again in its own light, with the Marshall Plan no longer obscuring it.

24 UNRRA train, Dubrovnik, then in Yugoslavia.

The UNRRA contribution went far beyond mere aid. A proper appreciation of UNRRA requires a revision of common assessments of why nations provide aid and development assistance.

Twenty-first century American policymakers and opinion formers, as well as the global aid and development community, seem unaware of UNRRA. Robert Orr edited *Winning the Peace: An American Strategy for Post-Conflict Reconstruction* while at the influential and mainstream Centre for Strategic International Studies and is now a senior UN official. Carol Lancaster is author of *Foreign Aid, Diplomacy, Aid, Domestic Politics*. Both argue for more effective and stronger US engagement in world issues, both unilaterally and through the UN. However, neither draws on the precedent set by American engagement with UNRRA. For Orr, the genesis or first generation of US experience is the occupation of Japan under General MacArthur, remarking that the Japanese experience 'helped to solidify a particularly American attitude that societies coming out of war could and should be rebuilt by the United States',[37] whereas the UNRRA experience was that such work should and could be done effectively by the people themselves with support from the United Nations as a collective body.

A classic academic account is provided by the American scholar Carol Lancaster, for whom the Marshall Plan is where the history of international development begins. Her argument is that development assistance has always been for narrow national reasons. The UNRRA experience provides a powerful precedent of the principle 'all for one and one for all', and Lancaster sees no development role in its work. But, the record outlined in this chapter is that UNRRA was indeed also a development agency. As Wilson described the work in Croatia, 'UNRRA brought in horses and cows, diving suits to enable wrecked ships to be refloated, twine for fishing nets and huge tanks to hold village water supplies in the Dalmatian Islands'.[38] In Italy, textile imports restarted the clothing industry and the income was reused in the programme. The operation there was led by an American, Spurgeon Keeney, a veteran of international relief efforts.

The work of UNRRA should be used more fully in contemporary discussion of post-conflict reconstruction and international aid. For example, the wartime commitments of national income to UNRRA provide an interesting precedent for the contemporary commitment of 0.7 per cent of GDP to development. War prevention was also the primary function of the economic institutions designed to come into operation post-UNRRA, and for which UNRRA did the short-term work. These began to be established at Bretton Woods and they are the subject of the next chapter.

CHAPTER 7

Money and trade: Bretton Woods and Havana – prosperity for all?

'The essential basis of enduring peace must be economic', said Henry Stimson, Roosevelt's Secretary of War.[1] For Stimson, and many others, this meant the global regulation of trade, currencies, banking and finance, rather than the 'free markets' of the deregulated twenty-first century.

Such a system of global regulation was agreed during World War II by all the United Nations, including the Soviet Union. In the decades after 1945, this system enabled the fastest and most egalitarian economic progress the Western world has known, also labelled 'the golden age of capitalism' (Table 4). This prosperity could have been greater and faster, especially in the developing world, if these agreements had been fully implemented.

The main agreements were made at a conference of 44 states at Bretton Woods, New Hampshire, USA in the summer of 1944. The were intended to build on UNRRA and lend lease. The first big US post-war loan was of $2.5 billion to France in February 1945 under the Lend-Lease programme, although most accounts of the end of Lend-Lease omit this major peacetime initiative.

The main global economic issues before the Bretton Woods conference had taken years to agree. The British, led by John Maynard Keynes, sought

TABLE 4 Economic growth 1950–2008 (average per capita growth rates),

	World	Western Europe*	OECD*	USA	Japan	LDCs
1950–1973	2.8	3.8	3.1	2.5	8.1	3.3
1973–1980	1.4	2.0	1.8	1.5	2.3	1.9
1980–1990	1.4	2.1	2.2	2.2	3.4	1.4
1990–2008	2.4	1.7	1.8	1.7	1.2	3.1

Adjusted to 1990 US$, using the Geary-Khamis PPPs method.
Source: Groeningen Growth and Development Centre, Total Economy Database, updated March 2010, at: http://www.conference-board.org/economics/database.cfm (*German data not available).

to protect the British Empire from competition from US industry, while many Americans favoured high taxes (tariffs) on all imports. The Soviet Union was suspicious of the West's economic and political objectives, and smaller nations feared Anglo-American domination.

Wartime economic cooperation was part of the process that kept the Allies together during and immediately after the war. But by the 1980s, the economic blueprints and structures bequeathed to us by the wartime decision-makers had been discarded, and their toolbox of unfinished policy instruments long left out of economics teaching. The development of cooperation for the post-war global economy was linked closely to the Lend-Lease programme and the hopes amongst America's Allies that it would use its economic power to provide loans for their economic recovery. Allied hopes of US economic assistance were not in vain. Stimson, like many of his generation, had been impressed by John Maynard Keynes's warning after Versailles that the 'economic consequences of the peace' would likely produce social hysteria, the collapse of civilization, and war:

> 'The [Versailles] treaty [of 1919] includes no provisions for the economic rehabilitation of Europe – nothing to make the defeated Central empires into good neighbours, nothing to stabilize the new states of Europe, nothing to reclaim Russia; nor does it promote in any way a compact of economic solidarity amongst the Allies themselves; no arrangement was reached at Paris for restoring the disordered finances of France and Italy, or to adjust the systems of the Old World and the New. ... It is an extraordinary fact that the fundamental economic problem of a Europe starving and disintegrating before their eyes was the one question in which it was impossible to arouse the interest of the four leaders'[2] [Henri Clemenceau for France, Woodrow Wilson for the USA, Lloyd George for Britain and Vittorio Orlando for Italy].[3]

Keynes resigned from the British delegation to Versailles and returned to academic life in Cambridge where he was inspired to write his *General Theory of Employment, Interest, and Money*, which he published in 1936. He only returned to government when the war he had prophesied broke out in 1939.

After 1918, economic disaster soon struck. In Germany in the 1920s, hyper-inflation mortally undermined the attempt to build a democratic republic from the ruins of monarchical rule left by the Kaiser, not least by destroying the savings of the middle-class. At the international level, the troubled Gold Standard regime ill-prepared major economies to cope with the Great Depression. The problem with the Gold Standard was that it placed the needs of international trading success over domestic growth. It had imposed a predominance of the external (trade) balance over internal policy autonomy to promote domestic investment and employment. When disaster hit in the form of the Great Depression, countries sought to increase exports and reduce imports by devaluing their currencies and putting up tariffs. This reduced world trade to everyone's disadvantage.

As the financial crisis took hold in 1930, Britain, France and the USA no longer thought about helping Germany and Central Europe with their still war-devastated economies. The resulting mass unemployment and poverty created the conditions in which both Communism and Nazism could prosper, with their offer of social protection and call for revolutionary change in the structure of society as long-term solutions. This enabled militarist demagogues like Hitler and Mussolini to move from irrelevance to dictatorial power as people lost faith in democratic institutions. Violent extremism thrives on desperation.

The need to avoid a repetition of the aftermath of World War I drove post-war economic policy-thinking amongst officials and the public in Europe and North America in the early 1940s. The global economy, as well as military security, had to be regulated if there was not to be a third world war. On this, there was broad agreement in the US and British Governments and the other Allies, including the Soviet Union.

What forms of regulation would be best, and for whom, became one of their central debates. As early as 1941, Roosevelt and Churchill agreed some far-sighted yet cautious language on free trade in the Atlantic Charter, which included these commitments in its eight-point programme:

> Fourth, they will endeavour, with due respect for their existing obligations, to further the enjoyment by all States, great or small, victor or vanquished, of access, on equal terms, to the trade and to the raw materials of the world which are needed for their economic prosperity;
>
> Fifth, they desire to bring about the fullest collaboration between all nations in the economic field with the objector securing, for all, improved labor standards, economic advancement and social security.

These commitments were also made clear in Article VII of the Lend-Lease agreements. For the British, the removal of tariff barriers presented a threat to the system of tariffs set up to protect Imperial and Commonwealth Trade in 1932. Now, in wartime, with the whole financial basis of the British economy in ruins, protection seemed essential to British officials to ensure post-war economic prosperity. Nevertheless, Hull wrote in September 1941 to John Winant, the US Ambassador in London, that,

> You should, therefore, take ... every suitable occasion that may present itself in the future, to impress upon British leaders our view that the prosperity and peace of the post-war world will depend upon the reduction of trade barriers and the reduction or elimination of preferences and discriminations.[4]

Subsequently, in May 1942, Hull publicly linked the US war effort to a new post-war economic system based on free trade:

> The United Nations have already resolved that, once victory is achieved, the economic relations among nations will be based on the principles and

objectives that have been tirelessly advocated by our Government on all ap-
propriate occasions in recent years. This must, of necessity, involve the rehabilitation, on a sound basis, not only of trade relations, but also of monetary,
financial and all other international economic relationships.

   The far reaching economic objectives of the Atlantic Charter cannot be obtained by wishful thinking. We in this country must realize that their achievement will be impossible if we follow policies of narrow economic nationalism,
such as our extreme and disastrous tariff policy after the last war. We must
realize that our own prosperity depends fully as much on prosperous conditions in other countries as their prosperity depends on ours.[5]

Hull was attempting to build a domestic political constituency in the
USA for these free-trade policies, which in limited form had been adopted
by the British in the period of their supremacy in the nineteenth century.
Stimson, a conservative Republican, agreed with Hull. Their shared view
represented that of many Americans regardless of party, though 'America-
Firsters' pursued a narrow view of the American interest. Stimson wanted
a settlement that involved no debts and no tariffs – especially in Europe.
'Central Europe after the war has got to eat. She has got to be free of tariffs
in order to eat', he wrote in his diary on 28 October 1943.[6] He rejected the
Republican success in passing legislation raising tariffs during the depression. In Britain, Keynes led the policy debate, seeking an open, balanced
and egalitarian global system while providing interim protection for the
Imperial trading system.

   There was keen public interest in most countries in what the proposals
of the main powers would be, but getting public backing required some
serious effort at public education. In 1945, Sigrid Arne warned her readers
sternly that a phrase such as 'currency depreciation' 'is the sort of term all
peoples may well have to understand to prevent a third world war'.[7] It
was clear to most people that stock markets and private banking did not
have the resources or the patience to fund the large long-term loans needed
to repair the damage of war and that nations needed their governments to
act for them economically as well as militarily.

   The international debate on economic policy reached a decisive conclusion at Bretton Woods, where the United Nations held the Monetary
and Financial Conference (UNMFC). This is the historical reference point
for the study of post-war economic planning. The UNMFC was the most
important part of a jigsaw of mutually supporting economic agreements,
which in turn formed part of the larger United Nations framework.

   The UNMFC amended and endorsed mainly Anglo-American proposals for the International Monetary Fund and World Bank, which provided
loans to governments and regulated exchange rates until the 1970s. These
two organizations would succeed UNRRA and be accompanied by a third
agreement on international trade. Although the trade agreement had been
anticipated from 1941, it was the last to be made after the negotiation of

the UN Charter. This agreement included the creation of an International Trade Organization (ITO). The ITO was negotiated in Havana as part of the UN World Trade Charter but this was never ratified by the US Senate. Nevertheless, there was agreement among the Western states to reduce tariffs under the General Agreement on Tariffs and Trade (GATT), and along with Bretton Woods, the GATT became a mainstay of the international economy.

Parallel efforts on labour, civil air routes and shipping accompanied those that created the IMF, World Bank and the GATT. But, from the start, the IMF, World Bank and GATT/Havana agreements and their implementation fell short of their founders' objectives. Happily, much that was positive was achieved in any case.

As delegates travelled to the Bretton Woods hotel in the summer of 1944, they had an added urgency as they hoped that the war in Europe could be over by Christmas. The Red Army was expelling the Germans from the last Soviet territory and heading for Berlin. In France, D-Day had finally happened. American, British, Canadian, Free French and Polish troops were fighting in Normandy. The Soviet press was euphoric about the success of the Western Allies.

The resort hotel at Bretton Woods appears to have been chosen for two reasons that illuminate the context of the times. A New Hampshire Senator, Charles Tobey, was strongly opposed to the Roosevelt Administration's proposals for a World Bank and regulation of currency. As the senior Republican on the banking and currency committee, he had great influence on whether any international agreement would be ratified by the US Senate. Staging the conference in Senator Tobey's state gave him kudos, boosted the local economy with the spending by several thousand delegates, press and staff, and also built local support for the proposed United Nations Bank. Coincidentally or not, Tobey came around to support ratifying the agreements. The reason for choosing the Bretton Woods hotel in particular appears to have been that is was one of only a few such places to accept Jews as guests.[8] Henry Morgenthau, the US Treasury Secretary and his assistant Harry White, to name but two participants, were both Jewish.

At Bretton Woods and in the preparations for the meeting, two states and two men dominated the debates and delegations: the USA, whose policy was shaped by White, and the UK, led by Keynes. In addition, the US-Soviet dealings on these economic issues influenced the development of the Allied effort as a whole.

Britain and the USA were not natural allies economically. Economic rivalry had been continuous since the war of independence in the 1770s. Until World War I, the USA had had a distinct sense of inferiority to the British. But escalating trade barriers and attempts by the two states to make their exports more attractive and imports less so by competitively devaluing their currencies had done nothing for prosperity and even less for the

25 Senior British and US Treasury officials, John Maynard Keynes and Harry Dexter White at the UNMFC, Bretton Woods, 1944.

attitude that the respective government officials had for each other. The American distrust of foreigners had been much reinforced by the failure of the Europeans (except for Finland) to repay their debts after World War I.

The British feared the Americans were seeking to keep them in a state of financial ruin after the war. For their part, Americans had a hard time accepting that the vaunted British Empire really was completely broke, and that Britain would need a lot of cash if it was not going to become so unstable as to provide fertile ground for extremists – not least the communists. It is easy to understand why the success of Soviet industrial organization in enabling the Red Army to defeat the German Army created a widespread admiration for the economic success of communism, regardless of the dictatorial methods used.

Roosevelt's ideas for helping Britain out cut little ice with Britons who believed that the economic conditions that the USA put on Britain in return

26 Keynes with Soviet and Yugoslav delegates at the UNMFC, Bretton Woods, 1944.

27 The US delegation to the UNMFC, Bretton Woods, 1944.

for Lend-Lease were exorbitant. Harold Wilson, Labour Prime Minister in the 1960s and 1970s, was one such. During the war he was a trade minister in Churchill's government. Twenty years later he still attributed Britain's post-war economic weakness to having to surrender patents on scientific inventions, including the jet engine, to the USA as giving away a generation of investment that could never be regained.[9] He wrote:

> Lend-Lease also involved Britain's surrender of her rights and royalties on a series of British technological achievements. Although the British performance in industrial techniques in the inter-war years had been marked by a period of more general decline, the achievements of our scientists and technologists had equalled the most remarkable eras of British inventive greatness. Radar, antibiotics, jet aircraft and British advances in nuclear research had created an industrial revolution all over the developed world. Under Lend-Lease, these inventions were surrendered as part of the inter-Allied war effort, free of any royalty or other payments from the United States. Had Churchill been able to insist on adequate royalties for these inventions, both our wartime and our post-war balance of payments would have been very different.[10]

As Warren Kimball has explained, US policy was indeed driven by strong pressure from conservatives and those unsympathetic to Britain to ensure that it paid 'to the utmost' and used up all its reserves of gold.[11] The negotiations leading up to the formal Lend-Lease agreement went on into 1942 and involved arguments over wartime trade in wheat and the limits the USA set on Britain's exports, as well as plans for the peace, as has been analysed extensively by Alan Dobson.[12] In the end, Article VII of the 1941 Mutual Aid agreement was left quite vague but it was picked up in the talks leading to Bretton Woods.[13] Lend-Lease also boosted US war industry and employment, as discussed in Chapter 3.

But the power imbalance between the USA and the UK was real and the congressional and public pressure in the USA real too. Kimball is one analyst of the period who is surprised not so much at concessions that the USA obtained, but that it did not press for more from the British. Additional demands could have included forcing the sale of extensive assets across South America to US corporations. Moreover, Roosevelt had no interest in annexing British Caribbean islands or other territory. He was well aware that weakening Britain would put even further global policing demands on the USA.

When the Bretton Woods conference came to an end, and many of these arguments were settled, the UNMFC agreements constituted the first global economic system. This system was made up of regulations given legal form in a treaty, though it was not ratified by the US Senate until July 1945, almost a year later.

Before examining the detail of these unprecedented agreements, it is important to consider that they came as part of an international process with other Allies, especially the Soviet Union, and were designed to combat the ideological competition still offered by the Nazis. There was little point in defeating them only to have the ideology of Germany as heroic and impoverished victim rear its head again.

In 1942 and 1943, post-war monetary schemes addressed ideas put forward by nations as diverse as Norway and China. Canada sought to mediate between the UK and US positions. The Soviet Union had been included fully in the discussions during 1943 and 1944.[14]

As the Anglo-American-led discussion of plans to regulate the global economy progressed, the time came to begin a formal process. Roosevelt did not intend to invite the United Nations to a conference without first agreeing it with Stalin – and he wanted the communists to join the capitalist system. In early 1944 he wrote to Stalin:

> In recent months a number of important steps have been taken by the Governments of the United Nations toward laying the foundations for post-war cooperative action in the various fields of international economic relations. You will recall that the United Nations Conference on Food and Agriculture, held in May 1943, gave rise to an Interim Commission which is now drafting recommendations to lay before the various governments for a permanent organization in this field. More recently, there has been established – and is now in operation – the United Nations Relief and Rehabilitation Administration. For nearly a year there have been informal technical discussions at the expert level among many of the United Nations on mechanisms for international monetary stabilization; these discussions are preparatory to a possible convocation of an United Nations Monetary Conference.[15]

Roosevelt described these discussions as based on a document agreed by the Big Three at the Moscow conference in September 1943: the 'Bases of our Program for International Economic Cooperation'. Stalin replied on 10 March,

> I consider as quite expedient the establishment at the present time of a United Nations apparatus for the working out of these questions and also for the establishment of conditions and order of consideration of various problems of the international economic collaboration in accordance with the decisions of the Moscow and Tehran Conferences'.[16,17]

Through this diplomatic strategy based on the preliminary United Nations Conferences, Roosevelt succeeded in his objective of the Soviet Union joining the international capitalist system at Bretton Woods. The conditions Stalin exacted have been itemized by Keynes's biographer, Robert Skidelsky. He cites Keynes's itemization of five points on which Stalin was given concessions: too large an influence in the IMF; too little cash and gold contributions; no likely need to actually move any gold out of Moscow; and flexibility on the currency exchange rate.[18] They displeased Keynes but are small when set against Stalin's agreement to join capitalism. For the critical point was that the Soviet Union agreed to join a system based on the private ownership of capital. 'The significance of the participation of the

Soviet Government in the Bretton Woods arrangements cannot be exaggerated. . . . The fact that instruments were drawn up in the field of monetary
cooperation which provided for concerted action of governments with
fundamentally different structures has been justifiably considered of decisive importance for future international intercourse', wrote Ervin Hexler
in 1946.[19] Hexner had been part of the US delegation to the UNMFC and
one of the committee reporters.

Stalin hoped that Lend-Lease would lead the way to a post-war loan,
as it had for the French, either through Lend-Lease or through the World
Bank and IMF. But it is too easy to simply assume that there had been no
shift towards the market economy in the Soviet Union. Jaques Sapir, the
French historian, observes of the Soviet Union's wartime economy that,

> The combination of economic specialisation (partly enabled by Lend-Lease)
> and Lend Lease itself was not enough by itself to carry the economy through to
> victory. The third piece of the puzzle was the application of what, in retrospect,
> appears to have been a far-reaching, multi-sided economic reform. A range
> of relaxations were permitted throughout the economy, beginning in 1942.
> Price mechanisms were allowed to govern a very large portion of retail trade,
> controls over the agricultural sector receded, and financial policy responded
> to the emerging reality of market mechanisms within the economic system.
>
> In large part, the economic and administrative adjustments of the war
> anticipated the debate of the 1950s and 1960s on Market Socialism. Already by
> 1947/8 the monetary reform and a brutal return to Stalinist practices (partic-
> ularly in Ukraine) re-established the pre-war state of affairs.[20]

Sapir's account is intriguing. If correct, it indicates that, as with the
renaissance of the Church discussed in Chapter 2, a combination of internal pressures, external ideas and pressure from Roosevelt may have had a
significant impact on Stalin's policies in such a way as to make a tangible
impact across the Soviet economy. In addition, Sapir's account that brutal economic Stalinism did not return until 1947–8 puts it sometime after
Churchill's Iron Curtain speech, indicating that even in the Soviet Union
market flexibility may have been continuing at this time.

The evidence of Soviet external and internal engagement with capitalism indicates a softening of economic Stalinism during and immediately
after the war. This provides evidence both that Roosevelt's policy towards
Moscow was not the 'one way street' his opponents alleged, and that, in
consequence, the opportunity to continue cooperation after the war was
greater than assumed in Western politics at the start of the Cold War.

The importance of Bretton Woods is often discussed as reducing the
rise of communism, but it also served to counter fascist ideology during
the war. As an Associated Press report from April 1944, when the Reich
still held north-west Europe in its grip, makes clear,

> The Nazis seem to be getting ready to proclaim some kind of 'Magna Carta' for
> Europe, with the double purpose of persuading Europeans their best chance

of escaping post-war social and economic chaos will be under German leadership while convincing the impoverished German masses they won't have to go Bolshevik to get social justice. Indications in this direction are seen in discussions of the post-war order appearing in the provincial German press and also in the program recently drawn up by Quisling economists and social theorists from all parts of Europe at a conference in Bad Salzbrunn. ... They frankly aimed at something halfway between 'the discredited methods of the capitalistic welfare policy and the disruptive anti-social slogans of class-war Marxism'. Their program accordingly looks like a compromise between the 1936 Stalin constitution, President Roosevelt's 'Four Freedoms', and Britain's postwar housing and social security plans. 'Our socialistic order', the article added, 'will recognize no fat profits of do-nothing directors. It will see to it that profits flow in increasing measure to the people who do the work'. Language such as this – especially the reference to the year 1932, when the Nazis were revolutionaries who had not yet achieved power – suggests that some of them are thinking the best way to recover from the disaster of a lost war is to try to win the post-war European revolution.[21]

These plans were made irrelevant by German military defeats within weeks of this Silesian conference. However, they illustrate the importance of the creation of UNRRA and the achievements of the UNMFC at Bretton Woods in preventing the economic chaos that those at this Nazi conference planned to exploit even after their military defeat.

When they were finalized in July 1944 at Bretton Woods, the UNMFC agreements met the expectations of many people in the Allied nations, though not defenders of the British Empire or American opponents of Roosevelt's domestic New Deal. The Bretton Woods agreements included four main regulatory mechanisms, all of which have relevance in the twenty-first century because they were designed to correct trade imbalances of the type that exists in 2010 between the USA and China. These mechanisms also fixed the rate at which currencies would be exchanged; created and funded a bank (the IMF) to manage and correct exchange rates; and created and funded an investment organization (the World Bank) to assist in post-war reconstruction, preventing wars and promoting long-term economic development.

This system was intended to provide the basis for global free trade without getting involved in micro-managing national governments' policies in the way the IMF and World Bank have recently done. The original plan at the global level was intended to prioritize full employment policies and industrial domestic production with the objective of social stability.

In 1942, both Keynes and White published plans for the post-war global economy. Keynes proposed an International Clearing Union and White an International Stabilization Fund (ISF) and an international bank. In April 1942, White's first draft – 'Preliminary Draft Proposal for a United Nations Stabilization Fund and a Bank for Reconstruction and Development of the

United and Associated Nations' – was intended as a clear transition from wartime to a peacetime alliance.

Both plans envisaged a par value (fixed-rate) system and elimination of discriminatory exchange arrangements (picking on individual countries for advantageous or disadvantageous treatment). Both provided that states could borrow money to balance the books if they faced a balance of payments crisis. But the means of providing this liquidity were different.

Importantly, the final deal at Bretton Woods included a process to ensure that surplus economies would use their resources to support deficit economies. In other words, if countries just keep their large currency reserves instead of using it to buy imports from poorer economies, the currency could be declared 'scarce'. This reversed the policy of the Gold Standard period by shifting the burden of international adjustments from deficit to surplus economies, rather than forcing deficit economies to carry the entire burden by reducing their imports. The policy of Bretton Woods was regarded as central to preserving peace through prosperity, and avoiding destructive spirals of competitive devaluations and protectionism.

The American plan required members to put in money and gold to create enough money (liquidity) to enable loans to be drawn from it by the nations the borrowing country was in deficit with. Thus, if the Belgians had a problem with having imported too much from France, they would borrow against the franc deposits that the French government had placed in the bank. The British plan called for a world system of accounting founded on the balance sheets of central banks, such as the Bank of England and the US Federal Reserve. Based on these accounts of the total global assets, the bank would issue credit notes – 'bancors'. The British proposal would have used the American gold and dollars to underwrite a global currency which would be used for loans.

The Americans rejected Keynes's plan as it appeared to place an unlimited requirement on them to honour all the deficits other countries had with them, while in their system the obligation was limited to the amount the USA deposited in the bank. The White plan also called for adjustments to the deposits nations made to the bank, depending on the growth in world trade.

Other key issues were debated all the way up to the first meeting of the IMF and the World Bank in Savannah, Georgia, in March 1946. These issues included an international currency, multilateral clearing, the right to leave the fund, the par value system and the transition period.

Keynes's plan would have created an international currency other than the dollar and it did not find favour with the Americans. White's plan was much more restricted and did not create general automatic convertibility between currencies. The Americans became focused on potentially being required to honour many tens of billions of debts. At this time, corporations obtained currency from banks and their central national banks rather than in an open market. Keynes considered the lack of a general multilateral clearing operation to be a huge problem as it could cause the breakdown of trade and with it, of course, political relations. During 1943, debate focused and then faded around an international currency unit – the 'unitas' – such that it and the clearing system never happened. Keynes's British colleagues were concerned that full convertibility of the pound sterling would create a rush to sell it for dollars, eliminating any British reserves of dollars and causing them potentially to reduce the dollar value of the pound.

Had Keynes's plan for an international currency union been carried forward, then a world of convertible currencies would probably have come about in the 1950s rather than the 1960s, when the European currencies became convertible with the dollar. Without currencies that could be exchanged with each other, dollars and gold would be the world currency, and as trade grew there would be a risk that there would not be enough to go around. This potential problem, of having to use too many dollars to prop up the international system, was an embarrassing and avoidable issue for the Americans that an international currency union would have overcome. The implementation of limited economic reforms may have restricted the power of the IMF to improve the European economies in 1946 and later, so failing to pick up from UNRRA and leaving problems in Europe that the Marshall Plan was created to solve, albeit on a bilateral rather than international basis.

In order to stave off this problem, White introduced a proposal that when a currency was scarce, the board of the IMF could determine which countries got to trade and limit exports. The most likely candidate would be the USA, whose products were available and much desired at the time. But a key selling point to US business and the general public was that the new UN bank and IMF would help US exports. White went so far in the ratification hearings before Congress as to guarantee that the dollar would never be declared scarce. To solve the problem, after 1945, US Treasury officials themselves rationed lending in dollars through the bank. The weakness of bank lending and of US loans in general to Europe left the European economies on the brink of disaster in the late 1940s, despite the best efforts of UNRRA's economic resuscitation 'paramedics'. One specialist on Bretton Woods observed: 'Had Keynes won his argument, loans would have been made in an international currency. As a result there would have been no scarce currency clause. And as a result of that, economic recovery in Europe would have been faster'.[22]

Another key objective of the IMF was to prevent a system of competitive devaluations as states sought to make their export goods more competitive by reducing the amount of foreign currency needed to buy them. This action-reaction cycle had occurred in the 1930s and was understood by most interested people to have caused the breakdown in US exports at that time. The solution adopted in the negotiations was to create an initial standard of exchange rates – 'par' – that might be changed. But the system did not survive the dollar crisis of the early 1970s, resulting from US deficits during the Vietnam War. A global currency might have solved the problem, as would the system of using the value of a group or basket of currencies as the measure of the rate of exchange. In 2009, the idea of a world currency began gradually to re-enter debate in *The Economist* and elsewhere.[23]

White wished the fund to go into operation immediately but Keynes and smaller countries' representatives favoured a transition period to dollar convertibility for the pound and other European currencies. As a result, the fund was not much used to assist either the development of trade or post-war reconstruction. When it was activated in the 1960s, priority turned to the developing world and by this time the idea that the World Bank's mission was to prevent wars through policies addressing high unemployment in stable economies had been cast aside. Even at Bretton Woods, there was political pressure from within the US State Department to block language supporting high employment and economic development internationally. Writing in 1996, a member of the Mexican delegation to Bretton Woods described his and the British insistence on preserving the language of Article I paragraph 3.[24] The purpose of international investment was 'thereby assisting in raising productivity, the standard of living, and conditions of labor in member countries in their territories'. The word territories was a compromise in which the colonized and future developing world squeezed in a mention for themselves. He thought it was Acheson who had sought the deletion. There is similar language in the agreement on the purposes of the IMF,

> 'To facilitate the expansion and balanced growth of international trade, and to contribute thereby to the promotion and maintenance of high levels of employment and real income and to the development of the productive resources of all members as primary objectives of economic policy.[25]

Never mind, 'this clause has been long forgotten', and as he critically observed, 'growth', then the new found 'sustainable development' and now simply 'zero inflation and structural adjustment are the obsession of bankers'.[26]

The agreements made at Bretton Woods did not have a great reception in the conservative and financial communities. The London Chamber of Commerce issued a damning pamphlet and in the USA, Thomas Dewey, the Republican candidate for President in the autumn of 1944, was opposed, as were influential senators including Robert Taft. On 1 July 1944, *The New York Times, Wall Street Journal* and the *Chicago Tribune* all attacked the idea that government should control exchange rates.

Treasury Secretary Morgenthau continued to argue that 'we cannot expect any American business man, nor business men of any nation, to take major financial risks, immediately upon the heels of a catastrophic war, without some assurance that steps have been taken to prevent their investments from being jeopardized by unduly fluctuating money values and severe exchange restrictions'. The purpose of the IMF would be just that, 'to promote exchange stability, assure multilateral payment facilities, help lessen disequilibrium and give confidence'.[27] Ratification in the Senate finally occurred in the summer of 1945 and was signed into law by Truman on 31 July. In the House of Representatives only Republicans voted against.[28] The Soviet Union declined to implement the IMF agreement, although it did send an observer to the first meeting of the new organization in Savannah, Georgia, the following March. Worsening relations with the West changed policy in Moscow towards the organizations that Roosevelt had persuaded the Soviet Union to join.

With United Nations agreement reached on questions of money and finance, the issues of world trade (that had proved to be vexatious in Anglo-American relations throughout the war) had still to be resolved and the USA did not initiate a UN negotiation on trade until well after the UNMFC at Bretton Woods. Many countries were keen to obtain direct US economic help through loans and a continuation of Lend-Lease. While the UNFMC offered future prosperity and UNRRA would help sort out the wreckage and feed the starving, neither would provide intermediate help in restarting economies. America's Allies looked for help in two ways, through a continuation of Lend-Lease and through direct, bilateral loans.

Papers in Roosevelt's presidential library indicate that he gave his personal agreement to the British and to the Soviet Union that aid would come in two forms: a continuation of Lend-Lease and in direct loans.[29] In the case of Lend-Lease, there was to be a phased reduction: the first phase would end with victory in Europe, the second with victory in Japan and the third would take place during the transition to peace. In the event, President Truman cancelled the first phase so abruptly that ships were unloaded at the dockside or turned around in mid-ocean. The offence caused and suspicions aroused in London and Moscow were intense. The insult to injury was that these countries felt that they had suffered grievous losses from enemy action while the USA was unscathed. Truman backtracked somewhat but most histories conclude that nothing was done to use lend lease for the peace.

The realism of turning Lend-Lease into a transitional arrangement for supporting the civilian economies was far greater than is generally assumed by scholars. The evidence for implementing phase three of Lend-Lease can be found in the agreement the USA made with France in late February 1945. Under the agreement, the USA agreed to supply France

with $2.5 billion of civilian industrial equipment, food, oil and other sup-
plies. Where these were not used directly in the war, they were to be treated
as a 30-year loan at $2\frac{3}{8}$ per cent interest. The statement was issued on behalf of Morgenthau for the Treasury Department, Joseph Grew, the Acting
Secretary of State and Leo Crowley, the Foreign Economic Administrator.
As was the habit of the time, the statement emphasized the effectiveness
of Lend-Lease 'in aiding the United Nations to progress to victory over
the common enemies'.[30] The *Wall Street Journal* was quick to support the
agreement but, claiming that a similar negotiation was under way with
Russia, urged Congress to oppose it on the grounds that Russia's need
for post-war reconstruction was less than that of France.[31] The value of
the French agreement was about two-thirds the value of the post-war loan
to Britain so painfully negotiated by Keynes as Prime Minister Attlee's
representative in talks with the Truman Administration.

There appears to have been no effective Congressional opposition to
the use of Lend-Lease in this way. Further research into the Lend-Lease
agreements made in early 1945 is needed. The USA made such agreements
with a number of late additions to the ranks of the United Nations. In the
light of the agreement with France, there is a need to look anew at the
negotiations under way at that time with Britain and the Soviet Union.

Nevertheless, the ability of the Roosevelt Administration to use Lend-
Lease as a mechanism for providing bilateral loans for economic development without needing Senate approval indicates that the same option
was far more of a possibility for Truman than scholars consider it to have
been. It is possible to attribute Truman's actions to a general hardening of
US public and Congressional opinion towards hand-outs to foreigners –
especially socialists and communists. And it is possible to regard his actions as a warning that, even before Japan had been defeated, he intended
a tougher and more confrontational approach to inter-Allied relations. It is
not credible to see this as an act of an innocent abroad. Truman had been
in the Senate and deeply engaged in wartime politics and was well aware
of the importance that Roosevelt placed on Lend-Lease as the foundation
and model of the new international system. Whatever else one can say
about Truman's actions, it was not the continuation of Roosevelt's policy
to which he had publicly committed himself.

The same was the case with respect to US loans. Both Churchill and
Stalin believed that they had agreement with Roosevelt for loans of around
$6 billion each. It was mostly to be spent, in the case of the Soviet Union,
on US equipment for manufacturing to support the civilian economy. Indeed, the *Wall Street Journal* reported, in early 1945, on a brochure of intended purchases produced by the Soviet purchasing agency in the USA,
with sponsored advertising by US corporations. The Soviet loan negotiations stuttered to a halt within months of Truman's taking office and never

appear to have been resumed seriously on the US side. In Britain, the last energy of Keynes's life was devoted to persuading the US Administration to extend a loan to the Labour government elected by the British in July 1945.

With regard to US international economic policy in mid-1945, it is hard to imagine Roosevelt, Hopkins and Hull allowing their careful plans for peace to be based on economic policy to fail with the end of Lend-Lease and ill-starred loan negotiations. Rather, the French-style Lend-Lease loan would have served to link UNRRA to the rapid implementation of the Bretton Woods institutions and then the Havana Charter. Large-scale economic assistance akin to the Marshall Plan would have been likely to have been initiated in 1945 rather than three years later on a rising tide of anti-communism. Clifford Matlock, a US Lend-Lease administrator, later observed that 'if Lend-Lease had been continued for a time, it would have in some measure anticipated the Marshall plan'.[32]

The Havana United Nations Conference on Trade and Employment of 1947 was the attempt to bring to fruition the conditions for a fair system of global free trade conceived by Hull and Roosevelt. From 1941, the Americans, British and Canadians discussed new trading systems under Article VII of the Mutual Aid (Lend-Lease) agreement and then the provisions of the Anglo-American loan agreement of 1945. In parallel, the USA began to use its huge financial reserves to float the IMF and World Bank.

In late 1945, the US Department of State issued a document calling for a UN conference on Trade and Employment as was agreed at Bretton Woods. This was endorsed at the inaugural meeting of the UN's Economic and Social Council in 1946.[33] There followed an intense debate within the 18-nation preparatory group in London, which met in a bomb-damaged Church House, off Whitehall. In the discussions, 'the raw expression of intense rivalry between the dominant United States and the declining world power of the United Kingdom emerged from time to time to mar the proceedings and was never far below the surface'.[34]

This preparatory group also reached agreement on the reduction of tariffs. The process was one whereby the principal traders (suppliers) of any given product reached a deal to which the rest adhered – a systematic application of the internationalization of power and of cartels.

The negotiations that took place at Church House did not include provisions on investment, employment, or restrictive business practices, or agreements on commodities or 'organizational' issues. However, these were all the subject of detailed agreement at the formal discussions of the UN Conference on Trade and Employment (UNCTE) that took place in Havana in the spring of 1947. Looking back at them from the early twenty-first century, what is startling about the Havana Charter is how naturally fair and radical it is compared to current debates in the World Trade Organization (WTO).

The Havana Charter's nine chapters and 106 articles are themselves evidence of how many topics governments were prepared to reach agreement on. Trade barriers, both formal and informal, were described and regulated. The principles of the charter also included the point that 'industrial stability [meaning full employment] and fair labor standards are essential to the expansion of world trade'.

In the Havana Charter specific provision was given that regulation of state-run trading should match that of private corporations. Export subsidies such as those that enable US, Japanese and European Union (EU) farmers to protect themselves from competition from poorer economies in world markets were to be phased out under the charter. These provisions are listed alongside more familiar ones regarding the protection of the interests of foreign direct investors in developing states.[35] The International Trade Organization was given the charter as a basis for negotiating specific agreements. It would have been governed by a quite democratic and veto-free Executive Committee of 18 states, eight of whom would have been the world's biggest economies. So, in this system, power would have been recognized but not given complete control.

By the time the negotiations were concluded, the Western powers had secured their main objectives through the GATT, and soon the careful compromises in the Havana Charter were attacked by protagonists on all sides for being just that. In the USA, right-wing anti-communism was in the ascendancy and new attacks on the rights of organized labour were happening. The Havana Charter languished before the US Congress for two years in the late 1940s and was then withdrawn by President Truman.[36] For US protectionists, there were too many concessions and commitments; for liberal or free traders, too many exemptions and loopholes. But what came to be called simply 'GATT' survived and prospered.[37] Wilcox's lament that the charge that GATT violated the principles of the Atlantic Charter and other wartime agreements had little impact in the USA, where increasingly any liberal policy was effectively branded as communist. This was a process Roosevelt had experienced but had been able to defeat, up to a point. But in the twenty-first century, a similar rhetoric continues to have a powerful political voice, at least in the USA.

One of the few international commentators to recommend the revival of the ideas of the Havana Charter to NGOs and the developing world is Susan George.[38] She has ruefully observed that the politics of the twenty-first century do not allow onto today's agenda, even that of trade unions and the development and aid community, the agenda of the 1940s.

The trade issues at the Havana conference are best discussed in conjunction with Bretton Woods to enable full consideration of the end of war economic debates, even though this does not follow the historical sequence of events. In addition to agreements at Havana and Bretton Woods, there were others on international labour and on civil aviation and shipping that took place in 1944 and 1945. They complete the range of negotiations aimed to create a comprehensive system of world economic governance as a means of war prevention, conceived when the war was at its height. The Atlantic Charter pointed to the need to improve labour standards and social security. This was one part of international public life where there was still a functioning and well-regarded League of Nations body, the International Labour Organization. The ILO delegates debated the future of Germany and three other issues: people before profits, full employment by the industrialized nations, and raising the living standards of the colonized peoples.

The Indian trade union leader Jamandas Mehta, supported by the Australian delegation, sought ILO committees to investigate how the British, Dutch and French Empires were helping 'raise up the colonial peoples'. But their efforts to hold the imperial leaders in London and Paris to account were fobbed off by the major powers.

The goal of full employment was agreed as an aspiration, but the idea of making it legally binding to ensure demand for raw materials was soon forgotten. Likewise, the idea of putting people first also remained an aspiration. The main product of the ILO meeting was the Philadelphia Charter, which served as a visionary set of norms that have helped shape the world – or utopian hot air, depending on your point of view. Its provisions included the basic assumption that lasting peace requires social justice, that labour is not a commodity and that all people have the right to equal economic opportunity, regardless of race, creed and sex.

The Aviation Conference in mid-1944 followed the by then traditional pattern whereby the US Government invited the other United Nations to debate an issue and then put forward its own plan for the outcome. This time the venue was Chicago, a traditional centre of isolationists, and for the first time the profits of private companies were explicitly on the agenda. The USA included non-United Nations countries, notably Portugal under the Salazar dictatorship, resulting in the Soviet Union boycotting the meeting. The outcome was the International Civil Aviation Organization, later recognized as a UN Specialized Agency that from 1944 agreed safety and management standards. The other main achievement was to allow airlines to freely overfly countries other than their own. At the time, for example, Dutch airlines could not cross the USA, and Italy sought to charge a fee for overflights. An Australia–New Zealand proposal for a single government-controlled airline for the entire planet had little support, though the motivation was not to create a tedious monopoly but to remove a possible cause of rivalry between nations.[39]

The main issue at the conference – whether to have complete free trade of the air – was never completely resolved. A Darwinian process of survival meant that the fittest and largest – which would naturally be the USA – would triumph; the alternative would have been the world body parcelling out the routes that airlines were permitted to fly. At that time, 'consumer' states without airlines wanted to ensure the lowest prices, whilst those with smaller airlines, such as the Europeans, wanted to make sure that they were not taken over by the USA.

Without the Chicago conference, the development of international air travel would have been more difficult and the tensions between the USA and its Western Allies greater. Had the whole process not been started until after 1945, it is likely that the result would have shifted even more in favour of the USA than was in fact the case.

Finally, in considering the international work for the global economy, a word or two must be said about the now less than glamorous world of shipping – which of course had been the key to Allied success. Without sufficient cargo vessels, the worldwide war effort could never have been supported by American supplies and the British would never have sustained the Empire and Commonwealth. At sea, the smaller nations, Greece, The Netherlands and Norway in particular, made a large contribution to the merchant fleet of the United Nations. A combination of sunken ships and American production created a huge US dominance in world shipping.

A British minister, Oliver Lyttleton, wrote with astonishment in 1942 after meeting with Roosevelt, that the President was prepared to sell off at a discount US merchant ships to Britain, Greece, The Netherlands and Norway to restore the proportion of national shipping tonnages that had existed before the U-boats decimated their fleets.[40] This, coupled with a desire to ensure the fastest possible economic recovery, led to the creation in 1944 of a United Shipping Authority. This programme does not appear to have happened and its managerial role soon lapsed, but some of its functions were developed into the UN's International Maritime Organization (IMO) created in 1948.

Open global markets became the central feature of the global economy in the second half of the twentieth century, with rapid growth especially in the 'trente glorieuse', the 30 years following the war. These policies were a direct and deliberate result of the policies developed by the United Nations during the war. The Bretton Woods/GATT system remained at its strongest up to the mid-1970s. Overall, the second half of the twentieth century was the most rapidly growing and prosperous period in history (average world growth rates between 1960 and 1980 were almost double that of 1980–2000). The major powers have not gone to war with each other since 1945 and while economic nationalism has been a factor, it has not been on the scale of the inter-war period. Thus, the work of the wartime United Nations was highly successful in achieving its economic objectives, at least amongst the Western industrialized states, despite the onset of the Cold War.

The main changes to the system have been the refocusing of the World Bank, in geographic, political and economic terms, on the developing world. Economically, the shift was away from full employment, rapid growth and industrialization as an objective of international security, towards structural adjustment, with loans increasingly being made conditional on rolling back the state's economic role and on liberal institutional and policy reforms.

The IMF never functioned as was originally intended and in the 1970s the USA unilaterally abandoned the fixed-rate exchange rate system to enable its domestic economy and electorate to be insulated from the economic impact of the Vietnam War. The GATT has morphed into the World Trade Organization without any revival of elements of the Havana Charter's International Trade Organization not conducive to the interests of Anglo-Saxon multinational corporations.

The limited agreements made at the end of World War II failed to cover a number of critical issues. These included anarchy in global financial markets beyond the influence of national central bankers, including those of the EU and the USA, and the increasing rich-poor divide in the industrialized world and between it and the Third World. The drive to improve the stock-market value of companies is incompatible with long-term planning – not least for environmental impact. The net result has been the creation of a dominant and uncontrolled financial and corporate elite that is apparently beyond popular control.[41]

As Robert Skidelsky, amongst others, has argued, the weakness in the global economic system is a direct function of the US attempt to maintain economic as well as political-military supremacy at the global level. The 'bancor' and a return to a fully multilateral approach as envisaged in the talks leading to Bretton Woods offers a soft landing for the USA and the global economy in the twenty-first century. The alternative may be a prolonged period of instability as the USA seeks to maintain its past pre-eminence. The dangerous conceit amongst Western leaders as to their political prowess was highlighted by Thomas Weiss, who pointed to the contrast between the British proposal to the UNMFC at Bretton Woods that the IMF should have a value of half of world imports and today's far smaller IMF resources. As the late Hans Singer pointed out: 'Today's Fund is only 2 per cent of annual world imports. The difference between Keynes's originally proposed 50 per cent and the actual 2 per cent is a measure of the degree to which our vision of international economic management has shrunk'.[42]

CHAPTER **8**

Security: Dumbarton Oaks, Yalta and San Francisco

In 1944, most Americans backed transferring the authority of Congress to declare war into the hands of the US delegate to the United Nations, for this was an explicit policy of Roosevelt's on which he was elected President that year. This was indicative of public support for the United Nations at the time and of a widespread sentiment around the world. It also provides a sense of the politics at a moment when America and its Allies defeated Hitler and formalized the new UN organization for peace and security that was to be the culmination of the war effort.

The completion of the UN Charter in San Francisco in June 1945 was a process of metamorphosis. The gradual growth of the peace-building elements of the United Nations finally flowered fully-formed as the armoured shell of the war-fighting alliance fell away, its job done. The meeting in San Francisco took place amidst the continuing conflagration of the war and the jockeying for position in the post-war world by all concerned.

A succession of diplomatic meetings led up to forming the new UN organization at San Francisco. Hopes of smooth progress were buffeted by events. There was disagreement between the Big Three over what they had agreed at Yalta. When the United Nations Conference on International Organization (UNCIO) opened in San Francisco in late April, it did so barely two weeks after the death of Roosevelt. Within weeks, Harry Truman, the new President, adopted a more confrontational approach to his Allies. He made headlines by claiming to have directly told the Soviet Foreign Minister to get on with implementing the Yalta agreements on Eastern Europe. He then abruptly terminated economic assistance through Lend-Lease to the other United Nations, without any follow-on programme, after Hitler's Reich finally surrendered on 8 May 1945.

This chapter discusses the relations between the Big Three in the period leading up to the San Francisco conference and how they worked with other countries. When Churchill, Roosevelt and Stalin met in the Black Sea resort of Yalta in early 1945, the question of a joint approach to the creation of the new organization was high on their agenda. Although the three had not met since November 1943 in Tehran, there were other, lower-level meetings that paved the way. The most important of these were the financial agreements made at Bretton Woods in July 1944, described in the previous chapter; the August 1944 agreement at Dumbarton Oaks on the post-war UN Organization, discussed below; and two other meetings. These were between Churchill and Roosevelt in Quebec in September and between Churchill and Stalin in Moscow that October. Since 1942, Roosevelt had pressed Stalin for one-to-one meetings but this never happened.

Within weeks of the success at Bretton Woods, a smaller conference was held at Dumbarton Oaks mansion, Washington, DC, to agree on a structure for a new international security organization. It was at this meeting that the four powers – Britain, China, the Soviet Union and the USA – formally proposed that the United Nations alliance create a global security organization of the same name. The American domestic background to these meetings was the 1944 US Presidential election campaign, intensifying after the summer party conventions chose the candidates: Thomas Dewey for the Republicans and Roosevelt for the Democrats.

Roosevelt did not duck the issue of post-war planning until after the election; on both economics and security he campaigned to conduct US policy through a permanent United Nations.[1] The result of Roosevelt's campaign was an extremely positive reaction from the voting public exemplified in their support for his proposal to provide war making powers to UN delegates. The intention was to prevent a repeat of the indecision of the 1930s in the new UN.

This positive attitude towards creating a permanent UN security organization was encouraged by the success of the meetings in Moscow and Tehran; the United Nations conferences on food, relief and economics; on the success of Lend-Lease; and, above all, on the triumphs of the armies of the United Nations on the battlefield, from Normandy and Eastern Europe to the Pacific. By this time, US public opinion was overwhelmingly in favour of the USA joining a new international organization for peace and security.

The earlier chapters of this book have demonstrated how, from its inception in 1942, government officials and private citizens usually considered it both desirable and likely that the wartime United Nations would merge into the post-war organization. The US State Department planning groups on the peace had begun well before US entry into the war. They were led by Sumner Welles, Roosevelt's favourite in the Department, and Leo Paslovsky. Welles was forced to resign in 1943 over privately made allegations that while drunk on an official journey he sought to pay for sex with a male railway steward.

Cordell Hull's proposal in January 1942 for a United Nations Supreme War Council was dropped as too ambitious. Nevertheless, the idea was in wide circulation amongst the press and diplomatic community. As the Anglo-American combined military and economic committees gathered momentum, so those on the outside sought to be included.

A United Nations Authority of all the United Nations, with a smaller big power Executive Committee, was proposed internally in the State Department in early 1942, but this was quashed by Roosevelt who wanted no diplomatic issue to allow the unilateralists an opportunity to get back into the debate.[2]

The work in the State Department continued in parallel with that of Roosevelt in the White House and other governments and organizations. The Chinese, smaller states, and many in Congress and the non-governmental groups all favoured the immediate creation of a UN Executive Committee, as discussed in the earlier chapters of this book.

For Britain, firm American involvement was fundamental to any new organization as they had been left holding the infant League of Nations when the USA renounced its responsibilities as parent. With this in mind, the Foreign Office under Eden tended to react by seeking to adapt proposals from the State Department and the White House and talk down Churchill's ideas, which concentrated on regional organizations and from time to time on an alliance of the English-speaking peoples. Churchill hankered for the vision of an Anglo-Saxon world Empire notably espoused by Cecil Rhodes. British officials, notably Gladwyn Jebb and Charles Webster, with the Foreign Office experience of running the League in their veins, worked on the details of the proposed Charter with their colleagues at State.[3]

The discussions within and between governments in private and in public also interacted with the debate in the US Congress. With the haunting memory of the Senate rejection of the League, the Administration was at pains to encourage Senate debate on international issues, as discussed in Chapter 4. A reference point for historians is the B2H2 resolution, named after the two Democrat and two Republican Senators proposing it: Senators Ball, Burton, Hill and Hatch. This resolution shaped the Congressional debate on the issue of an international organization through 1943 and 1944. It is rarely quoted. I do so here so that readers can make their own judgement.

Organization of United Nations; Senate Resolution 114, 16 March 1943.
That the Senate advises that the United States take the initiative in calling meetings of representatives of the United Nations for the purpose of forming an organization of the United Nations with specific and limited authority:
To assist in coordinating and fully utilizing the military and economic resources of all member nations in the prosecution of the war against the Axis.
To establish temporary administrations for Axis-controlled areas of the world as these are occupied by United Nations forces, until such time as permanent governments can be established.
To administer relief and assistance in economic rehabilitation in territories of member nations needing such aid and in Axis territory occupied by United Nations forces.

To establish procedures and machinery for peaceful settlement of disputes and disagreements between nations.

To provide for the assembly and maintenance of a United Nations military force and to suppress by immediate use of such force any future attempt at military aggression by any nation.

The resolution concludes by recommending that the new organization be capable of amendment and growth.[4]

Here we can see that the Senate was debating, from the early spring of 1943, the immediate creation of a United Nations organization that would be an integrated global mechanism for enforcing peace by military means if necessary, fighting wars, preventing conflict, and aiding and developing post-war activities.

While Roosevelt did not endorse this resolution publicly, as was discussed in Chapters 2 and 4, he was pursuing a very similar policy at home and abroad. For Roosevelt, the Congressional political debate was but one part of global political dynamics.

Until late in the war, the idea of making a general organization of the United Nations to coordinate military and economic affairs was resisted by the Big Three. Roosevelt regarded it as creating an unnecessary target for his opponents at home and did not publicly endorse the idea until after D-Day had succeeded.[5] Churchill was more concerned with US-UK bilateral agreements, and sought to elevate Australia and Canada as auxiliaries of the Empire and arrange regional rather than global structures. Stalin, having given strong support to the League of Nations, was now more concerned to secure a territorial buffer zone against further attacks from Germany.

As Soviet experience in joining the US-led new United Nations organizations grew during 1943 and 1944, Stalin appears to have begun some preparations to enable a stronger Soviet role. Noticing the US ability to whistle up support from within South America, and the British likewise from the white-run states of the Commonwealth, he set about some legalistic reform at home. The Soviet Constitution was a beautiful utopian façade and he created fresh embellishments. Each of the republics forming the Union was given a new constitution in 1944 providing for their independence in foreign policy, and on this basis Moscow began to lobby for 16 places on what was to become the General Assembly.

At Dumbarton Oaks it was agreed that the purpose and principles of the new organization were to suppress any international aggression and to foster conflict resolution and political, economic and social cooperation on the basis of equal sovereignty of nations. The organization was to consist of a General Assembly, a Security Council, an international court of justice and a secretariat.

The Security Council was to be an institutionalized form of the four powers that had led the war effort, plus France, where General de Gaulle's

28 Soviet postage stamp marking United Nations Day 1944.

personal leadership had led it from the humiliation of surrender in 1940 to restoration at the top level of international affairs. A Military Staff Committee was created at the UNCIO in San Francisco, and as late as 1947, states sent in lists of military units it might call upon. Churchill called for British air force units to form part of an air force under UN command, with the only restriction being that they not bomb Britain, in his famous Iron Curtain speech of 1946.

However, with Cold War animosity the committee was never used and since the Cold War ended it has not been regenerated. It has been at the Security Council's disposal but quite unused for nearly 70 years.

As the government debates on the creation of the UN organization gathered pace, so too did the efforts of the public and NGOs. The experience of the Senate rejection of the League of Nations always drove the way Roosevelt, Hull and other officials developed policy; similarly, it also influenced relations with the non-governmental world and public opinion. The

head of the US support group for the League of Nations, Charles Eichelberger, kept pressing the President and State Department. But even though
he had headed the Committee to Defend America, his association with the
League meant he was kept at arms length by a White House anxious not
to be seen putting new wine into old bottles contaminated with failure.
Rather, Eleanor Roosevelt went around boosting UN Committees all over
the USA – with counterparts overseas – and it was only in early 1945 that
the old League of Nations Association changed its name to become a UN
association, long after the multinational United Nations Information Organization had been created and the Four Freedoms Committee had come
up with the first United Nations flag in 1943.

After the Dumbarton Oaks proposals were agreed, the US State Department began a national publicity campaign for the new organization,
enlisting the help of a wide variety of NGOs. Across the USA, in countless
communities, its ideas were debated in detail. For contemporary practition-
ers and scholars of public diplomacy and the cooperation between social
movements and governments, this campaign and the United Nations Days
that led up to it provide a rich source of examples. The official history of the
US State Department records how that organization 'undertook a public
relations campaign to build support for the United Nations. As part of that
effort, the Department printed two million copies of the Dumbarton Oaks
proposals and an informative, eight-page guide to the draft United Nations
Charter. The Department worked in concert with interested groups to inform the public about the United Nations and even dispatched officials
around the country to answer questions on the proposed organization. By
the end of the effort, the Department of State had coordinated almost 500
such meetings'.[6]

The international circus of UN conferences is a feature of our times.
They are studied as if they are modern, post-Cold War phenomena. The
relation of government to these NGOs is also the subject of study and
comment. Measures such as the Millennium Development Goals and the
landmine ban come about through a combination of government and
non-governmental groups working together. It is useful to remember that
the UN organization itself was created in just such a fashion. The million spectators on the streets of San Francisco for the opening of the UN
conference that created the Charter were very much aware and engaged
because of the intense publicity campaign. And the US Government included 49 non-governmental representatives in its delegation, of which
just one was a woman. The Administration also made sure to include Senators and Congressmen.

The hopes for cooperation and peace emanating from Dumbarton Oaks
were challenged with the realities of human behaviour in Poland where
further tragedies unfolded in August 1944. Nazi extermination camps were

found for the first time by the Red Army, and in Warsaw, the resistance rose against the Germans only to be crushed with appalling loss of life. Inspecting the camps at Majdanek and Treblinka, journalists reported that they saw extermination chambers, mounds of skeletons and decaying corpses. In the vegetable garden of the camp guards, cabbages were being fertilized with human ashes from the crematoria.[7] The exposure of the extent of Nazi methods reinforced the public sense that the United Nations must establish a working peace.

In the battle for Warsaw, the Red Army was unable, and Stalin unwilling, to help the fighters who clearly opposed communism. At the time, most in the West believed that the Red Army could have liberated Warsaw and linked up with the resistance, and Stalin's temporary refusal to allow US planes that were trying to parachute supplies to land in Russia to refuel reinforced that belief. It appears though that the Germans pulled together a desperate resistance with tank units in order to prevent the Russians crossing the last major river barrier before Germany.

The Red Army had destroyed a huge German Army during late July, but was exhausted after suffering over a million deaths. This was the price of expelling the German Army from Byelorussia and Ukraine, killing 300,000 enemy soldiers in the process. The attack was designed to hit the Germans from the east in coordination with the D-Day landings in the west, so stretching German resources to the maximum.

Stalin accused the Polish forces in Warsaw, loyal to the government in exile in London, of failing to coordinate with him when they launched their uprising. The Warsaw rising was still underway when Churchill and Roosevelt met again in Quebec. With the Anglo-American-Canadian-French and Polish Armies racing for the German border, they needed to discuss the fate of post-war Europe and the final phase of the war against Japan. The press conference at the end of their meeting – which had included discussions with the Canadians – concentrated on the British commitment to send the Royal Navy to assist in the defeat of Japan once Germany was vanquished. In private they came close to agreeing a plan put forward by Treasury Secretary Morgenthau that Germany would be divided into two parts and all industrial capacity removed. The British also began to press for negotiations on a post-war loan and the continuation of Lend-Lease. Churchill also obtained a private agreement with Roosevelt on joint control of any use of the atom bomb – but this personal agreement by Roosevelt died with him.[8]

By the beginning of October 1944, the Nazis had destroyed hopes of a Christmas victory party. Their armies held the line on the Vistula River in Poland, and in Holland they defeated an attempt by American, British and Polish paratroopers to create a channel through German-held territory into the heart of Germany. Eight thousand British paratroopers were killed or captured fighting for the bridge over the Rhine River at Arnhem.

The Moscow meeting, initiated by Churchill, took place in mid-October. The meeting is best known now for the secret 'percentages agreements' under which Churchill and Stalin divided Eastern European countries between them.

In the United States, the Presidential election was tightening as it entered its final weeks. Roosevelt won votes from the internationalist Republicans with aggressive support for a United Nations organization a few weeks after Dumbarton Oaks. Roosevelt's proposal to put power into the hands of the US delegate at the UN succeeded on winning over the leading internationalist Republican, 38-year-old Senator Joseph H. Ball of Minnesota. Ball said: 'If Congress reserves the right to consider each particular case before American forces can act against aggressors, then other nations will make similar reservations [and] we will have no more certainty of international law enforcement than we had in the '20s and '30s'.[9] Ball was won over when on 21 October 1944 Roosevelt stated:

> To my simple mind it is clear that, if the world organization is to have any reality at all, our American representative must be endowed in advance by the people themselves, by constitutional means through their representatives in the Congress, with authority to act. If we do not catch the international felon when we have our hands on him, if we let him get away with his loot because the Town Council [he meant the Congress] has not passed an ordinance authorizing his arrest, then we are not doing our share to prevent another world war.

He made these remarks in the speech to the Foreign Policy Association referred to in Chapter 1.[10] In the aftermath of Ball's defection to the Democrats, *The Washington Post* carried a commentary sympathetic to the Republican Presidential candidate, Thomas Dewey, by one Merlo Pewsey. Pewsey's argument portrayed Dewey as agreeing with Roosevelt and argued that there was a bipartisan consensus in favour of Congress giving up war-making powers in case of action by the UN.[11]

The significance of the strength of American public support for a world security organization that included the Soviet Union increases when one understands that there was an unrelenting campaign by Republicans to smear all progressive policies as communism. Alongside Pewsey's article ran the news story ' "Communists Run New Deal" Bricker says', reporting a speech by the Republican Vice-Presidential candidate, Governor John Bricker of Ohio, in which he alleged that 'Franklin Roosevelt and the New Deal are in the hands of the radicals and the communists'. The argument was based on the idea that the Roosevelt Administration had support from labour unions and the labour unions had connections to the tiny American communist party. Rather, as in 2009 when President Obama was routinely accused of introducing communism into the USA, the accusation was based on a smear. The false association of foreign and domestic adversaries is an old political tactic, of a type that would have been applauded by Machiavelli as a basic tool of statecraft. The hollowness of the charge becomes clear when it is realized that those who made it rarely had anything critical to say of those American anti-Semitic fellow travellers of the Nazis, notably Hitler's 'inspiration', Henry Ford and Charles Lindbergh.[12]

With the arguments won and the war going well, the voters elected Roosevelt by 25 million votes to 22 million for Dewey. But still, the minority voted for candidates espousing virulent politics. After the election, in obviously poor health, Roosevelt continued to work for victory and a secure peace. The next summit with Churchill and Stalin was arranged for February in Yalta, a seaside resort on the Black Sea coast of the Crimea. The destruction in the area made a profound impression on Roosevelt, who had not previously seen such devastating impacts of the war.

Much scholarship has been devoted to this meeting at the Livadia Palace. The discussion here will focus on the main issues before the Allied leaders and the subsequent interpretation of what they agreed. Each leader had key objectives for the meeting.

All agreed that Germany must be prevented from becoming a threat 20 years on. All agreed on implementing the Dumbarton Oaks proposals for a United Nations organization. Stalin wanted to be sure that the Soviet Union would not be attacked again and so wanted territory to the west of Russia and the assurance which would come with control of the states in Eastern Europe. Churchill sought to restrict communist influence and secure the British Empire. Both Churchill and Stalin wanted American money for post-war development, while Roosevelt wanted Russian help against Japan.

But, as Sigrid Arne puts it, behind all these major specific issues there loomed 'the question about which the politically literate world was wondering; whether or not the world's great Communist power and the world's two great capitalist powers could reconcile their differences well enough to write a plan for restoring order to chaotic Europe'.[13]

To complicate matters, one of the issues the leaders had to manage was the development of the atom bomb. Some senior US officials saw the weapon as a card to play with the Soviet Union at this stage, according to the late Sir Joseph Rotblat, a Polish scientist who worked on the programme in the USA and who resigned when this became clear to him.[14] In hindsight, we know that the bomb worked. At the time, only very few people outside of the bomb-makers themselves knew of its existence, including Stalin through his spies. But no one knew for certain it would work.

The USA faced the prospect of having to invade Japan with very high casualties. The Germans had not surrendered until their capital city had been conquered one street at a time, fighting on long after their situation

IX The situation in the Pacific, December 1944.

was clearly hopeless. The Japanese fought with at least as much tenacity. In addition, Japan still had millions of men overseas, occupying some of China and much of South East Asia. A top priority for the USA, therefore, was to ensure that the Red Army moved forces across Siberia to be ready to attack the Japanese in China. This the Russians agreed to do, and in return were granted territorial concessions in North East Asia. The result, six months later in August, was a Soviet attack in Manchuria that destroyed the large but ill-equipped Japanese Army in a couple of weeks.[15]

The debate on Eastern Europe and Poland came to dominate politics and the development of renewed confrontation between the West and Russia. Stalin's policy had been to take land as a protection against attack. The Western Allies had kept Russia out of the management of Italian affairs from 1943, and although the Soviet Union was party to the armistice, the agreement was not made public until after the war. The tension between narrow and broad national interests was a feature of the wartime United Nations throughout its existence.

The Italian experience provided a precedent for other parts of Europe that the Soviet and Western Armies entered. The October 1944 'percentages' agreement between Stalin and Churchill was an extension of this approach and was naturally enough also a secret – and whatever the exact details were, was a de facto division of spheres of influence – in violation of the soaring rhetoric of the Atlantic Charter and the United Nations. Churchill's intervention in Greece pitted British soldiers against communist guerrillas as he tried to defeat them with the help of British-equipped royalist forces. There was international shock at his action and no support from Washington, but Stalin did nothing, honouring his deal with Churchill. In the House of Commons in January 1945, Churchill spoke of what he represented as the restoration of law and order as an unpleasant duty, carefully separating the Greek communists from Moscow: '. . . all forms of government would have been swept away and naked, triumphant Trotskyism installed. I think "Trotskyists" is a better definition of these people and of certain other sects, than the normal word, and it has the advantage of being equally hated in Russia'.[16]

Roosevelt's European policy was more open to left-wing influence in government. On 5 December 1944, Stettinius publicly criticized British opposition to the Italian leftist politician Count Sforza and declared a policy of non-intervention in the other liberated United Nations, not least Belgium and Greece. When the British appeared to be using American support against Greeks, US naval chiefs broke into the military chain of command to prevent US ships supplying the British forces in Greece, prompting a vitriolic phone call from Churchill to Hopkins. On New Year's eve, with the Battle of the Bulge raging around Bastogne, Churchill flew to Athens and managed to negotiate a truce in the developing Greek civil war.

For his part, Stalin had brutally seized territory. He took part in the Pact with Hitler under which he absorbed Eastern Poland – or from the Soviet perspective, took it back after it had been conquered by Poland in 1920. He absorbed the Baltic States, seen as traditionally part of the Russian Empire, and attempted to protect Leningrad (now St Petersburg) through the conquest of Eastern Finland. The Polish pre-war government had an explicit policy of breaking up the Soviet Union, and for its part saw its policy as a necessary defence against Russian/Soviet imperialism.[17] The discovery in 1943 by the Nazis of the murder by Stalin of 20,000 Polish officers and educated elite only aggravated the issue, not least for the six million Polish-American voters.

The statement of the Big Three on Poland at Yalta was regarded as a betrayal by the London-based Poles. Under the agreement, Poland lost territory inhabited largely by Ukrainians. Roosevelt and Churchill agreed to recognize Stalin's puppet government based in the city of Lublin as the provisional government and agreed a tortuous formula to produce democracy. The critical Yalta agreement on Poland states that the three foreign ministers were 'authorized as a commission to consult in the first instance in Moscow with members of the present Provisional Government and with other Polish democratic leaders from within Poland and from abroad, with a view to the reorganization of the present Government along the above lines. This Polish Provisional Government of National Unity shall be pledged to the holding of free and unfettered elections as soon as possible'.[18]

If such a statement were issued nowadays, critical observers would point to the leisurely and indecisive nature of the commitments. Certainly in Britain such language contains no real commitment. And as to elections, for the Western Allies, 'as soon as possible' turned out to be June 1946 in Italy.

As for the rest of the region, by the time of the Yalta conference, the Red Army had liberated most of Eastern Europe and a number of countries had signed armistice agreements. These ended hostilities and established the control of the Allies. The surrender documents made frequent reference to the United Nations.[19] In the Balkans, the British and Americans were involved with the Soviet Union in taking the surrender of each country.

Communist rule was not imposed as Soviet tanks entered the capitals of Eastern Europe. While there were purges and killing of political opponents, Stalin restrained the local communist parties from taking power, ensuring the formal existence of coalitions. With the exception of the Baltic states and Eastern Poland, Stalin did not make these countries part of the Soviet Union. And in Finland, which made peace in October 1944, there was no Soviet occupation despite the fact that this country had been a province of the Czarist Empire.

29 Churchill, Roosevelt and Stalin at the Yalta conference, February 1945.

Studies using recently available Soviet archives indicate flexibility in Stalin's policy in Eastern Europe into the later 1940s. The records of his confidants, such as the Bulgarian former leader of the Comintern, Georgi Dimitrov, show him as prepared to accept a Europe of non-communist governments.[20] The Yalta meeting issued statements on Liberated Europe and on Poland. In each case there was a commitment by the three to elections in all liberated countries. In Western Europe, post-war elections were held in France in October 1945 and in Italy in June 1946. In the immediate post-war years in Eastern Europe, elections of varying honesty were held in Bulgaria, Czechoslovakia, Hungary and Romania. Soviet critics saw this as part of a prepared plan to move successively from coalition government on to bogus coalition and thence to dictatorship.[21] The evidence now suggests that Stalin's policy was far more incremental and flexible.[22]

The three-power agreement on Germany at Yalta could not have created a clearer line between their values and those of the Nazis. Germany was to be subject to the authority of the three powers, and it was to pay $22 billion and surrender machinery and other wealth as required. A decision on war criminals would come later. However, the German people and even the Nazi party were not exterminated, enslaved or deliberately starved to death by either the Western Allies or the Soviet Union. What had changed? Had Stalin become more humane, sickened by the deaths of tens of millions in the war? Or had Churchill's supplies of tanks for the battle of Moscow in 1941, the gigantic US supplies under Lend-Lease and the participation of the Soviet Union in the peace-building conferences of the United Nations in 1943 and 1944 all persuaded Stalin that it was possible to work with the West in the long term, and indeed that it was essential if war was not to break out generation after generation with ever more deadly effect?

The Yalta conference also agreed that the US would issue the formal invitations to the other United Nations to a conference to create the new UN organization. It was to be held in San Francisco in April. When it came to decisions in the Security Council, each of the five major powers – Britain, China, France, the USA and the USSR – would have a veto. The precise nature of the veto became a major issue in San Francisco.

On his return from the Crimea, Roosevelt was treated as a hero. The media and the public generally regarded the agreements as a triumph, even if far from perfect. Clearly exhausted, he addressed Congress sitting down, the effort of standing, held up by metal frames around each leg, being too much for him.

One of the compromises Roosevelt made at Yalta was to allow two additional Soviet Republics, Ukraine and Byelorussia, to have seats in the General Assembly. At the Yalta conference the Western Allies whittled Stalin's proposal for 16 seats in the General Assembly allocated to each republic down to three, with an equal number for the USA. This cynical horse-trading made sense at the level of power politics, but to the American public – on the one hand seeking a utopian new world and on the other looking for any evidence of communist evil-doing – the outcome was a moral blemish or deformity, depending on your point of view. It had been concealed by Roosevelt for weeks after he had announced the results of the Yalta meeting. His assertion that it did not mean much as the General Assembly had little power, did not help his argument. Opponents of the UN seized on the issue to attack the moral stature of the new organization.

Fears of bad faith were also found in Moscow. In late March, US special intelligence agents – predecessors of the CIA – initiated discussions in Switzerland with the SS for the surrender of the German forces in Italy to the Anglo-Americans. General Marshall, the British Field Marshal Sir Harold Alexander and the State Department later informed Molotov of the overture, but refused to allow the Soviets to join the talks. They did not tell Roosevelt. The Soviet reaction was to fear a German deal with the West. In response, Stalin informed Roosevelt that Molotov was too busy to go to San Francisco. When he found out what had happened Roosevelt reassured Stalin at length.

Trying to recuperate, but still weak and losing weight, Roosevelt took a spring break at his favoured southern retreat of Warm Springs in Georgia, but continued to work. He recommended to Churchill the need to get along with Stalin. In correspondence with the Soviet leader he had emphasized that failure to implement the Yalta agreement on Poland would jeopardize all their efforts for peace. In reply, Stalin appeared to be conceding, agreeing that the three foreign ministers and not his puppet Lublin government select the new members of the government.[23]

Then, on the morning of 12 April, Roosevelt suffered a cerebral haemorrhage, fell unconscious and died later that day. The mourning and shock was universal in the Allied world. Hitler, in his Berlin bunker, fantasized about a reprieve from defeat, anticipating a major change in US policy on the model of events in German history following the death of the Russian Empress Elizabeth.[24]

On taking the oath of office, Truman announced that the planned United Nations Conference on International Organization (UNCIO) would go ahead as planned. Even had he favoured postponement, it would have been an administrative nightmare. The conference was huge. Its phone-book ran to 120 pages in the familiar format used for American towns of white and yellow pages.[25] A celebratory US postage stamp had been issued, and 5,000 delegates, staff, non-governmental groups and media were preparing for the opening.

In Moscow, Stalin and the Soviet people were deeply moved by the death of Roosevelt. The Soviet leader sent an anxious Molotov to find out more about the new US President's intentions. En route to San Francisco, Molotov had two meetings with Truman. The press reported that Truman had told Molotov bluntly to stick to the Yalta agreements on democracy in Eastern Europe, much to Molotov's shock. The Soviet Union and the West had yet to agree to turn the Yalta language on Poland into a real change in the Polish government organized by Stalin. Without an agreement on a new provisional government, Poland was not invited by the USA to participate in UNCIO. It is far from clear that at Yalta a deadline for the opening of UNCIO was set for the re-organization of the Polish Government, or that Roosevelt would have escalated the issue in this way.

In San Francisco, the power relations were clear even in the room allocations. The Big Five met in the penthouse suite of the Fairmont Hotel, chaired by Stettinius, who had become Secretary of State the previous December. Other delegations worked on the lower floors. Yet in contrast to the Versailles Conference of 1919, there were no Presidents or Prime Ministers overbearing the conference with their personalities and all the now 50 United Nations were present and voting, except for the Poles.

The conference proceedings are recorded in the multi-volume account of the United Nations Conference on International Organization. It is not

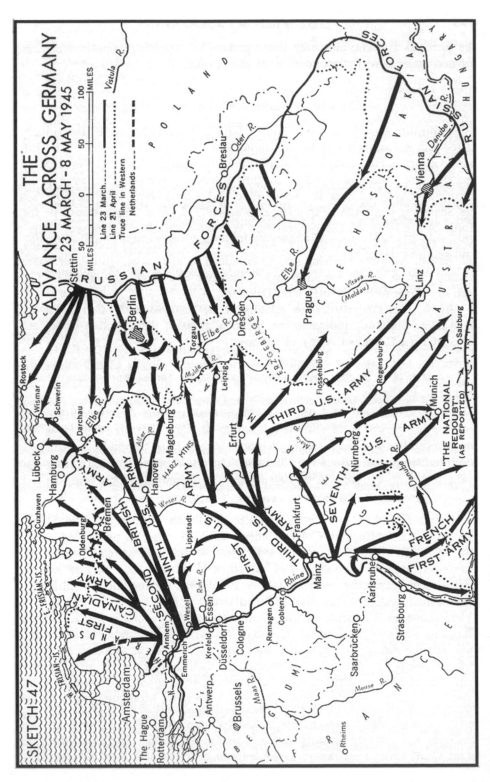

X The advance across Germany, 1945.

the purpose of this study to look in detail at the negotiation of the Articles of the Charter. A prodigious study by German lawyers from 1994 gives due weight to the smaller powers and provides a balance to those that focus overmuch on the role of the US.[26]

As the delegates considered and sought to amend the draft charter of Dumbarton Oaks, events in Europe and the Middle East crystallized some of the theoretical issues. 'General Eisenhower informs me that the forces of Germany have surrendered to the United Nations', announced President Truman in a radio broadcast on 8 May.[27] Yet on 12 May, Truman suspended Lend-Lease, long described as the foundation of United Nations cooperation. The shock internationally was tangible and a sign to all who needed it that Washington under Truman was different and less reliable than under Roosevelt.

In Moscow, 16 non-communist Polish politicians were thrown in jail. And in San Francisco, the Soviet Ambassador Andrei Gromyko sought to extend the veto power in the Security Council to stop a topic being debated. In early June, Truman asked Harry Hopkins to fly to meet with Stalin to resolve the Polish issue – and whilst there to manage the impasse over the veto. Feelings ran so high amongst the non-permanent members that it seemed the Charter might never be agreed. Stalin gave up on this, though not on the imprisonment issue. At this stage, both Washington and Moscow's commitment to internationalism was in question.

A Canadian diplomat at UNCIO recalled in his diary for 6 June 1945 that some of his colleagues were now so antagonistic towards the Soviet Union that 'Hume is much too ready to contemplate the immediate formation of two alliance systems. [There were British contingency plans in circulation for this.] X (an officer in the Department) is dangerously irresponsible. He has twice stated that, if there is to be a showdown with the Russians, it had better come before the German army is disbanded so that we can use it'.[28]

A further blow to international ideals came in Syria: General de Gaulle, enjoying the large Lend-Lease agreement, was killing locals seeking self-government, one of the prized ideals of the Atlantic Charter. It took Churchill to make De Gaulle stop his re-colonization, but it raised a question on the veto: would not France be able to stop UN action to help the Syrians? And indeed it could. Throughout the conference, the veto-less majority continually sought ways to limit the veto being given to the permanent members of the Security Council. The Australian, Herbert Evatt, and the Canadian, Lester Pearson, were at the forefront of these demands. The only substantive concessions were that nations with issues before the Security Council are allowed to attend and discuss the matter at hand.

The Economic and Social Council (ECOSOC) was made an integral part of the UN alongside the free-standing organizations created at Bretton Woods. Thus, the world was either to have duplicate institutions or a 'belt and braces' approach, so important did all concerned consider it to be to hold up the world economy.[29] The argument for the inclusion of a diverse range of social and economic policies was a security argument, not a moral one. The expression given this view at Dumbarton Oaks was:

> 'With a view to the creation of conditions of stability and well-being which are necessary for peaceful and friendly relations among nations, the Organization should facilitate solutions of international economic, social and other humanitarian problems and promote respect for human rights and fundamental freedoms'.

At this moment, when millions were still dying in the war, the most powerful states publicized the view that this range of issues was fundamental to international security. They did so having already achieved a great deal with respect to food security, war crimes, aid and economic development. The priority given to what is now called human security in the mid-1940s provides powerful reinforcement to those seeking to develop these agendas in the present century. More importantly, in the 1940s, these agendas rejected out of hand the deregulated approach to international economics that now prevails and which is rarely addressed even by proponents of securitization and human security.

Alongside ECOSOC, pre-prepared specialized agencies slotted into place. Notable among them were the Food and Agriculture Organization, the modest pathfinder of the UN system. In late March 1945, in one of his last acts as President, Roosevelt sent the constitution of the UNFAO to the Senate for ratification. Roosevelt wrote,

> We must strive to correct the conditions that predispose people toward war or make them the ready tools and victims of aggressors. We shall need also to work together as Nations toward achieving freedom from want. Our participation in the Food and Agriculture Organization will be an essential step in this collaboration. The Organization will seek its ends through the provision of international services in agriculture and nutrition which have heretofore been either lacking or inadequate.[30]

In addition, the UN Education, Scientific and Cultural Organization (UNESCO) was created with the energy of the exiled governments in London at meetings of education ministers; and the International Labour Organization was inherited from the defunct League of Nations, whose other assets were also transferred to the UN.

The UN Trusteeship Council had been intended by Roosevelt to manage decolonization. In the papers prepared for him for UNCIO, there was still language envisaging the end of the European empires.[31] But the idea of requiring dates to be set did not survive him – the Trusteeship system was

30 Key personalities amongst the UN delegates, San Francisco, 1945, including members of the delegations to the United Nations Conference on International Organization, left to right: American politicians Charles A. Eaton (1868–1953), Sol Bloom (1870–1949), Arthur H. Vandenberg (1884–1951), Tom Connally (1877–1963), the former French Prime Minister Joseph Paul-Boncour (1873–1972), British politician and Ambassador to America Edward Wood, 1st Earl of Halifax (1888–1959), US Secretary of State Edward Stettinius (1900–49), Russian Ambassador to America Andrei Gromyko (1909–89) and Wellington Koo (1887–1985), Chinese Ambassador to Britain.

little used for its purpose of assisting in decolonization and the peoples under European domination across Asia and Africa had to fight for their freedom in the hostile climate of the Cold War.

Many amendments to the Dumbarton Oaks text were debated by the delegations and a few by the now Big Five (with the inclusion of France) who were to be the permanent members of the Security Council. Their key amendment became Article 51, which provides for the right of self-defence for any member, until measures have been taken by the Security Council. This and the provision for regional security organizations, such as the USA had in Latin America, provided for other legitimate forms of security than just that provided by the Security Council.

Other political principles developed those of the 1942 United Nations Declaration. In particular, the emphasis on gender and racial equality has provided a basis for securing those rights around the world in a continuing effort . . . to this day.

After the agreement of the Charter, relations with the Soviet Union continued to sour, and the dropping of the atomic bomb on two Japanese cities opened a new chapter in world history. 'Stalin and Molotov feared the American monopoly of the atomic bomb, and believed that their only reply was to present a threat of the rapid conquest of Western Europe', wrote Allan Nevins, the biographer of Herbert Lehman, with a precision that has eluded countless historians of the period.[32] This dynamic alone was enough to set in train a whole series of political events beyond the scope of this book. However, the evidence suggests that as anti-communism became dominant in US-led politics, so more right-wing, fascist and even Nazi alliances were made by the Western powers. Accepting the need for anti-communism, was it necessary to construct it on such a right-wing political basis? The US-led United Nations provided the choice of a broader, progressive and more powerful agenda.

An early example of promoting a pro-Nazi regime in a political ploy against Moscow was the support given by the USA for the inclusion of Argentina in the United Nations at UNCIO. This became a trade-off with the inclusion of the Soviet republics of Ukraine and Byelorussia (Belarus). Despite international opprobrium, the USA supported the inclusion of Argentina. Ostensibly, the Latin American states acted independently in forcing the compromise whereby all three would be admitted to the UN. However, Sigrid Arne observed the operation of the US-led bloc during the United Nations conferences of the period:

> The situation was so obvious that at Bretton Woods one of the high Indian delegates remarked to an American, 'How do you Americans like your new empire?' . . . The very suggestion is extremely embarrassing to the State Department. But it is often obvious that Latin American delegates confer alone with United States delegates.[33]

Truman is often portrayed as an innocent in international politics when he became President. This is to underestimate him. Some observers credited him with organizing the B2H2 resolution in 1943 and through the committee he chaired on managing the war economy, he gained considerable insight into international affairs, which were in any case analysed daily in the press. He was clearly committed to a strong US role in the world, but he came from a more conservative and racist background than Roosevelt. As Mary Glantz, an historian of Roosevelt's relationship with Russia observed, 'In short, Harriman [US Ambassador to Moscow] persuaded the President [Truman] to adopt the very course that Roosevelt had been struggling against throughout the war. The formulation and implementation of foreign policy reverted to the very bureaucracy Roosevelt had ignored and mistrusted for twelve years'.[34]

31 The atomic bombing of Nagasaki, August 1945.

David Reynolds argues convincingly that Stalin wanted the wartime alliance to continue and had no great desire to foment revolution; his preoccupation was to rebuild the devastated economy and society of the Soviet Union. Even in private he opposed imposing the Soviet system in Germany, saying that this strategy was 'an incorrect one . . . an antifascist democratic parliamentary system must be established'.[35]

The US public's willingness to empower the United Nations in 1944 and 1945 was the peak of support for cooperative, multilateral internationalism. What came later in the Cold War was not a return to isolation but a more traditional policy of power politics in which a narrow view of power justified a rejection of the UN as the body through which foreign policy should be organized. The turn to a more conservative view of the national interest after World War II, albeit with global engagement, had taken such a hold by the end of the Cold War that, despite the collapse of communism, US foreign policy under the three Bush family and two Clinton presidential terms continued to see the UN as irrelevant to expanding US world power.[36] No one asked why America, in 2000, found Presidents Putin and Chirac tougher to deal with than Stalin and De Gaulle in the early 1940s.

Nevertheless, there was no going back to splendid isolation after 1945. The USA now rejected George Washington's advice to reject permanent alliances. The USA remained a member of the UN but also created NATO and other regional security agreements outside the traditional sphere of the Americas. The Marshall Plan and the encouragement of Western European integration under Washington's control were all beneficial. But at home, the progressive era of the Roosevelt Administration ended with the abrupt ascendancy of reactionary politics intent on keeping negroes and organized labour in their place, enhanced by the rhetoric of anti-communism.

After the UNCIO, in the face of gathering confrontation between the West and the Soviet Union, the nations set about implementing the Charter and creating the new organization. In doing so they were able to draw on the skills developed in the secretariat of the much-maligned League of Nations, distilled in a series of conferences organized by the Carnegie Endowment.[37] Public enthusiasm remained high as US cities competed to host the new organization. St Louis, home of Howard Hughes's Transworld Air Lines, even argued that it was ideally suited because it was equally remote from all areas of potential conflict.

The first meetings of the UN General Assembly and the Security Council were held in London, a city already home to a variety of United Nations organizations. There was a UN senior officers club next door to Chatham House in St James's Square; another United Nations officers club had been blitzed up by a Nazi missile but had managed to keep going;[38] the UNWCC operated from new offices on Berkeley Square and UNRRA's European operations were organized from Portland Place near the BBC.[39]

Conclusion

The United Nations was created to win World War II and secure the peace. For many of the leaders and citizens involved, this was a deliberate process, not an accident of history. Their success in winning the war in 1945 and in creating organizations which still function more than half a century later is unprecedented in international history. The story of the United Nations at war adds a valuable dimension to the history of America's 'Greatest Generation' and their counterparts in the other nations fighting the Axis.

The failure of the USA and European states to either invest themselves fully in the League of Nations or to confront the rise of the dictators put them in peril. In the United States, ideas of renewed international cooperation were critical to rallying the nation to meet this threat.

Roosevelt used a succession of speeches and political initiatives to overcome the anti-interventionists. The 'Arsenal of Democracy' and 'Four Freedoms' speeches paved the way for the Lend-Lease Act of March 1941. The Atlantic Charter issued with Churchill in August of that year served both to confront his critics at home and offer an agenda for a post-war world in which America would be involved, even though the USA was not yet at war.

After Pearl Harbor, Anglo-American military cooperation became formalized within the wider political-military alliance created by the Declaration by United Nations of January 1942. The United Nations was at this point the formal culmination of the earlier statements by Roosevelt and Churchill. The Atlantic Charter forms the political foundation of the Declaration by United Nations, supported by the Soviet Union, China and more than twenty other states.

From this point on until the creation of the UN Charter in 1945, the United Nations served its triple and mutually reinforcing functions. These functions were to rally domestic support in the USA and elsewhere, hold the, at times, fractious Allies together and create the structures for peace-building in the post-war world.

The United Nations Days of June 1942, 1943 and 1944 provided a globally unifying idea for both the military and political alliance. This sense of unity was needed not merely to combat the Axis's own propaganda, but to compensate for serious differences within the Alliance over D-Day and over the lack of any operational UN military machinery that involved all the Allies. Rather, the now familiar policy of a small group of powerful states pre-ordering the agenda for the later advice and consent of a wider group of states became the norm.

Lend-Lease became the foundation of United Nations collaboration. The Roosevelt Administration considered the active development of United Nations activities for the post-war period to be essential to ensuring continuing Congressional support for Lend-Lease. It is also clear that without Lend-Lease the outcome of battles, campaigns and the war itself would have been less favourable and could have been lost. Andrew Roberts' *The Storm of War: A New History of the Second World War* is a powerful corrective to those who think that victory was inevitable.

The politics of Lend-Lease thus represents the strongest link between internationalist ideas crystallized in the United Nations and the military progress of the war. The motor vehicles from Detroit which enabled the Red Army's rapid advances from 1943 epitomize this connection.

Detroit was also the scene of civil rights riots during the war. Their occurrence highlighted the contradiction between fighting for freedom abroad under the ideals of the United Nations whilst keeping African-Americans oppressed at home. Roosevelt's support for China and India as significant independent powers in the world raised expectations at home. Roosevelt's antipathy to empire had been implemented in his own 'good neighbour' foreign policy before the war, but his death cut short his attempt to impose a process of agreed timetables for the dissolution of the European empires in Africa and Asia.

More successful was his leadership in bringing the USA to engage with the other United Nations on a series of mainly economic initiatives for the post-war world. Through 1943, 1944 and into 1945, the US press contained reports of the development of a variety of programmes. There were United Nations conferences and organizations concerned with food and agriculture, relief and reconstruction, finance and trade and, finally, global security. By the time of his election for a fourth term in November 1944, Americans had become so disenchanted with Congress's contribution and so concerned to empower the still-to-be-formed UN organization they supported Roosevelt's plan to move Congress's war-making powers into the hands of the US delegate at the UN.

Nor should it be thought that this debate was one that Americans were having only with themselves. States as varied as China and New Zealand sought a functioning UN Council in 1942. Anthony Eden urged every support for United Nations programmes, understanding Roosevelt's strategy of using these initiatives to bind the USA into the post-war system. Nevertheless, Eden and his colleagues sought means of slowing the decline of British power, and small states bridled at the impositions of the Big Four, but few either wanted a return to the League of Nations where everyone had a veto, or to the anarchic balance of power that had existed prior to 1914.

The Soviet Union too had joined in most of the organizations for the post-war world, including those agreed at Bretton Woods. The critical meetings of Soviet, US and British leaders in Moscow and Tehran in the autumn of 1943 and at Yalta in February 1945 operated within the United Nations framework and provided public diplomatic affirmation of aims for the war and the peace.

While these meetings brought the most powerful together, weak states also needed and made use of the United Nations' ideas and alliance. Of all the organizations of the wartime UN, the one concerned with war crimes, the UNWCC, owed most to the work of the weaker states. It was the Czechs and the Poles, together with the non-governmental organizations, that persuaded first the British and then the Americans that such a body was needed. It and the December 1942 statement on the extermination of the Jews are important parts of the Allied, United Nations, response to the Holocaust.

The slogan 'United Nations in War and Peace', much used in the USA, was turned into the most effective fighting and peace-building alliance the world has known. In the present century there continues to be an effort to strengthen the UN. A rhetorical flourish from Churchill provides reinforcement to this work and an apt ending. In September 1944, while the battle of Arnhem raged, Churchill had a private conversation with one of his top commanders, Admiral Cunningham, on the proposed United Nations organization. He replied to Cunningham, who had dared to say that the UN would not amount to anything, by saying, 'It is the only hope of the world'.[1]

Chronology

1937

July 7 Japan begins invasion of China at Beijing.

1938

March 12 Anschluss: Germany absorbs Austria.
September 30 Germany occupies the mainly ethnic German province of Sudetenland in Czechoslovakia with acquiescence of Britain, France and Italy.

1939

March 15 Czechoslovakia broken up; Slovakia declares independence and Germany takes over remaining Czech areas (Bohemia and Moravia).
May–September Soviet Union defeats Japanese army in Mongolia.
July Britain, France and Soviet Union fail to reach an alliance against Germany.
August 23 German-Soviet alliance: the Molotov-Ribbentrop Pact.
September 1 Germany invades Western Poland.
September 3 Britain and France declare war on Germany.
September 17 Soviet Union invades Eastern Poland.
November 30 Soviet Union invades Finland; armistice in March 1940.

1940

April-June Germany invades Denmark and Norway on April 9, and on May 10 The Netherlands, Belgium and France.
May 10 Winston Churchill chosen as British Prime Minister by the House of Commons.
May 26–June 4 British and French soldiers evacuated to England from Dunkirk.
June 10 Italy attacks Britain and France.
June 22 France surrenders; central and southern France remain unoccupied under pro-Nazi regime in Vichy; France retains its overseas Empire.
June Soviet Union invades the Baltic states.
July–September Germany fails to destroy British Royal Air Force in the Battle of Britain and postpones invasion of England.
September 14 US Congress passes limited draft of men into the army.
September 22 Japan occupies Vietnam.
September 30 Germany, Italy and Japan form Tripartite Pact: the Axis.

November 5 Roosevelt elected US President for third term with 54% of the popular vote.

October 28 Italy attacks Greece, unsuccessfully.

1941

December 7–February 9 British defeat Italian army in Libya.

March–May Germany helps Italy counterattack and invades Egypt.

March 11 US Lend-Lease Act becomes law; German submarines threaten essential supplies to Britain.

April 6–18 Germany and its allies invade Yugoslavia and Greece.

May 2–31 Iraqi nationalists fail to expel the British, despite German help.

June 22 Germany and its European allies attack the Soviet Union.

August 1 US bans sale of oil to Japan.

August 9–14 Churchill and Roosevelt meet aboard warships near Newfoundland; they issue the Atlantic Charter.

August 16 US Congress keeps trained draftees in the service.

August 15–September 17 British and Soviets occupy Iran.

September 24 Allies, including the Soviet Union, endorse the Atlantic Charter at a meeting in London.

November 23 Britain completes defeat of Italy in Ethiopia and Somalia.

December 5 Soviet counterattack pushes Germans back from Moscow.

December 7 Japan attacks US at Pearl Harbor and the Philippines, and British and Dutch colonies in East Asia.

1942

January 1 Roosevelt and Churchill, with Stalin, issue the Declaration by United Nations, supported by 23 other states; US and Britain create combined organizations for fighting the war.

January–March Japan conquers Singapore and Malaya by January 31 and starts bombing Australia on February 19; Japanese control Java, Burma and New Guinea by March 9, and Philippines by March 11.

May 30 Roosevelt and Soviet Foreign Minister Molotov meet in Washington, DC.

May 30 1,000 British bomber planes attack Cologne in one night.

June 4–7 Japanese Navy defeated by the US fleet at Midway.

June 14 United Nations Day celebrated throughout the Allied world.

June 20–25 Roosevelt and Churchill meet in Washington, DC.

July German and Italian Armies get to within 150 miles of Cairo at El Alamein.

August 12–17 Churchill and US Ambassador Harriman meet Stalin in Moscow.

August German Army drives towards Stalingrad and the Caucasus.

October–November British defeat Germans and Italians in Egypt and Anglo-American forces land in North West Africa.

November 3 Republicans make gains in US Congressional elections.

November 19 Red Army counterattacks at Stalingrad.

December 17 United Nations Declaration on the extermination of European Jews in Poland.

1943

January 14–24 Roosevelt and Churchill meet in Casablanca and issue 'unconditional surrender' ultimatum to the Axis.

February 3 German Army surrenders at Stalingrad.

March German submarines again threaten to cut off Britain.

May 13 German and Italian Armies in North Africa surrender.

May 12–27 Roosevelt and Churchill meet in Washington, DC.

May 18–June 3 United Nations Conference on Food and Agriculture at Hot Springs, Virginia.

May 23 Germans accept they cannot win the submarine war in the Atlantic.

June Stalin learns D-Day postponed until 1944 and withdraws the Soviet Ambassadors from London and Washington.

July–August German Army's last major attack in the Soviet Union fails at Kursk.

August 17–24 Roosevelt and Churchill meet in Quebec.

September Anglo-American armies land in Italy; Italy switches sides in the war.

October 18–November 1 British, US and Soviet Foreign Ministers meet in Moscow.

October 20 United Nations War Crimes Commission created.

November 9 United Nations Relief and Rehabilitation Administration (UNRRA) formed.

November 23–26 Roosevelt, Churchill and Chiang Kai-shek meet in Cairo.

November 28–December 1 Roosevelt, Churchill and Stalin meet in Tehran.

1944

May Japan abandons invasion of India.

June 5 Rome liberated.

June 6 D-Day: Anglo-American and Canadian Armies land in France.

June 12 Germany begins V1 missile attacks against England.

June 15 US begins bombing Japanese home islands.

June 22 Soviet Union begins offensive that destroys the German Armies in the centre of the Eastern Front by the end of July.

July 1–15 United Nations Monetary and Financial Conference held at Bretton Woods, New Hampshire, USA.

July 22 Red Army finds German extermination camp at Majdanek.
August 21–29 Five-power meeting at Dumbarton Oaks, Washington proposes a permanent United Nations.
August 1 Warsaw uprising begins.
August 25 US Army liberates Paris.
September 8 Germany begins V2 ballistic-missile attacks against England.
September 12–16 Roosevelt and Churchill meet in Quebec.
October 9 Churchill and Stalin meet in Moscow.
November 7 Roosevelt elected US President for fourth time.
December 16–January 25 Last German attack in the West: Battle of the Bulge.

1945
February 4–11 Roosevelt, Churchill and Stalin meet at Yalta in the Crimea.
April 12 Roosevelt dies; Truman becomes US President.
April 25–June 26 United Nations Conference on International Organization creates UN Charter.
May 8 Germany surrenders.
July Labour Party wins British election; Attlee replaces Churchill as Prime Minister.
July 17–August 2 Truman, Churchill, then Attlee, and Stalin meet in Potsdam, Berlin.
August 6 & 9 USA drops atomic bomb on Hiroshima and then on Nagasaki.
August 9 Soviet Union attacks Japanese army in China.
August 14 Japanese forces in Manchuria surrender.
September 2 Japan formally surrenders; end of World War II.

Glossary of the United Nations in World War II

DUN   Declaration by United Nations of January 1942, initially supported by 26 states (Washington DC, 1942).

UN   UN refers both to the signatories of the Declaration of January 1942 and to the organization created at UNCIO.

UNCIO   United Nations Conference on International Organization (San Francisco, 1945).

UNCTE   United Nations Conference on Trade and Employment (Havana Charter, 1947).

UNFAO   United Nations Food and Agriculture Organization 1945, (first an Interim UN Commission established at Hot Springs, Virginia in 1943).

UNIB   United Nations Information Board (New York, 1942). This has UN Information Offices in New York and London and elsewhere and became an Organization in 1944.

UNMFC   United Nations Monetary and Financial Conference (Bretton Woods, 1944).

UNRRA   United Nations Relief and Rehabilitation Administration 1943–48 (created at a conference in Atlantic City, 1943 and subsequently had global operations).

UNWCC   United Nations War Crimes Commission (London, 1943–48).

Appendix: Selected Gallup Polls, 1938–45

Table of polling categories of US public opinion
  1: European War
  2: Neutrality
  3: Germany
  4: Armed Forces
  5: The Draft
  6: Lend-Lease
  7: Disarmament or Peace Conference
  8: Joint War Council and Allied Leadership
  9: Peace Organization
 10: Post-war Peace
 11: Anti-Lynching Law

Tables 1–11, compiled from categories and questions in: Gallup, George H., The Gallup Poll: Public opinion, 1935–71 (New York, Random House, 1972).

TABLE 1 European War.

Question	Date and response	Date and response	Date and response
If England and France go to war against Germany, which side do you think will win?	30/09/1938 England and France....86% Germany..............14%	25/04/1941 England..............57% Germany and Italy......11% Stalemate..............8% No opinion..............24%	
If England and France go to war against Germany do you think the United States can stay out?	02/10/1938 Yes..............57% No..............43%		
Do you believe there will be a war between any of the big European countries this year?	30/01/1939 Yes..............44% No..............56%	19/05/1939 Yes..............32% No..............68%	
If there is such a war, do you think the United States will be drawn in?	30/01/1939 Yes..............57% No..............43%	20/08/1939 Yes..............76% No..............24%	
If Germany and Italy go to war against England and France, do you think we should do everything possible to help England and France win, except go to war ourselves?	22/02/1939 Yes..............69% No..............31%		
In case a war breaks out, should we sell Britain and France food supplies?	13/03/1939 Yes..............76% No..............24%		
Should we send our army and navy abroad to help England and France?	13/03/1939 Yes..............17% No..............83%		

TABLE 1 European War (Continued).

Question	Date and response	Date and response	Date and response
Should we sell them [England and France] airplanes and other war materials?	09/04/1939 Yes............................66% No.............................34%		
In case Germany and Italy go to war against England and France should we lend money to England and France to buy airplanes and other war materials from the United States?	19/05/1939 Lend money...............31% Do not lend money.....69%		
If England, France and Russia were involved in a war with Germany and Italy, which side do you think would win?	19/06/1939 England, France, Russia.......................83% Germany and Italy.......17%		
What should be the policy in the present European War? Should we declare war and send our army and navy abroad to fight Germany?	06/10/1939 Yes...............................5% No...............................95%	29/05/1940 Yes...............................7% No...............................93%	
Do you think the United States will go into the war in Europe, or do you think we will stay out of the war?	25/10/1939 Will go in....................46% Will stay out...............54%	16/02/1940 Will go in....................32% Stay out.....................68%	27/04/1941 Will go in....................82% Stay out.....................18%
If it appears that Germany is defeating England and France, should the United States declare war on Germany and send our army and navy to Europe to fight?	21/02/1940 Yes............................23% No.............................77%		

TABLE 1 European War (Continued).

Question	Date and response	Date and response	Date and response
If it looked as though England and France would lose the war unless we loaned them money to buy war supplies here, would you favour or oppose lending them money?	04/03/1940 Favour..............55% Oppose.............45%		
If it appears that England will be defeated by Germany and Italy unless the United States supplies her with more food and war materials, would you be in favour of giving more help to England?	18/11/1940 Yes................90% No.................10%		
If England and France are unable to pay cash for airplanes they buy in this country, do you think we should sell them planes on credit supplied by our Government?	24/05/1940 Yes................51% No.................49%		
If the question of the United States going to war against Germany and Italy came up for a national vote within the next two weeks, would you vote to go into the war or to stay out of the war?	07/07/1940 Go to war...........14% Stay out...........86%	29/06/1941 Go to war...........24% Stay out...........76%	
If there is starvation in France, Holland and Belgium this winter, should the United States try to send food to those countries in our ships?	02/09/1940 Yes................38% No.................62%		

TABLE 1 European War *(Continued).*

Question	Date and response	Date and response	Date and response
Do you think our country's future safety depends on England winning this war?	03/01/1941 Yes.............................68% No...............................26% No opinion.................6%		
Do you think the United States should send part of our army to Europe to help the British?	21/04/1941 Yes.............................17% No...............................79% No opinion.................4%		
Should the United States navy be used to guard ships carrying war materials to Britain?	23/04/1941 Yes.............................41% No...............................50% No opinion.................9%		
Should the United States enter the war now?	09/07/1941 Yes.............................21% No...............................79%		
If the United States does enter the war against Germany and Italy, do you think it will be necessary to send our army to Europe to fight?	18/08/1941 Yes.............................65% No...............................30% No opinion.................5%		
Which of these two things do you think is the most important – that this country keep out of the war or that Germany be defeated?	05/10/1941 Keep out of war........30% Germany be defeated....70%		

TABLE 2 Neutrality.

Question	Date and response	Date and response	Date and response
Our present Neutrality Law prevents this country from selling war materials to any countries fighting in a declared war. Do you think the law should be changed so that we could sell war materials to England and France in case of war?	14/04/1939 Yes............57% No............43%	04/10/1939 Yes............62% No............38%	
If you were voting for President, which type of candidate (on card) do you think you would be more likely to vote for: (A) A candidate who promises to keep us out of war and refuses to give any more help to England and France than we are now giving them, even if they are being defeated by Germany; or (B) a candidate who promises to keep us out of war, but is willing to give England and France all the help they want, except sending our army and navy.	10/05/1940 Refuses help............34% Aid except troops............66% By Political Affiliation Refuse help/Aid except troops Democrats............32%/68% Republicans............36%/64%		
President Roosevelt has taken action making it possible for England and France to buy some airplanes that were being used by our army and navy. Do you approve or disapprove of this action?	30/06/1940 Approve............80% Disapprove............20% By Political Affiliation Approve/Disapprove Democrats............85%/15% Republicans............76%/24%		
General Pershing says the United States should sell to England 50 of our destroyer ships that were built during	19/08/1940 Approve............62% Disapprove............38%		

TABLE 2 Neutrality (Continued).

Question	Date and response	Date and response	Date and response
the last World War and are now being put back in service. Do you approve or disapprove of our Government selling these destroyers to England?			
England needs destroyer ships to replace those that have been damaged or sunk. The United States has some destroyers that were built during the last World War and are now being put back in active service. Do you think we should sell some of these ships to England?	05/09/1940 Yes..............60% No...............40%		
Which of these two things do you think is the most important for the United States to try to do – to keep out of the war ourselves or to try to help England win, even at the risk of getting into the war?	23/09/1940 Keep out..............48% Help England..........52%	15/01/1941 Roosevelt Voters in 1940 Keep out................38% Help England...........62% Wilkie voters in 1940 Keep out.................40% Help England...........60%	07/04/1941 Keep out..............33% Help England..........67%
Do you think the United States should lend money to Greece for the purchase of arms, airplanes and other war materials?	29/11/1940 Yes..............60% No...............40%		
Should the Neutrality Law be changed so that American ships can carry war supplies to England?	08/12/1940 Yes..............40% No...............60%	01/10/1941 Yes..............46% No..............40% No opinion..........14%	

TABLE 3 Germany.

Question	Date and response	Date and response	Date and response
Do you think the United States will have to fight Germany again in your lifetime?	23/10/1938 Yes...............48% No................52%		
Would you join a movement in this country to stop buying German-made goods?	18/12/1938 Yes...............61% No................39%		
If Germany should defeat England, France and Poland in the present war, do you think Germany would start a war against the United States sooner or later?	29/09/1939 Yes...............63% No................37%		
Do you think the Allies should supervise the education and training of German youth after this war?	02/09/1944 Yes...............66% No................19% No opinion......15%		

TABLE 4 Armed Forces.

Question	Date and response	Date and response	Date and response
Should the United States build a larger navy?	16/10/1938 Yes............71% No............29%	12/11/1939 Yes............88% No............12%	
Should the United States build a larger army?	16/10/1938 Yes............65% No............35%	12/11/1939 Yes............86% No............14%	
The army has asked Congress to change the law that says drafted men cannot be sent to fight outside of North or South America or this country's possessions. Do you think Congress should give the army the right to send drafted soldiers to any part of the world?	07/11/1941 Yes............42% No............53% No opinion............5%		

TABLE 5 The Draft.

Question	Date and response	Date and response	Date and response
Should the Constitution be amended to require a national vote before the country could draft men to fight overseas?	27/03/1939 Yes................61% No.................39%	10/09/1939 Yes.................51% No..................49%	
Do you favour increasing the size of our army and navy now by drafting men between the ages of 21 and 31 to serve in the armed forces for one year?	30/08/1940 Yes................71% No.................29%		
Would you be in favour of starting now to draft American women between the ages of 21 and 35 to train them for jobs in war time?	18/12/1940 Yes................48% No.................52%		
Do you think the draft is being handled fairly?	29/12/1940 Yes................92% No.................8%	05/01/1944 Yes.................75% No..................25%	
Do you think drafted men should be kept in active service for longer than one year, or should they be released at the end of one year?	06/08/1941 Should be kept..........50% Should be released......45% No opinion................5%		

TABLE 6 Lend-Lease.

Question	Date and response
Do you think Congress should pass the President's Lend-Lease Bill?	10/02/1941 Yes................54% No....................22% Qualified..........15% No opinion..........9% By Political Affiliation Democrats Yes................69% No....................13% Qualified..........10% No opinion..........8% Republicans Yes................38% No....................30% Qualified..........23% No opinion..........9%

TABLE 7 Disarmament or Peace Conference.

Question	Date and response	Date and response	Date and response
Would you favour a conference of the leading nations to reduce the size of all armies and navies at this time?	15/03/1939 Yes.............43% No...............57%		
Would you like to see the heads of the leading nations of the world meet in a new peace conference to settle the claims of Germany and Italy?	23/04/1939 Yes.............73% No...............27%		

TABLE 8 Joint War Council and Allied Leadership.

Question	Date and response	Date and response	Date and response
Do you think the United States, Britain, Russia and their Allies should form a joint war council that would plan all war operations against the Axis powers?	10/01/1942 Yes................80% No...................10% No opinion...........10%		
If such a council is formed, should the army, navy and air force of every country, including the United States, be controlled by the war council?	Yes..................68% No....................15% No opinion............17%		

Do you think that Roosevelt and Churchill should have the final decision on the military and naval plans of the war, or do you think these plans should be decided by the military and naval leaders of the United Nations?	7/8/42
	Roosevelt and
	  Churchill.........21%
	Military and naval
	  leaders....64%
	Undecided............15%		

Have you heard or read about the Crimean Conference between Stalin, Churchill and Roosevelt?	10/03/1945 Yes..................70% No....................30%		
Those who have heard or read about the Crimean Conference were then asked: On the whole, is your opinion of what was accomplished at the conference favourable or unfavourable?	Favourable...........61% Unfavourable..........9% No opinion............30%		

TABLE 9 Peace Organ zation.

Question	Date and response	Date and response	Date and response
Do you think the time will come when there will be a strong international army or police force for maintaining world peace?	06/09/1939 Yes............................30% No.............................70%		
Should the countries fighting the Axis set up an international police force after the war is over to try to keep peace throughout the world?	05/06/1942 Yes............................76% No.............................12% No opinion...............12%		
Do you think the United States should join a world organization with police power to maintain world peace?	08/04/1945 Yes............................81% No.............................11% No opinion...............8%		
How important do you think it is that we join such a world organization – very important, fairly important or not too important?	08/04/1945 Very important...........83% Fairly important.........11% Not too important.......3% No opinion................3%		

TABLE 10 Post-War Peace.

Question	Date and response	Date and response	Date and response
If England and France defeat Germany, should the peace treaty be more severe on Germany or less severe than the treaty at the end of the last war?	09/12/1939 More severe..........58% Less severe..........36% About the same..........6%		
Have you given any thought to what should be done to maintain world peace after the present European war is over?	28/01/1940 Yes..........34% No..........66%	05/03/1941 Yes..........34% No..........66%	
Would you like to see the United States join a league of nations after this war is over?	09/06/1941 Yes..........51% No..........49% Roosevelt voters in 1940 Yes..........53% No..........47% Wilkie Voters in 1940 Yes..........43% No..........57%	06/07/1942 Yes..........73% No..........27%	
Asked a cross-section of people listed in *Who's Who in America*: Would you like to see the United States join a league of nations after the war is over?	02/08/1941 Yes..........61% No..........23% No opinion..........16%		
Do you think the United States should have joined the League of Nations after the last war?	23/08/1941 Yes..........37% No..........37% No opinion..........26%		
If peace could be obtained today on the basis of Germany holding the countries it has conquered so far, and with Britain keeping the British Empire as it now stands, would you be in favour of such a peace?	28/06/1941 Yes..........29% No..........62% Undecided..........9%		

TABLE 10 Post-War Peace (Continued).

Question	Date and response	Date and response	Date and response
Should the Government take steps now, before the end of the war to set up with our Allies a world organization to maintain the future peace of the world?	24/03/1942 Yes.................64% No....................24% No opinion......12% By Political Affiliation Republicans Yes.................63% No....................24% No opinion........9% Democrats Yes.................65% No....................23% No opinion......12%		
If a new council or union of nations is formed after the war to take the place of the old League of Nations should this country join?	02/07/1944 Yes.................72% No....................13% No opinion......15% By Political Affiliation Democrats Yes.................74% No....................10% No opinion......16% Republicans Yes.................70% No....................15% No opinion......15%		
Asked of Britons: Should the United Nations adopt the principle of using force against aggressor nations when this war has ended?	15/11/1944 Yes.................77% No....................10% No opinion......13%		

TABLE 11   Anti-Lynching Law.

Question	Date and response
Under the proposed federal law against lynching, the Federal Government would (1) fine and imprison local police officers who fail to protect a prisoner from a lynch mob, and (2) make a county in which a lynching occurs pay a fine up to $10,000 to the victim or his family. Do you approve or disapprove of this law?	19/02/1940 Approve.................55% Disapprove.............45% South only Approve.................45% Disapprove.............55% Negroes only Approve.................89% Disapprove.............11%

Notes

Introduction

1. Lord Byron's *Childe Harold's Pilgrimage*, Stanza 35 of Canto III.
2. 'Flag Day', editorial, *The Washington Post*, Washington, DC, 17 June 1943, p.16.
3. http://www.state.gov/r/pa/ho/pubs/fs/55407.htm.
4. Sources are on http://www.presidency.ucsb.edu/ws/.
5. Stimson and Bundy, 1947: *On Active Service for Peace*, p. 565.
6. Arne, 1945: *United Nations Primer*, p. 4.
7. Wilcox, 2008: *Target Patton*, p. 112.
8. Reynolds, 2006: *From Cold War to World War*, p. 328.
9. Schlesinger, 2005: *My Dear Mr. Stalin*, p. xiii.
10. Kagan, 2003: *Of Paradise and Power, America and Europe in the New World Order*. See also review article by Ivo Daalder at http://www.nytimes.com/2003/03/05/books/books-of-the-times-americans-are-from-mars-europeans-from-venus.html?pagewanted=2.
11. Nye, 2004: *Soft Power*; and http://www.foreignaffairs.com/articles/59888/joseph-s-nye-jr/the-decline-of-americas-soft-power.
12. *The New Encyclopaedia Britannica* (Chicago, 2010), Macropedia, Vol. 29, p. 1023.

Chapter 1

1. http://georgewbush-whitchouse.archives.gov/news/releases/2002/01/print/20020129-11.html.
2. Roosevelt, Radio Address from the White House, 5 October 1944, at http://www.presidency.ucsb.edu/ws/index.php?pid=16574&st=communism&st1.
3. http://www.presidency.ucsb.edu/ws/index.php?pid=16456&st=united+nations&st1=.
4. http://www.presidency.ucsb.edu/ws/index.php?pid=16456&st=united+nations&st1=.
5. Watson, 1950: *Chief of Staff: Prewar Plans and Preparations*, p. 137.
6. Archive of the Committee to Defend America by Aiding the Allies is held at Princeton University. See: http://diglib.princeton.edu/ead/getEad?eadid=MC011&kw=.
7. Doenecke, 2000: *Storm on the Horizon* provides a detailed examination of America First.
8. The Republican Platform for the 1940 US Presidential Election: http://www.presidency.ucsb.edu/ws/index.php?pid=29640.
9. See Conn and Fairchild, 1960: *Framework of Hemisphere Defense*, ch. II; and Matlof and Snell, 1953: *Strategic Planning for Coalition Warfare, 1941-42*, chs. I-II.
10. Gaskin, 2005: *Blitz: The story of 29th December 1940*.
11. Roosevelt, Press Conference, 17 December 1940, available at http://www.presidency.ucsb.edu/ws/index.php?pid=15913.
12. Roosevelt's Annual Address to Congress – The 'Four Freedoms', available at http://docs.fdrlibrary.marist.edu/od4frees.html.

13. 'Ford and GM Scrutinized for Alleged Nazi Collaboration'. *The Washington Post*: pp. A01. 1998-11-30 (http://www.washingtonpost.com/wp-srv/national/daily/nov98/nazicars30.htm); Edwin Black's 2007 article discusses both Ford and GM's role, http://www.hnn.us/articles/38829.html.
14. http://www.naval-history.net/WW2CampaignsAtlanticDev.htm.
15. *New York Times*, 24 June 1941, p. 1.
16. Wayne Coy, Roosevelt's Special Assistant for Defense, reported that in July 1941 the US produced just two heavy bombers; cited in McJimsey, 1987: *Harry Hopkins*, p. 197.
17. Associated Press, 'House Opens Draft Debate', *Oakland Tribune*, 8 August 1941, p. 1.
18. Associated Press, 'Group Appeals to Congress to Avoid War', *Titusville Herald* (Pennsylvania), 6 August 1941, p. 1.
19. Associated Press, 'House Asked to Vote Indefinite Service Extension', *The Paris News* (Texas), 8 August 1941, p. 1.
20. http://www.trumanlibrary.org/oralhist/bendet1.htm#22.
21. Arne, 1945: *United Nations Primer*, p. 1.
22. Sherwood, 1948: *Roosevelt and Hopkins*, p. 314; General Alan Brooke, then commander of Britain's home defences, recorded in his diary that he was quite comfortable that invasion was not imminent before this visit but after the visit he became much more concerned that he was making the correct judgements on 29 July. Danchev and Todman, 2001: *War Diaries 1939-1945 Field Marshal Lord Alan Brooke*, p. 172.
23. http://www.nato.int/docu/basictxt/b410814a.htm.
24. For examples of the debate on colonialism, see Chand, Anup, *India and the Atlantic Charter* (Lahore: Ripon Press, 1943); Sorensen, 1942: *India and the Atlantic Charter*; Smith, 1942: *The Atlantic Charter and Africa from an American Standpoint*.
25. Mandela, 1994: *Long Walk to Freedom*, p. 110.
26. Arne, 1945: *United Nations Primer*, p. 4.
27. Doenecke, 2000: *Storm on the Horizon*, p. 236.
28. Doenecke, 2000: *Storm on the Horizon*, p. 237.
29. ibid., p. 236.
30. ibid., p. 238.
31. Sumner Welles, Under Secretary of State, Memorandum of Conversation, at Sea, 11 August 1941, available at http://avalon.law.yale.edu/wwii/at09.asp.
32. British Cmd. 6315, Misc. No. 3 (1941): Inter-Allied Meeting Held in London at St. James's Palace of September 24,1941, Report of Proceedings; and Department of State Bulletin September 21, 1941, pp. 233–5.
33. Doenecke, 2000: *Storm on the Horizon*, p. 327.
34. ibid., p. 326.
35. Roberts, 2006: *Stalin's Wars*, p. 116; Roberts quotes an order from Stalin to this effect.

Chapter 2

1. 'United Nations', *The Economist*, 31 January 1942, p. 1.
2. Sherwood, 1948: *Roosevelt and Hopkins*, p. 446.
3. Ward, 1995: *Closest Companion*, pp. 384–5.
4. Sherwood, 1948: *Roosevelt and Hopkins*, p. 458.

5. ibid., p. 453.

6. *ibid.*, pp. 448–9.

7. Miner, 2003: *Stalin's Holy War*, p. 82.

8. See http://knol.google.com/k/russian-church-and-stalin#.

9. Sherwood, 1948: *Roosevelt and Hopkins*, pp. 452–3. This includes a photograph of the paper where Roosevelt drew arrows re-ordering the nations.

10. Foreign Relations of the United States (FRUS) 1942, Vol.1, pp. 27–8.

11. Jenkins, 2003: *Churchill*, p. 676.

12. UK National Archives, Foreign Office, War, General, Confidential, (16209) L 2136/2136/405, 1 June 1942.

13. http://www.yale.edu/lawweb/avalon/wwii/italy03.htm.

14. Typewritten index to Chatham House's collection of newspaper clippings, British Library, Colindale.

15. Danchev and Todman, 2001: *Field Marshal Lord Alan Brooke, War Diaries 1939–1945.*

16. Conn and Fairchild, 1960: *Framework of Hemisphere Defense*, p. 135.

17. ibid., p. 329.

18. Matlof and Snell, 1953: *Strategic Planning for Coalition Warfare, 1941–42*, p. 98.

19. Gallup, 1972: *The Gallup Poll: Public Opinion, 1935-1971*, V1, pp. 316–7.

20. Hall, 1955: *North American Supply, History of the Second World War*, p. 354.

21. ibid., p. 346.

22. 'Co-ordination of the Allied War Effort, Agreements between the Prime Minister and the President of the United States of America' (Great Britain), Parliamentary Papers, Cmd. 6332, 1942.

23. UK National Archives, ADM/15758.

24. UK National Archives, COS (42) 335, 6 July 1942.

25. UK National Archives, Ministry of Fuel and Power POWE 33/1411.

26. UK National Archives, War Cabinet, JP (42) 1017 (S), 17 December 1942.

27. 'The Organisation for Joint Planning' (Great Britain), Parliamentary Papers 1941–42, Cmd. 6351, 1942.

28. Wild, Payson Sibley, Jr., 'Machinery of Collaboration between the United Nations', *Foreign Policy Report*, July 1, 1942.

29. Late News, front page of the *Evening Capital* in Annapolis, Maryland, 7 January 1942.

30. https://www.airforcehistory.hq.af.mil/PopTopics/chron/42mar.htm.

31. *The Times*, 18 April 1942.

32. Eade, 1952: *The War Speeches of Winston Churchill*, Vol. 2, pp. 180–5.

33. Marshall, George C., Chief of Staff of the US Army, Unity of Command of the United Nations and Admiral Ernest J. King, 'Conduct of the War by the United Nations', in Krout, 1942: Proceedings of the Academy of Political Science, Vol.XX, May 1942.

34. http://carlisle-www.army.mil/usawc/Parameters/1995/filibert.htm; also http://search.eb.com/dday/article-9400217.

35. The full description reads: 'Upon a field of heraldic sable (BLACK), representing the darkness of Nazi oppression, is shown the sword of liberation in the form of a crusader's sword, the flames arising from the hilt and leaping up the blade. This represents avenging justice by which the enemy power will be broken in Nazi-dominated Europe. Above the sword is a rainbow emblematic of hope containing all the colors of which the National Flags of the Allies are

composed. The heraldic chief of azure (BLUE) above the rainbow is emblematic of a state of peace and tranquility, the restoration of which to the enslaved people is the objective of the United Nations'. *History of Chief of Staff to Supreme Allied Commander* (US Army Center of Military History Historical Manuscripts Collection (HMC) file number 8-3.6A CA). Available at: http://www.army.mil/cmh-pg/documents/cossac/Cossac.htm.

36. General Eisenhower, Order of the Day, 6 June 1944, SHAPE.
37. http://www.eisenhower.archives.gov/research/Digital_Documents/DDay/ddaypage.html.
38. Canadian Army, Report No. 146, Historical Section, Canadian Military Headquarters, Operations Of First Canadian Army In North-West Europe, 31 Jul–1 Oct 44, (Preliminary Report) Para.8.
39. Lyttleton, 1942: *My American Visit: Some Random Notes*.
40. Clapper, Raymond, *Wisconsin State Journal*, 8 January 1942. NB Just a week after the Declaration, sub-editors had not got used to capitalizing 'United Nations', and the format of this quote respects the original.
41. Conn *et al.*, 1964: 'Guarding the United States and Its Outposts', p. 82.
42. Conn and Fairchild, 1960: *Framework of Hemisphere Defense*, pp. 158–60.
43. 'Viscount Halifax to Foreign Office', No. 2413 24, April 1942, repeated 6th May 1942.
44. Arne, 1945: *United Nations Primer*, p. 14.
45. 'Flag Day', *The Washington Post*, 14 June 1942, pp. 1 and 10; 'President's Flag Day Address', *The Washington Post*, 15 June 1942, p. 2.
46. Photo caption, *Edwardville Intelligencer* (Illinois), 15 June 1942, p. 1.
47. 'United Nations Day', *Coshocton Tribune* (Ohio), 14 June 1942, p. 12.
48. 'United Nations Day', *McKean County Democrat* (Smethport, Pennsylvania), 21 May 1942, p. 2.
49. Sherwood, 1948: *Roosevelt and Hopkins*, p. 577.
50. Associated Press, *Charleston Gazette* (North Carolina), 15 June 1942, p. 2.
51. *Dunkirk, New York Evening Observer*, 15 June 1942, p. 2.
52. Associated Press, 'Flag Day sees expression of Allied Unity', *Wisconsin Rapids Daily Tribune*, 15 June 1942, p. 2.
53. 'United Nations', *Daily Gleaner* (Kingston, Jamaica), 15 June 1942, p. 1.
54. Imperial War Museum, collections record ID Number: COI 145 Item Name: United Nations: a record of the first United Nations Day in Great Britain, 14th June 1942.
55. http://archives.un.org/unarms/doc/archivalcollections/4_unitednations_informationorganization.doc.
56. *The Washington Post*, 17 March 1943, p. 20.
57. 'United Nations Flag Flown in Washington', *Schenectady Gazette* (New York), June 15, 1943, p. 5.
58. UK National Archives, Halifax to Foreign Office, No. 1283, 17 March 1943.
59. http://select.nytimes.com/gst/abstract.html?res=FA0810F83D5C167B93C6A8178DD85F478485F9.
60. 'Flag Change Protested; Sons of Revolution Assail Use of Four Freedoms Banner Overseas', *New York Times*, 1 July 1943, p. 20.
61. ID Number: NMV 735 A Item Name: *British Movietone News* issue 735A (8 July 1943), Imperial War Museum collections record.
62. UK National Archives, PREM 4/32/13: Brendan Bracken to the PM 3 June 42 submitting draft, 1943, PREM 4/32/13 Hodge of MoI to Peck parades London

Cardiff and Edinburgh, some concern at war cabinet over stretch of resources on Whit Monday and getting into an annual event. Coordinated with the United Nations Office in London. UK National Archives, Halifax to Foreign Office, No 2341, 19 May 1943; UK National Archives PREM 4/32/13 AS Hodge of the Ministry of Information to JH Peck at Downing St.

63. Russian Stamps, *Lethbridge Herald* (Alberta), 10 April 1945.
64. Advertisement in *The Times*, 9 September 1944.
65. Advertisement in *The Times*, 19 April 1945.
66. Advertisement in *The Times*, 25 January 1943.
67. *The Times*, 11 September 1943.
68. *The Times*, 23 December 1943.
69. *The Times*, 30 July 1945.
70. *New York Times*, 8 June 1944.
71. 'THE FORM & ORDER OF THE SERVICE OF THANKSGIVING FOR THE VICTORY IN EUROPE OF THE ARMS OF THE UNITED NATIONS', Liturgies, Church of England (Cambridge University Press, 1945).
72. Liberal Jewish Synagogue (London, 19 August 1945).
73. London School of Hygiene and Tropical Medicine, Finance and General Purposes Committee Minutes, 12 May 1943: 'United Nations Courses – University of London. Reported that a part of the United Nations courses organised by the University of London was being held in the School and a small office had been allocated to the organising staff. As from 1st March 1943, the university would pay £7.10.0 per quarter towards the upkeep of the room, £7.10.0 for the use of the telephone excluding trunk calls and a charge of £2.10.0 per day for the lecture theatre. The lecture theatre would be required for about 3 days each month. Approved'. With thanks to Victoria Killick, Archivist & Records Manager, London School of Hygiene and Tropical Medicine.
74. *The Times*, 21 September 1943.
75. *The Times*, 5 December 1942.
76. http://lilt.ilstu.edu/mcuna/history/history.htm.
77. See for example, Samuel, 1993: *American Catholics and the formation of the United Nations*.
78. http://www.unausa.org/site/pp.asp?c=fvKRI8MPJpF&b=383535.
79. Commission to Study the Organization of Peace, 1943: The United Nations and the Organization of Peace: third report and papers presented to the Commission.
80. RIIA, 1943: 'War and Peace in the Pacific', a preliminary report of the Eighth Conference of the Institute of Pacific Relations on wartime and post-war co-operation of the United Nations in the Pacific and the Far East, Mont Tremblant, Quebec, December 4–14, 1942.
81. Lorwin, 1943: *Postwar Plans of the United Nations*.
82. Linton, 1942: *Salute to Valor: Heroes of the United Nations*.
83. www.pages.judyposner.com/60/PictPage/1921384955.html, accessed 20 September 2005.
84. Rich, 1944: *Art of the United Nations*.
85. Veal, 1944: *Recipes of the United Nations*.
86. *The Times*, 9 September 1944.
87. Sherwood, 1948: *Roosevelt and Hopkins*, p. 598.

Chapter 3

1. 'Letter from President Roosevelt', Report to Congress on Lend Lease Operations (Washington, DC, US GPO, June 1942).
2. See http://www.bea.gov/national/xls/gdplev.xls.
3. Stettinius, 1944: *Lend-Lease*, p. 101.
4. ibid., p. 165.
5. Leighton, 1955: *Global logistics and strategy 1941–1943*.
6. Report to Congress on Lend Lease Operations, (Washington DC, US GPO, June 1942), Chapter 3 'Lend Lease and the Peace'.
7. ibid.
8. Hall, 1955: *North American Supply, History of the Second World War*, p. 420, Table 14.
9. Ratner, 1970: 'An Inquiry into the Nazi War Economy', pp. 466–72; Ratner states that many German factories were still on a 'one normal shift system' late in the war, p. 471.
10. Conversation with Jerry Kuehl.
11. Levering, 1976: *American Opinion and the Russian Alliance, 1939–1945*, p. 43.
12. Stettinius, 1944: *Lend-Lease*, p. 260; Hall, 1955: *North American Supply*, p. 391.
13. Stettinius, 1944: *Lend-Lease*, p. 260–1.
14. Stettinius, 1944: *Lend-Lease*, p. 190.
15. Roosevelt, Press Conference, 17 February 1942, available at http://www.presidency.ucsb.edu/ws/index.php?pid=16223&st=lend-lease&st1=.
16. 'Fuehrer Conferences on matters Dealing with the German Navy' (13 April 1942), annex to report by Doenitz, in Motter, 1969: *The Persian Corridor and Aid to Russia, The Middle East Theatre, US Army in World War II*, p. 5.
17. Stettinius, 1944: *Lend-Lease*, p. 210–1.
18. Beevor, 1998: *Stalingrad*, p. 225.
19. Harriman and Able, 1975: *Special Envoy to Churchill and Stalin, 1941–1946*, p. 278.
20. Stettinius, 1944: *Lend-Lease*, p. 208.
21. ibid., p. 207.
22. Vorsin, 1997: 'Motor Vehicle Transport Deliveries through "Lend Lease"', p. 154–5.
23. Motter, 1969: *The Persian Corridor*, p. 161.
24. Vorsin, 1997: 'Motor Vehicle Transport', p. 158.
25. Motter 1969: *The Persian Corridor*, p. 496, Table 9.
26. Vorsin, 1997: 'Motor Vehicle Transport', pp. 153–75.
27. Beevor, 1998: *Stalingrad*, p. 112.
28. Beevor and Vinogradova, 2006: *A Writer at War: Vasily Grossman*, p. 122–3.
29. Lebedev, 1997: *Aviation Lend-Lease to Russia*, p. 71.
30. Motter, 1969: *The Persian Corridor*, p. 498, Table 10.
31. Lebedev, 1997: Aviation Lend-Lease to Russia, p. 70.
32. Petrov, 2002: *Red Stars 4: Lend-Lease Aircraft in Russia*. The first US P-47 Thunderbolt fighter plane sent to the USSR was funded by the 'Sovereign Senators, Knights of Pithias, New York Lodge No.463', pp. 81 and 196.
33. Van Tuyll, 1989: *Feeding the Bear: American Aid to the Soviet Union, 1941–1945*, p. 157, Table 10.
34. Flynn, 1998: *The Roosevelt Myth*, p. 356.
35. Sapir, 1997: 'The economics of war in the Soviet Union during World War II', p. 231.
36. Van Tuyll, 1989: *Feeding the Bear*, p. 140.

37. Schlesinger, 2005: *My Dear Mr. Stalin*, p. xii.
38. *The Economist* cxliv, 2 January 1943.

Chapter 4

1. The movie *Casablanca* went on general release on 23 January 1943, having premiered the previous November. I have found no evidence that the release was timed to coincide with the summit; it appears to have been a happy accident.
2. *The Paris News* (Texas), 24 January 1942, p. 1.
3. *The Observer*, 17 January 1943, p. 3.
4. Willkie, 1943: *One World*, pp. 175–6.
5. Sherwood, 1948: *Roosevelt and Hopkins*, pp. 695–7.
6. McJimsey, 1987: *Harry Hopkins*, p. 294, ref 8; 'Stalin to FDR May 26, June 11, 1943', in Stalin's correspondence with Churchill, Attlee, Roosevelt, and Truman 1941–45 (London: Lawrence & Wishart, 1958) Vol.II, pp. 66, 70–1; Mastny, 1972: 'Stalin and the Prospects of a Separate Peace in World War II', p. 1378; Sherwood, 1948: *Roosevelt and Hopkins*, p. 734.
7. Bullock, 1964: *Hitler: A Study in Tyranny*, pp. 691–4.
8. 'Towards a Full Alliance', *The Economist*, 27 February 1943, p. 258.
9. Eden, Anthony, 'The Four Power Plan', Cab 66/30/46 WP (42) 516 8 Nov 1942.
10. The Washington Post, 24 March 1943, p. 13.
11. Ray Tucker, McClure Newspapers, *San Mateo Times* (California), 23 January 1943, p. 4.
12. *Hayward Review* (California), 5 January 1943, p. 6i.
13. *New York Times*, 11 March 1943, p. 1.
14. 'FDR statement to Congress on the 2nd Anniversary of Lend-Lease', 11 March 1943 (US GPO 1943).
15. Office of Lend-Lease Administration, 1943: 'All for one, One for all: the Story of Lend-Lease'.
16. *New York Times*, 11 March 1943, p. 1.
17. *The Economist*, 20 March 1943, p. 361.
18. Sherwood, 1948: *Roosevelt and Hopkins*, p. 720.
19. Schlesinger, 2005: *My Dear Mr. Stalin*, p. xii.
20. Ward, 1995: *Closest Companion*, p. 207.
21. Acheson, 1970: *Present at the Creation*, pp. 64–5.
22. UK National Archives, 'Viscount Halifax to Foreign Office 5 June 1943', PREM 4.28/10.
23. Hull, 1948: *Memoirs of Cordell Hull*, p. 1642.
24. ibid.
25. Roosevelt, Franklin D, 'Letter to delegates to the Conference on Food and Agriculture', 18 May 1943.
26. Franklin D. Roosevelt, 7 June 1943; see http://www.presidency.ucsb.edu/ws/index.php?pid=16406&st=food&st1=.
27. 'Documents Relating to the Food and Agriculture Organisation of the United Nations August 1–December 14, 1944, UNCFA Hot Springs VA May 1943', Parliamentary Papers, session 1943–1944, Cmd. 6590 (London, 1945).
28. The Work of the FAO (Washington, DC: United Nations Interim Commission on Food and Agriculture, August 1945).
29. Bose, 2009: 'The Two Faces of Empire', *History Today* 58/10, pp. 17–9.

30. Sen, 1969: *Burke on Indian Economy*; and Langford, 1991: *The Writings and Speeches of Edmund Burke*, passim.
31. 'Willkie Says War Liberates Negroes', *New York Times*, 20 July 1942, p. 28.
32. Wille MacMahon, 2003: *Reconsidering Roosevelt on Race*.
33. Appendix I, Table 11.
34. 10 December 2002, http://archives.cnn.com/2002/ALLPOLITICS/12/09/lott.comment/.
35. Sherwood, 1948: *Roosevelt and Hopkins*, p. 733.
36. Eden, Anthony, 'The "Four Power" Plan', Cab 66/30/46 WP (42) 516, 8 November 1942.
37. UK National Archives, PREM.4/30/4 Hush-Most Secret From: QUADRANT 15 September 1943.
38. '(US) DRAFT UNITED NATIONS DECLARATION ON NATIONAL INDEPENDENCE', in UK National Archives, PREM.4/30/4 Hush-Most Secret From: QUADRANT 15 September 1943.
39. *The Economist*, 22 May 1943, p. 645.
40. Sherwood, 1948: *Roosevelt and Hopkins*, p. 734.
41. ibid., p. 737.
42. Arne, Sigrid, *United Nations Primer: The Key to the Conferences* (New York: Farrar and Rinehart, 1945).
43. *The Evening Independent* (St Petersburg, Florida), 15 October 1943, p. 1, available at http://news.google.com/newspapers?id=e40LAAAAIBAJ&sjid=I1UDAAAAIBAJ&pg=2134,4535374&dq=truman+lend-lease&hl=en.
44. Sherwood, 1948: *Roosevelt and Hopkins*, p. 748.
45. http://avalon.law.yale.edu/wwii/moscow.asp.
46. Kimball et al. 1994: *Allies at War*, p. 367.
47. Sherwood, 1948: *Roosevelt and Hopkins*, p. 591.

Chapter 5

1. 'Trial of Obersturmbannfuhrer Rudolph Franz Ferdinand Hoess, Supreme National Tribunal of Poland', in UNWCC, 1992, p. 128.
2. Dear David .... Basically, you must send your application to the Permanent Mission to the United Nations of the country of which you are citizen. The Permanent Mission to the UN of your country will send your application to the UN Secretary-General for review. Once we will have received an answer, we will inform you. Your application falls under the 3(b) Research by Individual. As a matter of result, you will not be allowed to take notes, make photocopies or pictures. (See in the PDF unwcc_application_new (the third one): page 4. "the Applicant understands that access will be permitted only in the areas reserved therefore in the United Nations archives building, that the United Nations Secretariat cannot provide copies of materials to which access is granted nor may the applicants may cause such copies to be made, and no official materials is to be removed from the concerned area".) Best Regards, Rémi DUBUISSON (Mr.) Associate Information Management Officer, UN Archives and Records Management Section, 30 July 2010.
3. Wright, Lord: History of UNWCC, Commission No. 7150, p. 496.
4. http://yourarchives.nationalarchives.gov.uk/index.php?title=War_Crime_Trials.
5. Kochavi, 1998: Prelude to Nuremberg, Allied War Crimes Policy and the Question of Punishment, p. 4.

6. *The Times*, 12 November 1940.
7. *The Times*, 20 December 1940.
8. Bathurst, 1945: *The United Nations War Crimes Commission*, pp. 565–8.
9. German Atrocities (HMSO for the Soviet Embassy, London, 7 November and 6 January 1942); see also, Punishment for War Crimes (HMSO: London, 1942), and Chapter V of the Official History of the UNWCC, http://www.enotes.com/genocide-encyclopedia/united-nations-war-crimes-commission.
10. Wright, Lord: History of the UNWCC, Commission No. 7150, Chapter 5.
11. Foreign Relations of the United States, 1942, Vol. 1: General, British Commonwealth, The Far East, p. 45ff.
12. Hull, 1948: *The Memoirs of Cordell Hull*, p. 1184.
13. Kochavi, 1998: *Prelude to Nuremberg*, p. 55.
14. 'Declaration on Persecution of the Jews', 17 December 1942, in United Nations Documents 1941–45 (Royal Institute for International Affairs: London, 1946).
15. Borgwardt, 2005: *A New Deal for the World*, pp. 218–20.
16. House of Commons, Official Report, London, 17 December 1942.
17. Kochavi, 1998: *Prelude to Nuremberg*, p. 222–30.
18. House of Lords, 23 March 1943.
19. Kochavi, 1998: *Prelude to Nuremberg*, p. 135.
20. ibid., p. 140–3.
21. Lankevich, 1990: *Archives of the Holocaust*, Vol. 1, pp. ix–xviii.
22. Kochavi, 1998: *Prelude to Nuremberg*, p. 235.
23. Wright, Lord: *History of the UNWCC*, p. 14.
24. Cited in Kochavi, 1998: *Prelude to Nuremberg*, p. 147.
25. See for example, Associated Press, *Port Arthur News*, Texas, 30 January 1944, p. 3.
26. http://avalon.law.yale.edu/20th_century/kbpact.asp.
27. Kochavi, 1998: *Prelude to Nuremberg*, pp. 157–8.
28. ibid., pp. 222–30.
29. Maxwell Fife, 1948, in *War Crimes Trials*, Vol. I, pp. xviii–xix.
30. Wright, Lord: History of the UNWCC, p. 165.
31. Wright, Lord: History of the UNWCC, p. 142.
32. Kochavi, 1998: *Prelude to Nuremberg*, p. 455, cites Truman Executive Order No.9547 fn (1).
33. Kochavi, 1998: *Prelude to* p. 133.
34. Wright, Lord: Chairman UNWCC, Law Reports of Trials of War Criminals, Introduction to Vol. V, (London: UNWCC, HMSO, 1948).
35. See for example, Widney Brown and Grenfell, 2003: Melbourne Journal of International Law VI/4, 2003.
36. 'Klaus Barbie and the United States Government', Report to the Attorney General of the United States, submitted by: Allan A. Ryan, Jr., Special Assistant to the Assistant Attorney General, Criminal Division, United States Department of Justice (US Government Printing Office: Washington, D.C., 20402, 1983).
37. Simpson, 1995: *Money, Law, and Genocide in the Twentieth Century*, p. 13.
38. Ministry of Justice, Ethiopia, Documents on Italian War Crimes submitted to the United Nations War Crimes Commission by the Imperial Ethiopian Government, 2 vols, Addis Ababa, 1949; evidence of International Committee of the Red Cross delegate, Vol. II, p. 31.
39. Badoglio's memoirs of the invasion were published in translation as *The War in Abyssinia* by Methuen in London in 1937.

40. Conversation with John Stanleigh.
41. Ambrose, 1998: *Citizen Soldiers*, pp. 342–4.
42. Kochavi, 1998: *Prelude to Nuremberg*, p. 115.
43. See for example, Blumenthal and McCormack, 2008: *The Legacy of Nuremburg: Civilising Influence or Institutionalised Vengeance?*

Chapter 6

1. *The Guardian*, 11 July 1944, report of study by the distinguished medical scientist, Professor R. M. Gordon.
2. 'Agriculture and Food in Greece', Operational Analysis Paper No. 19 (UNRRA European Regional Office, Portland Place, London W2, 1947), p. 32.
3. Woodbridge, 1950: *The History of UNRRA*; this official history provides the data in the paragraph.
4. *ibid.*, Vol. 1, p. 506.
5. Jacoby, Harold Stanley, *From Dar el Shifa to Dar es Salaam* (privately published, USA, 1992).
6. Hirschmann, 1949: *The Embers Still Burn*, pp. 146–7.
7. Official Report, House of Commons, 21 August 1940.
8. Acheson, 1970: *Present at the Creation*, p. 65.
9. Eden, Anthony, Cab/66/24/42 W.P. (42) 212, May 20 1942.
10. Wood, 1958: *Welfare and Peace in Political and External Affairs*, p. 348.
11. 'UNRRA', *Time*, 6 December 1943.
12. Danchev, 1993: *Oliver Franks: Founding Father*.
13. Woodbridge, 1950: *The History of UNRRA*, Vol. 3, p. 500.
14. Woodbridge, 1950: *The History of UNRRA*, Vol. 1, p. 125.
15. UK National Archives, Prem. 4/29/4 Prime Minister's Personal Minute Serial No. M(R)8/4.
16. UNHCR, 'Global Trends 2008: Refugees, Asylum-seekers, Returnees, Internally Displaced and Stateless Persons', available at http://www.unhcr.org/4a375c426.html, p. 2.
17. UNHCR, 'Figures at a glance', 2009, available at http://www.unhcr.org/pages/49c3646c11.html.
18. Woodbridge, 1950: *The History of UNRRA*, Vol. 3, Tables 9–14.
19. Woodbridge, 1950: *The History of UNRRA*, Vol. 2, p. 522ff.
20. *ibid.*, p. 516.
21. Supreme Headquarters Allied Expeditionary Force, Headquarters 'Guide to the Care of Displaced Persons in Germany', May 1945 revision, Part 1, Section 1; cited in Woodbridge, 1950: *The History of UNRRA*, Vol. 2, p. 522ff.
22. 'U.S. Zone History Report, Camp Self-Government', Appendix A, R. Taylor, 'Camp Self-Government, District I'; and Appendix B, Virgil Payne, 'Camp Self-Government, District III'; cited in Woodbridge, 1950: *The History of UNRRA*, Vol. 2, pp. 523–4.
23. http://www.merck.com/mmpe/sec14/ch177/ch177c.html.
24. Wilson, 1947: *Aftermath*.
25. Woodbridge, 1950: *The History of UNRRA*, Vol. 2, p. 230.
26. *ibid.*, p. 248.
27. *ibid.*, p. 252.
28. *ibid.*, pp. 424–37.
29. Tucker, 2005: *Tractors and Chopsticks: My Work with the UNRRA Project in China, 1946 to 1947*.

30. Armstrong-Reid and Murray, 2008: *Armies of Peace*, Appendix C.
31. Wilson, 1947: *Aftermath*, pp. 159–60.
32. *New York Times*, 6 February 1946, cited in Hirschmann, 1949: *The Embers Still Burn*, p. 232.
33. Quoted in Hirschmann, 1949: *The Embers Still Burn*, p. 228.
34. *ibid.*, p. 147.
35. *ibid.*, p. 90.
36. Acheson, 1970: *Present at the Creation*, p. 201.
37. Orr, 2004: *Winning the Peace: An American Strategy for Post-Conflict Reconstruction*, p. 186.
38. Wilson, 1947: *Aftermath*, p. 211.

Chapter 7

1. Stimson and Bundy, 1947: *On Active Service for Peace*, p. 567.
2. Keynes, 1919: *The Economic Consequences of the Peace*, p. 226.
3. Stimson and Bundy, 1947: *On Active Service for Peace* (New York: Harper, 1947).
4. http://avalon.law.yale.edu/wwii/at14.asp.
5. Cordell Hull, statement for *Foreign Trade Week*, May 1942, in *America's Economic Policy for the war and the peace* (London: Hutchinson & Co., 1942).
6. Stimson and Bundy, 1947: *On Active Service for Peace*, p. 567.
7. Arne, 1945: *United Nations Primer*, p. 68.
8. Margaret De Vries in Kirshner, 1995: *The Bretton Woods System: Retrospect and Prospect After Fifty Years*, p. 9.
9. *Pittsburgh Post-Gazette*, January 25, 1977.
10. Wilson, 1986: *Memoirs: The Making of a Prime Minister 1916–1964*, pp. 122–3.
11. Kimball, 1969: *The Most Unsordid Act: Lend-Lease 1939–1941*, pp. 235–6.
12. Dobson, 1986: *US Wartime Aid to Britain 1940-1946*.
13. See Gaddis, 1965: *American Diplomacy During the Second World War, 1941-1945*.
14. Hexner, 1946: *American Journal of International Law* 40/3, pp. 637–40.
15. Butler, 2006: *My Dear Mr. Stalin*, p. 208.
16. Butler, 2006: *My Dear Mr.Stalin*, pp. 208–10.
17. Stalin's correspondence with Churchill, Attlee, Roosevelt, and Truman 1941–5 (London: Lawrence & Wishart, 1958).
18. Skidelsky, 2000: *John Maynard Keynes: Fighting for Freedom 1937–1946*, p. 356.
19. Hexner, 1946: *The American Journal of International Law*, 40/3, p. 637.
20. Sapir Jacques in Kershaw and Lewin, 1997: *Stalinism and Nazism*, p. 231.
21. 'Nazis Making plans for Post-war Europe', AP's Wade Werner reported from Lisbon. *The Dothan Eagle*, Alabama, 19 April 1944.
22. Raymond S. Mikesell in Kirshner, 1995: *The Bretton Woods System*, p. 24.
23. http://www.economist.com/daily/news/displaystory.cfm?story_id= 14842922&fsrc=nwl.
24. Kirshner, 1995: *The Bretton Woods System*, p. 36.
25. United Nations Monetary and Financial Conference, Final Act Cmd 6546 HMSO London 1944.
26. *ibid.*, p. 37.
27. Henry Morgenthau, Congress, *Nevada State Journal*, 22 April 1944, p. 6.
28. De Vries, in Kirshner, 1995: *The Bretton Woods System*, pp. 16–7.
29. FDR Presidential Library online: Safe Files Box 5 Europe pp. 79–81 http://docs. fdrlibrary.marist.edu/fdrbx.html.

30. http://www.jewishvirtuallibrary.org/jsource/ww2/francelend.html.
31. 'Lend-Lease Beyond War', *Wall Street Journal*, 2 March 1945, p. 6.
32. http://www.trumanlibrary.org/oralhist/matlock.htm.
33. Simon Reisman in Kirshner, 1995: *The Bretton Woods System*, pp. 82–6.
34. Kirshner, 1995: *The Bretton Woods System*, p. 84.
35. Wilcox, 1949: *A Charter for World Trade*, pp. 53–62.
36. Hart, 1995: *Also present at the creation, Dana Wilgress and the UNCTE at Havana.*
37. William Diebold in Kirshner, 1995: *The Bretton Woods System*, pp. 152–70.
38. www.stwr.org/imf-world-bank.
39. Arne, 1945: *United Nations Primer*, pp. 85–92.
40. Lyttleton, 1942: *My American Visit: Some Random Notes.*
41. Kirshner, 1995: *The Bretton Woods System*, pp. ix–xiii.
42. Weiss, 2009: *International Studies Quarterly*, 53:2, pp. 253–271.

Chapter 8

1. Roosevelt speech to Foreign Policy Association, 21 October 1944.
2. Hoopes and Brinkley, 1997: *FDR and the Creation of the U.N.*, pp. 49–51.
3. Sir Adam Roberts in Louis, 2001: *Still More Adventures with Britannia*, pp. 229–47.
4. Discussion of Truman Committee origins of B2H2, http://www.trumanlibrary. org/oralhist/judd.htm, Truman Library Oral History Interview with Dr Walter H. Judd , member of Congress from Minnesota, 1943–62, April 13, 1970 by Jerry N. Hess.
5. Roosevelt Press statement, 15 June 1944, FRUS 1944 I, p. 643.
6. http://www.state.gov/r/pa/ho/pubs/fs/55407.htm, Office of the Historian, Bureau of Public Affairs, US Department of State, October 2005.
7. *Frederick Post*, Frederick, Maryland, August 31, 1944, pp.1 and 7.
8. http://www.cfo.doe.gov/me70/manhattan/international_control_1.htm, accessed June 2010.
9. 'Ball Pledges His Support to Roosevelt', *Washington Post*, 24 October 1944, p. 1.
10. http://www.presidency.ucsb.edu/ws/index.php?pid=16456&st=&st1=.
11. Merlo Pusey, *The Washington Post*, 31 October 1944, p. 7.
12. 'Ford and GM Scrutinized for Alleged Nazi Collaboration', *The Washington Post*, 30 November 1998, pp. A01, available at http://www.washingtonpost.com/ wp-srv/national/daily/nov98/nazicars30.htm.
13. Arne, 1945: *United Nations Primer*, p. 93.
14. Rotbalt, 1985: *Bulletin of Atomic Scientists*, 41/7, pp. 16–9.
15. Glantz, 2003: *The Soviet Strategic Offensive in Manchuria, 1945: "August Storm".*
16. UK, House of Commons Debate, HC Deb 18 January 1945, Vol. 407, cc.376–493.
17. Woytak, 1984: *East European Quarterly*, XVIII/3 (September), pp. 273–8. Woytak cites Edmund Charaszkiewicz who wrote in Polish.
18. Protocol of the Proceedings of the Crimea Conference, Yalta, 11 February 1945 (London, Foreign Office, HMSO, 1945).
19. See Appendix.
20. Dimitrov, 2007: *Soviet Foreign Policy, Democracy and Communism in Bulgaria 1941– 1948*, pp. 69–128.
21. Seton-Watson, 1960: *Neither War Nor Peace: The Struggle for Power in Post-War Europe.*
22. Mastny, 1980: *Russia's Road to the Cold War: Diplomacy, Warfare and the Politics of Communism, 1941–1945.*

23. Butler, 2006: *My Dear Mr. Stalin,* pp. 310–20.
24. http://www.britannia.com/history/euro/3/4_1.html.
25. Telephone Directory, The United Nations Conference on International Organization, San Francisco, California, Pacific Telephone and Telegraph Co., Third Issue, 25 April 1945.
26. Simma *et al.,* 1994: *The Charter of the United Nations: A Commentary;* and for example, Goodrich Leland and Hambro, 1946: *Charter of the United Nations Commentary and Documents* which provides an article by article comparison with the Dumbarton Oaks proposals.
27. http://www.trumanlibrary.org/publicpapers/index.php?pid=34&st=&st1=.
28. Reid, 1983: *On Duty: A Canadian at the Making of the United Nations, 1945–1946,* p. 57.
29. Hull, 1948: *The Memoirs of Cordell Hull,* p. 1642.
30. Transmittal to Congress of a Report by the United Nations Interim Commission on Food and Agriculture. 26 March 1945, available at http://www.presidency.ucsb.edu/ws/index.php?pid=16598&st=&st1=.
31. FDR archives, Hyde Park, Safe Files, Box 5 a69d15-29.
32. Mazower, 2009: *No Enchanted Palace: The End of Empire and the Ideological Origins of the United Nations.*
33. Nevins, 1963: *Herbert H. Lehman and His era,* p. 290.
34. Arne, 1945: *United Nations Primer,* p. 59.
35. Glantz, 2005: *FDR and the Soviet Union,* p. 177.
36. Reynolds, 2009: *America, Empire of Liberty,* p. 376, cites Banac, 2003: *The Diary of Georgi Dimitrov, 1933–1949,* pp. 338 and 372, entries for 28 Jan and 7 June 1945.
37. See for example this discussion of the US 1992 Defense Guidance by Paul Wolfowitz and its implementation under the Clinton Administration, available at http://www.defense.gov/transcripts/transcript.aspx?transcriptid=2594.
38. Conferences on 'Training for International Administration, Experience of the League of Nations Secretariat' and 'Experience of International Administration' discussed in Ranshofen-Wertheimer, 1945: *The international secretariat : a great experiment in international administration.*
39. *The Times,* 20 June 1944 p. 1.
40. See: Google map 'united nations in wartime London', by Lazerowitz A.

Conclusion

1. Moran, Lord, Winston Churchill, *The Struggle for Survival 1940–1965* (London: Constable, 1996), p. 186.

Bibliography

This bibliography consists of an introductory note, a bibliography of publications concerning, or by, the United Nations published in the years 1942–5, a selected bibliography of UK official papers from 1942–5 and a selected general bibliography.

Primary sources that are available online include parts of the national archives of Australia, Canada, New Zealand and Great Britain. So too are the edited volumes of the Foreign Relations of the United States (FRUS). Nevertheless, while the FRUS was long a leader in the field, today the comparative difficulty of accessing the original US Government files is a problem for research. Susan Butler's compendium of the Roosevelt-Stalin correspondence is a wonderful volume. The daily debates of the British Parliament (Hansard) and the US Congress are now also digitally accessible. The US presidential libraries of Dwight D. Eisenhower, Franklin D. Roosevelt and Harry S. Truman; the American Presidency Project (americanpresidency.org), established by John Woolley and Gerhard Peters at the University of California, Santa Barbara; the 'ibiblio' project of the University of North Carolina and Yale's Avalon Project all provide invaluable resources.

Secondary digital sources include newspapers by individual title, at newspaperarchives.com and through Google. These newspapers often include primary material, including government statements that are otherwise hard to find. The British Library holding of Chatham House's contemporary newspaper clippings is a rare resource especially of non-English papers. Academic search engines such as JSTOR list many publications from the war years with United Nations in the title and thousands of text references. But lastly it is important to mention the second hand book shops such as Nemona Collectables, Zubal Books, Vashon Island Books, Early Republic Books and The Book Abyss that provided copies of valuable texts that do not exist online.

There are a multitude of memoirs and studies on the period covered here that would require a further volume or two to even list.

Publications by or about the United Nations published in 1942–5

Addinsell, Richard, *March of the United Nations* (London: Keith Prowse and Co., 1943).

American Bible Society, *The Bible and the Nations*. Excerpts from letters and addresses of Franklin Delano Roosevelt, presented by the American Bible Society to the delegates of the United Nations Conference on International Organization, San Francisco, May 1945 (New York, 1945).

American Council on Public Affairs, Education and the United Nations: A report of the Joint Commission of the Council for Education in World Citizenship and the London International Assembly (Washington, DC, 1943).

American Jewish Committee, *A World Charter for Human Rights*. The story of the consultants to the American delegation to the United Nations Conference on International Organization and their historic achievement (New York, 1945).

Amery, Leopold Charles Maurice Stennett, 'British Links with Europe: Inaugural Address' (London: University of London, United Nations University Centre, 1945).

Anderson, Violet, 'The United Nations Today and Tomorrow', Addresses given at the Canadian Institute on Public Affairs, 21–28 August 1943 (Toronto: The Ryerson Press, 1943).

Arne, Sigrid, *United Nations Primer: The Key to the Conferences* (New York: Farrar and Rinehart, 1945).

Arnold-Foster, W., *Charters of the Peace: A commentary on the Atlantic Charter and the Declarations of Moscow, Cairo and Tehran* (London: Victor Gollancz, 1944).

Arnold-Foster, W., *Today and Tomorrow: Britain and the Peace* (London: War Office, 1944).

Bathurst, M. E., *The United Nations War Crimes Commission* (American Society of International Law, 1945).

Bennett, Francis, United Nations Victory Waltz, music score available at the National Library of Australia collection (c.1945).

Beveridge, William, *The Price of Peace* (London: Pilot Press, 1945).

Bidwell, Percy W., *The United States and the United Nations: Views on Postwar Relations* (New York: Council on Foreign Relations, 1943).

Bonnet, Henri, *The United Nations: What they are, what they may become* (Chicago: World Citizens Association, 1942).

Bonnet, Henri, *Outline of the Future: World Organization Emerging from the War* (Chicago: World Citizens Association, 1943).

Bronson, Leisa and Elaine Exton, *Reading List on The Four Freedoms* (Washington, DC: Women's Division Democratic National Committee, 1943).

Cang, Joel, *The Who's Who of the Allied Governments: United Nations Who's Who in Government and Industry* (London, 1941).

Chapman, C. C. and McNamara, Ray, Hymn of the United Nations (c.1942).

Chiang, Mayling Soong, *We Chinese Women: Speeches and Writings during the first United Nations Year* (New York: John Day, 1943).

Church of England, *The Form & Order of the Service of Thanksgiving for the Victory in Europe of the Arms of the United Nations* (Cambridge: University Press, 1945).

Cleaver, H. Robinson, *United Nations: March* (London: Radio Music Pub. Co., c.1942).

Commission to Study the Organization of Peace, The United Nations and the Organization of Peace: third report and papers presented to the commission, February 1943 (New York: The Commission, Carnegie Endowment, 1943).

Cooledge, Sherman, The United Nations music score (c.1943).

Crichlow, Clyde, Song of the United Nations (c.1943).

Culbertson, Ely, *Total Peace: What makes Wars and How to Organize Peace* (New York: Doubleday, Doran and Co., 1943).

Cunard, Nancy and Padmore, George, *The White Man's Duty: An Analysis of the Colonial Question in the Light of the Atlantic Charter* (London: W.H. Allen and Co., 1942).

Currie, Eve, *Journey Among Warriors* (New York: Doubleday, Doran and Co., 1943).

Davis, Forrest, *The Atlantic System: The Story of Anglo-American Control of the Seas* (London: George Allen and Unwin, 1943).

Dutt, Rajani Palme, *Britain in the World Front* (New York: International Publishers, 1943).

Eaton, Howard O., *Federation: The Coming Structure of World Government* (Norman, OK: University of Oklahoma Press, 1944).

Eckersley, Charles E., *English for the Allies*, Specially written for soldiers, sailors and airmen of the United Nations (London: Longmans and Co., 1942).

Edwards, Corwin D., Kreps, Theodore J., Lewis, Ben W., Machlup, Fritz, and Terrill, Robert P., *A Cartel Policy for the United Nations* (New York: Columbia University Press, 1945).

Eichelberger, Clark M., *Proposals for the United Nations Charter: What was done at Dumbarton Oaks?* (New York: Commission to Study the Organization of Peace, 1944).

Einzig, Paul, *Can We Win the Peace?* (London: Macmillan and Company Ltd., 1942).

Eliot, George Fielding, *Hour of Triumph* (New York: Reynal and Hitchcock, 1944).

Fernand, Collin, *The Economic Solidarity of the United Nations* (Antwerp, 1945).

Finley, Lorraine Noel, *National Anthems of the United Nations and Associated Powers Music Book* (Boston: Boston Music Company, 1945).

Fisher, Agnes, *Once Upon a Time: Folk Tales, Myths and Legends of the United Nations* (Edinburgh: Thomas Nelson and Sons, 1942).

Frost, Frances, *Legends of the United Nations* (New York: McGraw-Hill Book Co., 1943).

Goris, Jan-Albert (ed.), *United Nations Series: Belgium* (Berkeley, CA: University of California Press, 1945).

Green, Peter, *Prayers for the United Nations* (London: Hodder and Stoughton, 1943).

Grew, Joseph C., *Report from Tokyo: A Warning to the United Nations* (London: Hammond, Hammond and Co., 1942).

Harris, Wilson, *Problems of the Peace* (Cambridge: Cambridge University Press, 1944).

Harrison, W. E. C. and Reid, A. N., *Contemporary Affairs: Canada and the United Nations* (Toronto: Ryerson Press, 1942).

Hendrikson, Alan K., 'FDR and the World Wide Arena', in Woolner D. et al. eds. *FDR's World: War, Peace and Legacies* (New York: Palgrave Macmillan, 2008), pp. 35–63.

Holborn, Louise W. (ed.), *War and Peace Aims of the United Nations: 1 September 1939–31 December 1942* (Boston, MA: World Peace Foundation, 1943).

Hulme, Clifford, *San Francisco Conference* (London: Kemsley Newspapers, 1945).

Ivanyi-Grunwald, Bela and Bell, Alan, *Route to Potsdam: The Story of the Peace Aims, 1939–1945* (London: A. Wingate, 1945).

Jackson, J. Hampden, *The Atlantic Charter: An Outline for Study Circles* (London: W.E.A., 1943).

Jennison, Keith Warren, *Dedication: Text and Pictures of the United Nations* (New York: Henry Holt and Co., 1943).

Johnsen, Julia E., *The Eight Points of the Post War World Reorganization* (New York: H.W. Wilson Company, 1942).

Johnsen, Julia E., *World Peace Plans* (New York: H.W. Wilson Company, 1943).

Kerner, Robert, Joseph (ed.), *United Nations Series: Czechoslovakia. Twenty Years of Independence* (Berkeley, CA: University of California Press, 1945).

King, Cecil, *Atlantic Charter* (New York: Studio Publications, 1943).

Kirk, Grayson, *United Today for Tomorrow: The United Nations in War and Peace* (New York: The Foreign Policy Association, 1942).

Krout, John A, *Transportation in Wartime and the United Nations* (New York: Academy of Political Science, 1943).

Landheer, Bartholomew (ed.), *United Nations Series: The Netherlands* (Berkeley, CA: University of California Press, 1943).

Liberal Jewish Synagogue, *Service of Thanksgiving for the Victory of the United Nations in the European War* (London, 1945).

London International Assembly, Education and the United Nations: Report of a Joint Commission of the London International Assembly and Council for Education in World Citizenship (London, 1943).

Lorwin, Lewis L., *Postwar Plans of the United Nations* (New York: The Twentieth Century Fund, 1943).

Macnutt, Frederick B., *Four Freedoms, Atlantic and Christian* (Leicester: W. Thornley and Son, 1944).

Marchant, James, *World Waste and the Atlantic Charter* (Oxford: Blackwell, 1943).

Matthews, Basil, *United We Stand the Peoples of the United Nations* (New York: Little Brown and Co., 1943).

Matthews, Walter R., *'The Fellowship of Nations'*, Address delivered at the United Nations Service of Thanksgiving and Prayer in connection with the Universal Week of Prayer (London: World's Evangelical Alliance, 1944).

McKay, George Frederick, A Hymn for the United Nations (1944).

Mitrany, David, *The United Nations Charter: Peace Aims, Pamphlet 31* (London: National Peace Council, 1945).

Moore, Douglas, *Prayer for the United Nations* (New York: H.W. Gray Co., 1943).

Morton, Henry V., Atlantic Meeting: An account of Mr Churchill's voyage in *HMS Prince of Wales*, in August 1941, and the conference with President Roosevelt which resulted in the Atlantic Charter (London: Methuen and Company Ltd., 1944).

Moss, W. H., Soldiers of the United Nations. Music score (c.1944).

Muzumdar, Haridas T., *The United Nations of the World: A Treatise on How to Win Peace* (New York: Universal Publishing, 1942).

Nash, Sir Walter, Relations of the United Nations in Defence of the Pacific, Address at the meeting of the Study Committee of the Empire Parliamentary Association, 5 August 1942 (London, 1942).

National Peace Council, *Allied Peace Aims* (London, 1942).

Pacific Telephone and Telegraph Co. Telephone Directory, The United Nations Conference on International Organization, San Francisco, California, Third Issue, 25 April 1945.

Peaslee, Amos J., *A Permanent United Nations* (New York: G.P. Putnam's Sons, 1942).

———, *United Nations Government* (New York: G.P. Putnam's Sons, 1945).

Poteat, Edwin McNeill, *Four Freedoms and God* (New York: Harper and Brothers, 1943).

Renel, Henri, *United Nations Solo-Instrumental Polka Series* (New York: Charling Music Corp., c.1945).

Reston, James, *Prelude to Victory* (New York: Pocket Books Inc., 1942).

Rich, Daniel Cotton, *Art of the United Nations* [an illustrated catalogue of an exhibition held 16 November 1944 to 1 January 1945] (Chicago: Art Institute of Chicago, 1944).

RIIA, War and Peace in the Pacific: A preliminary report of the Eighth Conference of the Institute of Pacific Relations on wartime and post-war co-operation of the United Nations in the Pacific and the Far East, Quebec, 4–14 December 1942 (London: Royal Institute of International Affairs, 1943).

RIIA, *International Security: A Selection of Authoritative Statements by Spokesmen of the United Nations, 1939–February 1944* (London: Royal Institute of International Affairs, 1944).

Rudhyar, Dane, *The Faith That Gives Meaning to Victory* (Hollywood, CA: Foundation for Human Integration, 1943).

Salter, Arthur, *The United Nations and the Atomic Bomb* (Oxford: Oxford Joint Committee, 1945).

Savage, Lorna, *The United Have Declared: The Documents Issued by the United Nations* (Toronto: Canadian Institute of International Affairs, 1944).

Schmitt, Bernadotte Everly (ed.), *United Nations Series: Poland* (Berkeley, CA: University of California Press, 1945).

Schnapper, M. B. (ed.), *United Nations Agreements* (Washington, DC: American Council on Public Affairs, 1944).

Shaw, Martin (ed.), *National Anthems of the United Nations and France* (London: J.B. Cramer and Co., 1943).

Shoemaker, Don C., *American Testament: 'Toward United Nations' – A Memorial to Franklin Delano Roosevelt* (Asheville, NC: Stephens Press, 1945).

Shotwell, James T., *The Great Decision: On the Problems of Peace* (New York: Macmillan, 1944).

Smith, Edwin W., *The Atlantic Charter and Africa from an American Standpoint. A study by the Committee on Africa, the War, and Peace Aims.* (New York: Committee on Africa, 1942).

Sorensen, Reginald, *India and the Atlantic Charter* (London: The India League, 1942).

Spaull, Hebe, *This is the United Nations* (London: Barrie and Rockliff, 1945).

Stone, Julius, *The Atlantic Charter: New Worlds for Old* (Sydney: Current Book Distributors, 1943).

Straight, Michael, *Make This The Last War: The Future of the United Nations* (New York: Harcourt Bruce and Co., 1943).

Stronski, Stanislaw, *The Atlantic Charter: No Territorial Guarantees to Aggressors, No Dictatorships* (London: Hutchinson & Co., 1944).

Thomas, Norman Mattoon, *A Socialist Looks at the United Nations* (Syracuse, NY: Syracuse University Press, 1945).

Thomson, D., Meyer, E., Briggs, A., *Patterns of Peacemaking* (New York: Oxford University Press, 1945).

Treharne, Bryceson, *National Anthems of the United Nations and Associated Powers* (Boston, MA: Boston Music Company, 1943).

United Nations Association of Great Britain and Northern Ireland, *United Nations Association News Sheet*, October 1945 to December 1947 (London, 1945–7).

————, *International Outlook* (London: November 1945 to March 1946).

————, *The London Bulletin* (London: Regional Council, November 1945 to January 1949).

United Nations Information Office, *Germany's Record and World Security* (New York: 1944).

United Nations Information Organization, *Helping the People to Help Themselves: The Story of the United Nations Relief and Rehabilitation Administration* (London: HMSO, 1944).

————, *An Introduction to the United Nations* (London: HMSO, 1945).

————, *The United Nations Today and Tomorrow* (London, HMSO, 1945).

————, *Allied Plan for Education: The Story of the Conference of Allied Ministers of Education* (London: HMSO, 1945).

————, *Today's Children, Tomorrow's Hope: The Story of Children in the Occupied Lands* (London: HMSO, 1945).

————, *Towards a World of Plenty: The Story of the Food and Agriculture Organisation of the United Nations* (London: HMSO, 1945).

Veal, Irene, *Recipes of the United Nations* (London: John Gifford, 1944).

Visson, Andre, *The Coming Struggle For Peace* (New York, Viking, 1944).

Warman, Erik and Moiseiwitsch, Maurice, *Valour without Frontier: Outstanding Stories of Heroes of the United Nations* (London: Argus Press, 1943).

Wallace, Henry A., *The Price of Free World Victory* (New York: L.B. Fischer, 1942).

Welles, Sumner, *The World of the Four Freedoms* (New York: Columbia University Press, 1943).

————, *The Time for Action* (New York: Harper and Brothers, 1944).

————, *The Time for Decision* (New York: World Publishing Company, 1945).

Welles, Sumner (ed.), *An Intelligent American's Guide to the Peace* (New York: Dryden Press, 1945).

Wells, Linton, *Salute to Valor: Heroes of the United Nations* (New York: Random House, 1942).

Williams, Ernest T., *Lasting Peace and a Better World: A Plan to Achieve Them* (Parkstone, UK: Victory Fellowship, 1943).

————, *The United Nations and a New World Organization* (Parkstone, UK: Victory Fellowship, 1944).

Willkie, Wendell L., *One World* (New York: Simon and Schuster, 1943).

Willkie, Wendell L., Herbert Hoover, Henry A. Gibson, and Sumner Welles, *Prefaces to Peace* (New York: Simon and Schuster, 1943).

————, *Emblems of the United Nations: Their Flags and Coats-of-Arms* (London: Alliance Press, 1943).

————, *Music for All Ranks, Men and Women, of the United Nations Forces: Cairo, Egypt, November 19th, 1941 to VE-Day, May 8th, 1945* (Cairo: Schindler's Press, 1945).

————, *Philadelphia-Cradle of Liberty. A Pictorial Introduction of the City of Brotherly Love to the Delegates of the United Nations Conference on International Organization* (Philadelphia: Citizens' Committee of Philadelphia, 1945).

————, *Proposed United Nations Headquarters, Navy Island at Niagara Falls on the International Boundary Between Canada and the United States* (Buffalo: Baker, Jones and Hausauer, 1945).

————, *Saint Louis Invites the United Nations* (Saint Louis: Chamber of Commerce, 1945).

————, *United Nations Organization: Boston Answers Seven Questions* (Boston, MA, 1945).

Specialized Agencies & Conferences

United Nations Charter

————, A Commentary on the Charter of the United Nations signed at San Francisco on the 26 June 1945. Foreign Office, Parliamentary Papers Cmd. 6666 (London, 1945).

_____, Charter of the United Nations: report to the President on the results of the San Francisco conference by the chairman of the United States delegation, the Secretary of State (Washington, DC: US Department of State, 1945).

_____, United Nations Charter: The text and a commentary (London: National Peace Council, 1945).

_____, Security provisions in the charter of the United Nations and the covenant of the League of Nations (London: HMSO, 1945).

_____, The Charter of the United Nations (London: United Nations Association of Great Britain and Northern Ireland, 1945).

United Nations Conference on International Organization (UNCIO)

_____, Committees and Commissions of the Conference Members of the Delegations Officers of the Secretariat (San Francisco, 1945).

_____, Documents of the United Nations Conference on International Organization, San Francisco, 1945 (New York: United Nations Information Organization, 1945).

_____, Program. Closing plenary session. The United Nations Conference on International Organization. San Francisco, 26 June 1945 (Washington, DC, 1945).

_____, Charter of the United Nations and Statute of the International Court of Justice, together with interim arrangements concluded by the governments represented at the United Nations Conference on International Organization (Berkeley, CA: California University Press, 1945).

_____, Charter of the United Nations and Statute of the International Court of Justice, together with Interim Arrangements concluded by the Governments represented at the United Nations Conference on International Organization (Berkeley, CA: University of California Press, 1945).

_____, Comments and proposed amendments concerning the Dumbarton Oaks proposals. Submitted by the delegations to the United Nations Conference on International Organization (San Francisco, 1945).

_____, The United Nations Conference on International Organization, San Francisco, 1945 (Washington, DC: US Government Printing Office, 1945).

_____, United Nations Conference on International Organization: Officers of the Conference, Committees and Commissions of the Conference, Members of the Delegations, Officers of the Secretariat. Revised to 4 May 1945 (Washington, DC: US Government Printing Office, 1945).

_____, United Nations Conference on International Organization. Report on the conference held at San Francisco 25 April to 26 June 1945 by the Rt. Hon. Peter Fraser, Chairman of the New Zealand Delegation (Wellington: New Zealand Department of External Affairs, 1945).

_____, Documents adopted by the United Nations Conference, San Francisco, 26 June 1945 (London: United Nations Information Organization, 1945).

United Nations Educational, Scientific and Cultural Organization (UNESCO)

_____, Conference of Allied Ministers of Education. Draft Proposals for an Educational and Cultural Organization of the United Nations (London: His Majesty's Stationery Office, 1945).

_____, Final act of the United Nations conference for the establishment of an educational, scientific and cultural organization. Presented by the Secretary of State for Foreign affairs to Parliament, Cmd. 6711 (London: HMSO, 1945).

United Nations Food and Agriculture Organization (UNFAO)
————, United Nations Conference on Food and Agriculture, Provisional List of Members of Delegations. Officers of the Secretariat (Washington, DC, 1943).
————, Final act of the United nations conference on food and agriculture, Hot Springs, Virginia, United States of America, 18 May to 3 June 1943. Presented by the Secretary of State for Foreign affairs to Parliament, Cmd. 6451 (London: HMSO, 1943).
————, United Nations Conference on Food and Agriculture, Hot Springs, Virginia, 18 May to 3 June 1943. Final act and section reports (Washington, DC, 1943).
————, Official Directory, First Session of the Conference (Quebec City, 1945).
————, Documents relating to the Food and Agriculture Organization of the United Nations, 1 August to 14 December 1944, Foreign Office Parliamentary Papers, Cmd. 6590 (London, 1945).
————, Constitution of the Food and Agriculture Organization of the United Nations (with annexes). Quebec, 16 October 1945. Presented by the Secretary of State for foreign affairs to parliament, Cmd. 6955 (London: HMSO, 1945).
————, The Work of FAO. A general report to the First Session of the Conference of the Food and Agriculture Organization of the United Nations (Washington, DC, 1945).

United Nations Monetary and Financial Conference (UNMFC)
————, Report of the London Chamber of Commerce on the Final Act of the United Nations Monetary & Financial Conference (London: F.H. Doulton and Co., 1944).
————, United Nations' Monetary and Financial Conference, Bretton Woods, 1–22 July 1944. Final Act. Parliamentary Papers, Cmd. 6546 (London: HMSO, 1944).
————, US Department of the Treasury, Articles of Agreement: International Monetary Fund and International Bank for Reconstruction and Development. United Nations Monetary and Financial Conference, Bretton Woods, New Hampshire, 1–22 July 1944 (Washington, DC: US Department of the Treasury, 1944).
————, Joint Statement by Experts on the Establishment of an International Monetary Fund of the United and Associated Nations, 21 April 1944 (Washington, DC: US Department of the Treasury, 1944).
————, United Nations Monetary and Financial Conference, Bretton Woods, New Hampshire, 1–22 July 1944. Final act and related documents (Washington, DC: US Department of State, 1944).
————, Report of the Indian delegation to the United Nations Monetary & Financial Conference at Bretton Woods, 1–22 July 1944. Final act (Delhi: Manager of Publications, 1944).
————, United Nations Monetary and Financial Conference Bretton Woods, New Hampshire, 1–22 July 1944. Documents supplementary to the Final act (Delhi: Manager of Publications, 1945).
————, United Nations Monetary and Financial Conference, Bretton Woods, New Hampshire, 1–22 July 1944. Documents supplementary to the final act. Parliamentary papers Cmd. 6597 (London: HMSO, 1945).
————, Money and the Post-War World: The Story of the United Nations Monetary and Financial Conference, Bretton Woods (London: HMSO, 1945).

United Nations Relief and Rehabilitation Administration (UNRRA)
_____, Agreement for United Nations Relief and Rehabilitation Administration, Washington, 9 November 1943. Presented by the Secretary of State for Foreign Affairs to Parliament. Cmd. 6491 (London: HMSO, 1943).
_____, Resolutions and reports adopted by the Council at its first session, held at Atlantic City, New Jersey, USA, 10 November to 1 December 1943. Presented by Secretary of State for Foreign affairs to Parliament Cmd. 6497 (London: HMSO, 1943).
_____, United Nations Relief and Rehabilitation Administration, First Session of the Council: Selected Documents (Atlantic City, 1943).
_____, Belgium: Welfare Services (London: UNRRA European Regional Office, 1944).
_____, *Bulletin of Communicable Diseases and Medical Notes, 1944–46* (London: UNRRA European Regional Office, 1944–6).
_____, Report of the Director General to the second session of the Council (Washington, DC, 1944).
_____, Supplementary report of the Director General to the second session of the Council from 17 July through 15 September 1944 (Washington, DC, 1944).
_____, Resolutions adopted by the Council at its second session, held at Montreal 16–26 September 1944. Presented by the Minister of State to Parliament Cmd. 6566 (London: HMSO, 1944).
_____, First Session of the Council of the United Nations Relief and Rehabilitation Administration. Selected Documents. Atlantic City, NJ, 10 November to 1 December 1943 (Washington, DC: US Government Printing Office, 1944).
_____, United Nations Relief and Rehabilitation Administration. Journal: Second session of the Council (Washington, DC, 1944).
_____, Luxembourg: Welfare Services (London: UNRRA European Regional Office, 1944).
_____, Relief and Rehabilitation in China (Washington, DC, 1944).
_____, The Netherlands: Welfare Services (London: UNRRA European Regional Office, 1944).
_____, Italy: Welfare Services (London: UNRRA European Regional Office, 1945).
_____, Medical Manual. Health and medical care of displaced persons (London: European Regional Office, 1945).
_____, Norway: Welfare Services (London: UNRRA European Regional Office, 1945).
_____, Poland: Welfare Services (London: UNRRA European Regional Office, 1945).
_____, Program of Operations. Presented by the Director General to the third session of the Council (Washington, DC, 1945).
_____, Report of the Director General to the Council for the period 1 April to 30 June 1945 (London: Burrup Mathieson and Co., 1945).
_____, Resolutions adopted by the Council at its third session, held in London 7 –24 August 1945. Presented by the Minister of State to Parliament Cmd. 6682 (London: HMSO, 1945).
_____, Out of Chaos (Washington, DC: UNRRA, 1945).
_____, UNRRA Review of the Month. April 1945 to January 1947 (London: UNRRA European Regional Office, 1945–7).

————, Weekly Bulletin of Epidemiological Information, June 1945 to November 1946 (London: UNRRA European Regional Office, 1945–6).

United Nations War Crimes Commission (UNWCC)
————, Punishment for War Crimes: Collective notes presented to the Governments of Great Britain, the USSR and the USA, and relative correspondence (London: United Nations Information Office, 1943).

Selected UK government files concerning the United Nations 1942–5

ADM 1/13457   CEREMONIAL (88): Allied National Days and United Nations Day: recognition and celebrations. 1940–4. MO9666/1943.

ADM 1/13961   ADMIRALTY (5): United Nations plan: Admiralty comments. 1943. CS22/1943.

ADM 1/15758   ADMIRALTY (5) and FOREIGN COUNTRIES (52): Vandenburg report on the aircraft situation of the United Nations: American request for statistics. 1942–4.

ADM 1/16378   ADMIRALTY (5) and FOREIGN COUNTRIES (52): Departmental and inter services discussions on United Nations Control Commission for Finland: directive on Naval matters to Admiralty representatives. 1944–5. MO58103/1944.

ADM 274/4   Wartime instructions for Merchant Ships: volume 2, Merchant Ships' Code, produced by the US Navy Department and Admiralty for benefit of United Nations' merchant shipping. 1 January to 31 December 1944. SP 2405 (2).

AIR 2/6551   OVERSEAS: USA (Code B, 42/7): United Nations Exposition, Chicago: British Exhibit. 1942–5. C11607/42.

AIR 8/651   United Nations Air Forces Conference. May 1942. ID3/858(D).

AVIA 22/916   Relief supplies to United Nations Relief and Rehabilitation Administration: policy and procedures to be adopted. 1944–5. 238/20 Part I.

AVIA 26/520   United Nations Beacon frequency drift unit Mks. I and II: table of curves, figures and diagrams. 1943. T 1518.

AVIA 38/1233   United Nations Relief and Rehabilitation Administration. 1943–7. NAS/H/15/7.

BT 11/5130   INTERNATIONAL ORGANISATIONS (CODE 13): INTERNATIONAL TRADE ORGANISATION OF THE UNITED NATIONS: Imposition of import restrictions to safeguard balance of payments. 1945–6. CRT 328/1946.

BT 11/5197   INTERNATIONAL ORGANISATIONS (CODE 13): INTERNATIONAL TRADE ORGANISATION OF THE UNITED NATIONS: Preparatory Committee on Trade and Employment: Commercial policy proposals (spring conference). 1945–7. CRT 2745/1947.

BT 28/1019   United Nations and North Africa: retreading of tyres. December 1942 to July 1943. M/805/23

BT 58/362   United Nations Forces Fellowship. 1944. COS 455/44.

CAB 115/578   United Nations Relief and Rehabilitation Administration: functions. 1943. 34/1/5J Part I.

CAB 120/184   United Nations Conference on World Organisation, San Francisco, April 1945: preparations for UK delegation. March to June 1945. 402/43.

CAB 120/185   United Nations Conference on World Organisation, San Francisco, April 1945: arrangements for preliminary Dominions' Ministers meeting in London. March to April 1945. 402/43/1.

CAB 121/162   United Nations conference at San Francisco on the establishment of an international organisation. April 1945. February to 17 August 1945.

CAB 121/32   United Nations' bases, post-war Vol. I .July 1943 to March 1946.

CAB 122/1208   United Nations strategic policy in the Balkan-Eastern Mediterranean region. 1943. 13/9/7 K.

CAB 122/1528   United Nations shipping statistics. 1944. 18/31.

CAB 122/459   Relations with United Nations Relief and Rehabilitation Administration. 1943–4. 3/25/3 Part 1.

CAB 122/460   Relations with United Nations Relief and Rehabilitation Administration. 1944. 3/25/3 Part 2.

CAB 122/468   Property of United Nations other than US and UK and property of their nationals in areas to be liberated. 28 March 1944.

CAB 122/545   Release of Radar equipment and information to United Nations forces under British or US Theatre Commanders, and co-belligerents and certain neutrals. 1944–6. 05/09/2007.

CAB 122/604   World Organisation: United Nations Conference, San Francisco. 1945. 6/25/2 Part 1 and 2.

CAB 123/225   Establishment and scope of the United Nations Relief and Rehabilitation Administration (UNRRA). 1943. 150/1.

CAB 142   United Nations Relief and Rehabilitation Administration: United Kingdom and British Commonwealth Delegations: Minutes and Papers. 1943–6.

CAB 21/1598   United Nations: organisations dealing with European problems. 1943–5. 56/34.

CAB 21/2753   Dumbarton Oaks: proposals and charter of United Nations. July 1943 to July 1949. 60/3 Part I.

CAB 21/3871   Protection of monuments and works of art in territories entered by the forces of the United Nations (UN). August 1943 to October 1955. 32/238.

CAB 65/26/29   1. Naval, Military and Air Operations: Air Operations: Home Theatre; Malta; Pacific. Naval Operations: Shipping Losses; The Russian Convoy. Military Operations: Burma; Libya; Russia. 2. USSR. 3. Italy: Repatriation of civilians from Ethiopia. 4. United Nations Day. 26 May 1942. WM (42) 68.

CAB 65/27/2   1. Naval, Military and Air Operations: Air operations: Malta, Egypt. Naval operations: Russian Convoy. Military operations: Egypt, Russia. 2. Middle East: Fall of Tobruk. 3. Czechoslovakia: Relations with Czechoslovak Government. 4. War Criminals: Proposed United Nations Commission on Atrocities. 6 July 1942. WM (42) 86.

CAB 65/41/39   1. Food and Agriculture: Permanent United Nations Organisation. 23 March 1944. WM (44) 39.

CAB 65/42/41   1. United Nations Reconstruction and Development Bank. 2. Ethiopia. 3. Arrangements for Repatriation of certain Germans. 4. War Criminals: Treatment of Major Enemy War Criminals. 5. War Criminals: United Nations War Crimes Commission. 6. By-Elections: Suggested Temporary Release of Party Agents from the Services. 28 June 1944. WM (44) 83.

CAB 65/44/31   3. Food and Agriculture: Permanent United Nations Organisation. 30 November 1944. WM (44) 160.

CAB 66/24/43   United Nation's Day. Memorandum by the Secretary of State for Foreign Affairs. 20 May 1942. WP (42) 213.

CAB 66/26/7   Treatment of War Criminals. Proposed United Nations Commission on Atrocities. 1 July 1942. WP (42) 277.

CAB 66/30/8   United Nations Relief and Rehabilitation Administration. Memorandum by the Secretary of State for Dominion Affairs, the Secretary of State for Foreign Affairs and the President of the Board of Trade. 22 October 1942. WP (42) 478.

CAB 66/33/31   The United Nations Plan. Memorandum by the Secretary of State for Foreign Affairs. 16 January 1943. WP (43) 31.

CAB 66/33/39   The United Nations Plan. Memorandum by the Secretary of State for India. 25 January 1943. WP (43) 39.

CAB 66/33/44   The United Nations Plan. Memorandum by the Secretary of State for Dominion Affairs. 28 January 1943. WP (43) 44.

CAB 66/35/40   United Nations Day. Memorandum by the Minister of Information. 5 April 1943. WP (43) 140.

CAB 66/37/29   United Nations Relief and Rehabilitation Administration. Memorandum by the President of the Board of Trade. 2 June 1943. WP (43) 229.

CAB 66/38/50   United Nations Plan for Organising Peace. Memorandum by the Secretary of State for Foreign Affairs. 7 July 1943. WP (43) 300.

CAB 66/39/21   Post-War Settlement and the United Nations Plan. Memorandum by the Secretary of State for Dominion Affairs. 19 July 1943. WP (43) 321.

CAB 66/40/21   United Nations Plan. Judicial and Arbitral Machinery. Memorandum by the Secretary of State for Foreign Affairs. 16 August 1943. WP (43) 371.

CAB 66/42/11   United Nations Relief and Rehabilitation Administration. Instruction to United Kingdom Representatives. Joint Memorandum by the Minister of Production, President of the Board of Trade and Minister of State. 18 October 1943. WP (43) 461.

CAB 66/44/29   Questions arising out of the Council Meeting of UNRRA. Memorandum by the Secretary of State for Foreign Affairs. Includes: United Nations Relief and Rehabilitation Administration, resolutions and reports adopted by the Council at its first session, held at Atlantic City, New Jersey, USA, 10 November to 1 December 1943 (folios 170–214). 21 December 1943. WP (43) 579.

CAB 66/50/44   United Nations War Crimes Commission. Memorandum by the Lord Chancellor. 2 June 1944. WP (44) 294.

CAB 66/51/38   The Proposed United Nation's Bank for Reconstruction and Development. Memorandum by the Chancellor of the Exchequer. 20 June 1944. WP (44) 338.

CAB 66/54/19   The United Nations Relief and Rehabilitation Administration. Directive by the Prime Minister. 26 August 1944. WP (44) 469.

CAB 66/56/39   Second Session of the Council of the United Nations Relief and Rehabilitation Administration. Memorandum by the Minister of State. 19 October 1944. WP (44) 589.

CAB 66/63/39   The United Nations Relief and Rehabilitation Administration. Memorandum by the Minister of State. 21 March 1943. WP (45) 184.

CAB 66/67/18   An Educational and Cultural Organisation of the United Nations. Memorandum by the Minister of Education. 7 July 1945. CP (45) 68.

CAB 78/19   United Nations Relief and Rehabilitation Administration: Papers 1–18. 1943. Series GEN 29.

CAB 78/6/7/8/9   United Nations Conference on Food and Agriculture: Papers 1–100. 1943. Series GEN 8.

CAB 79/22/1 5   Revision of Directive for 'Rapid Military Communications of the United Nations'.

CAB 79/37/3 1. Situation in Greece. COS(45)493(O). 2. British Missions to Norway. COS(45)485(O). 3. Rubber Position of the United Nations. 4. Future of Combined Intelligence Objectives Sub-Committee. 5. Fire Support of Seaborne Landings. TWC(45)28. 6. Meeting with Admiral Mountbatten. 26 July 1945. COS(45)184th.

CAB 79/72/15 1. Post Hostility Planning Organisation. 2. United Nations Bases. PHP(44)8(Final). 3. Conversations with the United States concerning Middle East oil. 4. Preparations for the visit of Dominion Prime Ministers. JP(44)87(Final). PHP(44)19(Final). COS(44)282(O). 30 March 1944. COS(44)(O)105th.

CAB 79/72/8 1. Post War Planning. PHP(43)24a(Final). 2. United Nations Bases in Relation to General Security Organisation. PHP(44)8(Final). 23 March 1944. COS(44)(O)98th.

CAB 80/37/35 Revision of Directive for 'Rapid Military Communications of the United Nations'. Memorandum by Wireless Telegraphy Board. 6 July 1942. COS(42)335.

CAB 80/43/60 UNITED NATIONS BASES IN RELATION TO A GENERAL SECURITY ORGANISATION. Note by Vice Chiefs of Staff. 3 April 1944. COS(44)60.

CAB 80/43/68 UNITED NATIONS BASES. Note by Secretary. 7 April 1944. COS(44)68.

CAB 80/48/12 RUBBER POSITION OF THE UNITED NATIONS. Copy of a letter dated 23 April 1945, to the Secretary, Chiefs of Staff Committee from the Ministry of Production. 23 April 1945. COS(45)85.

CAB 80/48/54 THE UNITED NATIONS CONFERENCE ON INTERNATIONAL ORGANISATION. Report by the Representative of the Chiefs of Staff with the United Kingdom Delegation. 13 June 1945. COS(45)127.

CAB 80/51/40 US VIEWS ON THE FUNCTIONS AND ORGANISATION OF THE MILITARY STAFF COMMITTEE OF THE UNITED NATIONS. Note by the Secretary. 12 December 1945. COS(45)320.

CAB 84/51/35 UNITED NATIONS PLAN OF CAMPAIGN. IN 1943. Terms of Reference. 17 December 1942. JP(42)1017(S).

CAB 84/53/115 POLICY TO BE ADOPTED BY UNITED NATIONS TOWARDS JAPAN. 27 April 1943. JP(43)166.

CAB 84/53/96 POLICY TO BE ADOPTED BY UNITED NATIONS TOWARDS JAPAN. 25 April 1943. JP(43)148(S) (Draft).

CO 537/1225 International Labour Office, Relationship to the New World Security Organisation (United Nations). 1945–6. 12263/17.

CO 852/510/12 Rubber (Malaya): establishment of United Nations Organisation. 1943. 19206/3.

CO 852/510/4 United Nations Relief and Rehabilitation Administration (UNRRA). 1943. 19203 Parts I and II.

CO 852/510/8 United Nations Relief and Rehabilitation Administration (UNRRA): Far Eastern Regional Committee. 1943. 19203/8.

CO 852/584/2 United Nations Monetary and Financial Conference. 1944. 19037/18/1.

CO 852/584/3 United Nations Monetary and Financial Conference: Bretton Woods Agreement. 1945. 19037/18/1.

CO 859/44/6 United Nations Education Conference, 15 June 1942. 1942–3. 12025/15.

CO 859/68/6 United Nations Conference on Food and Agriculture, 1943. 1943–4. 12620.

CO 859/68/7   United Nations Conference on Food and Agriculture, 1943: Colonial food policy. 1943. 12621.

CO 875/18/6   United Nations Day, 14 June 1942. 9119.

CO 875/18/7   United Nations Day, 14 June 1943. 9119.

CO 875/18/9   United Nations Flag Day: Empire Youth Sunday. 1943. 9119/2.

CO 968/167/1   Jews and other refugees in colonies and neutral countries: transfer of refugee camps in colonies to United Nations Relief and Rehabilitation Administration. 1944. 14821/61.

DO 35/1130   NATIONAL DAYS ETC.: United Nations Day 1943–4. 1943–6. H.532/4.

DO 35/1203   Co-operation between Governments of United Nations in War effort, by Prime Minister of Canada, 1943. 1943–6. WC59/1.

DO 35/1288   Proposal for discussions between Field Marshal Smuts, Prime Minister of the Union of South Africa, and an Indian delegate to the United Nations meeting in San Francisco, on the question of the position of the Indians in South Africa. 1943–6. G 715/23.

DO 35/1841   United Nations plan for post-war settlement and Dominion participation and representation on international bodies. 1943–6. WR 208/19.

DO 35/1847   Communications with Dominions Governments on steps necessary after Moscow conference towards a United Nations organisation. 1943–6. WR 208/38.

DO 35/1885   Australian proposals for paragraph in United Nations charter on domestic jurisdiction. 1943–6. WR 208/262.

DO 35/1897   United Nations declaration on national independence, especially of Colonies. 1943–6. WR 213/8.

FO 366/1472   Financial position of the United Nations War Crimes Commission. 1945. X 310.

FO 370/977   Press-cuttings for United Nations War Crimes Commission. 1944. Files 310.

FO 371   Foreign Office: Political Departments: General Correspondence from 1906–1966.

FO 371/30384   Brazilian citizens serving in the armed forces of the United Nations. 1942. File 9457.

FO 371/30857   United Nations Declaration signed at Washington on 1 January 1942. File 4 (topp. 2381).

FO 371/30858   United Nations Declaration signed at Washington on 1 January 1942. File 4 (pp. 2493–end).

FO 371/30870   Request for a list of the Allies and those who come within the term of United Nations. 1942. File 1205.

FO 371/30922   United Nations Commission for investigating war crimes. 1942. File 61 (pp. 10989–11700).

FO 371/31504   United Nations Relief and Rehabilitation Administration. 1942. File 12 (pp. 709–1400).

FO 371/32577   List of the United Nations. 1942. File 11981.

FO 371/33651   Economic mobilization: adherence to the United Nations Declaration. 1943. File 166.

FO 371/34401   United Nations flag: proposals for 1943. File 3008.

FO 371/34410   Adherence of Colombia to United Nations Declaration. 1943. File 14260.

FO 371/35396   United Nations Plan. 1943. File 402.

FO 371/35420   United Nations Forum. 1943. File 834.

FO 371/35423   Post-war problems: proposed United Nations conference. 1943. File 903.

FO 371/35470   United Nations Information Board. 1943. File 5905.

FO 371/36331   French adherence to United Nations Declaration. 1943. File 8791.

FO 371/38452   Peruvian Chamber of Deputies applauds efforts of United Nations. 1944. File 1216.

FO 371/38657   Proposed United Nations Bar Association. 1944. File 733.

FO 371/39032   Full list of the United Nations. 1944. File 4779.

FO 371/40527   Preparatory work by United Nations Relief and Rehabilitation Administration. 1944. File 41.

FO 371/40685   Future World Organisation: United Nations plan. 1944. File 180.

FO 371/40768   Proposed United Nations Economic Steering Committee. 1944. File 2162.

FO 371/40786   Proposed United Nations flag. 1944. File 3680.

FO 371/40840   Offer from a composer of a 'United Nations Anthem'. 1944. File 6531.

FO 371/40969   Property of United Nations nationals in Italy. 1944. File 673.

FO 371/42010   Question of French adherence to United Nations Declaration. 1944. File 3774.

FO 371/42854   Transfer of refugee welfare functions to United Nations Relief and Rehabilitation Organisation. 1944. File 37.

FO 371/42866   Maintenance of Polish refugees by United Nations Relief and Rehabilitation Organisation. 1944. File 97 (pp. 1729–end).

FO 371/43210   Report on delegations from Northern countries at United Nations Relief and Rehabilitation Administration Conference. 1944. File 440.

FO 371/44970   Ecuadorean adherence to the United Nations Declaration: declaration of war on Japan. 1945. File 589.

FO 371/45027   Adherence to the United Nations declaration by Latin American countries. 1945. File 817.

FO 371/45829   Reparation claims of United Nations. 1945. File 3812.

FO 371/46045   Egyptian delegation to United Nations. 1945. File 4390.

FO 371/50707   Dumbarton Oaks proposals for the establishment of a World Organisation: preparations for San Francisco Conference: United Nations Conference on International Organisation. 1945. File 12.

FO 371/50802   United Nations Information Organisation. 1945. File 165.

FO 371/50832   United Nations renegades and quislings. 1945. File 584.

FO 371/50840   Adherence to United Nations Declaration by countries who declared war only against Japan. 1945. File 980.

FO 371/50849   Signing by countries of United Nations Declaration. 1945. File 1928.

FO 371/50935   Military Staff Committee of United Nations Organisation: functions and organisation. 1945. File 6469.

FO 371/50950   United States delegation to the United Nations: position of the Republicans. 1945. File 7694.

FO 371/50956   United Nations and World Peace. 1945. File 8368.

FO 371/50958   United Nations Educational and Cultural Conference. 1945. File 8746.

FO 371/51009   Establishment and work of the United Nations War Crimes Commission: lists of war criminals. 1945. File 29.

FO 372/3623   United Nations Day 1943, celebration of. 1943. 5256.

FO 372/3888   United Nations Day celebrations. 1944. 4316.

FO 643/35 External Affairs, America: Joint Declaration by United Nations; War Crimes. 1942–4. 8.00E+01.

FO 770/77 Peace Treaty with Romania covering United Nations vessels. 1945–6. 5408/1.

FO 800/921 United Nations War Crimes Commission: minutes of meetings. 1944–5. 77 XIII Part 1.

FO 93/1/219 Declaration by United Nations. 1 January 1942 .

FO 93/1/251 Final Act. United Nations Conference on Food and Agriculture. 3 June 1943.

FO 93/1/254 Final Act and Articles of Agreement. United Nations Monetary and Financial Conference. 1–22 July 1944.

FO 954/19A Palestine: To Lord Halifax (Foreign Office dispatch No 658). US Government's proposal for a joint or United Nations statement on Palestine. 11/06/1943. Pal/43/11.

FO 954/22A Post War Plans and Reconstruction: Foreign Office telegram to Washington, No 1632. President to Prime Minister No 476. Need for United Nations machinery for joint planning. 24/02/1944. Pwp/44/2.

FO 954/22A Post War Plans and Reconstruction: Prime Minister telegram to Field Marshal Smuts No 916. United Nations Conference. 25/09/1944. Pwp/44/23.

FO 954/22A Post War Plans and Reconstruction: Washington telegram No 940. President's statement about United Nations meeting to discuss post war food problems. 25/02/1943. Pwp/43/8.

FO 954/30C USA: Washington telegram No 2429. Organisers of United Nations fortnight wish to be addressed by Mr. Attlee or Lord Cranborne. 11/04/1945. US/45/77.

FO 954/31B War (General): Prime Minister to President, No 68. (a) Is in entire agreement with President's 'Plan of the United Nations', (b) India. 12/04/1942. W(g)/42/42.

INF 1/928 Propaganda, press and censorship organisations in territories reoccupied by the United Nations. June 1942 to December 1945. File No. X 260.

INF 1/984 United Nations Information Organisation: original resolution. 1944–5. File No. X 305.

INF 2/44/672 Photograph referenced as INF 2/44/2900. 'Desert Air Force Fly Past'. Photograph shows: 'The RAF Ensign was prominent among the flags of the United Nations which made a colourful spectacle at the Fly Past of the Desert Air Force'. British Official Photograph. 1945.

INF 2/45/323 'Convoy'. Cover note to photographs 2 to 50. (INF 2/45 items 329–377) 'A Collection of Photographs Produced by the Ministry of Information'. The ships of the Merchant Navy form the supply line of the United Nations. In war time that line is subjected to continuous assault. c.1940–6.

INF 3/345 POSTERS: Unity of Strength – Inter-allied posters: United Nations for freedom from fear. (Child playing with parents) Artists signature: White. 1939–46.

INF 6/344 United Nations Day 1942. 1942–51. Folder No. CFU 218.

INF 6/346 We Sail at Midnight (United Nations background – a story of joint production) 1942. 1942–3. Folder No. CFU 221.

IR 40/8164 United Nations information organisation; entitlement to diplomatic privilege for tax purposes. 1944–8. T2023/10/45.

LCO 2/2972 German Atrocities Publication of the Bryce Committee report on allegations made during the 1914–8 War and the setting up of a similar Committee during the present war United Nations War Crimes Commission. 1940–4. 3201/20 (part 1).

LCO 2/2976   United Nations War Crimes Commission Proposed establishment of War Crimes Court. 1944. 3201/20 (part 3A).

LCO 2/2977   United Nations War Crimes Commission Draft Convention for the surrender of war criminals and other war offenders. 1944–5. 3201/20 (part 4).

LCO 2/2978   War Crimes Inter-Departmental Committee presided over by Lord Finlay: Winding up of United Nations War Crimes Commission. 1945–7. 3201/20 (part 5).

LCO 53/78   Proposed United Nations War Crimes Commission to try war criminals: correspondence, including memorandum by the Law Officers dated 15 April 1942, dealing with Superior Orders for amendment to chapter XIV of the Manual of Military Law. 1942–52. 263(1).

MAF 128/605   Food and Agriculture Organisation of United Nations: Interim Commission. 1941–5. A/GD 44.

MAF 83/1544   Relationship of United Nations Relief and Rehabilitation Administration to Combined Food Board. November 1943 to July 1945.

MAF 83/604   Draft agreement and brief for a United Nations Relief and Rehabilitation Administration. July to November 1943. XR/601.

MAF 83/620   Preparation for first Council meeting of United Nations Relief and Rehabilitation Administration. September 1943 to January 1944. XR/600.

MT 59/1964   CSAB United Nations shipping statistics. 1942–4. OIL Ref: Annexe III.

MT 59/2007   United Nations tanker requirements. October 1942 to June 1944. OIL Ref: 548 Pt.1.

MT 59/2008   United Nations tanker requirements. June 1944 to August 1945. OIL Ref: 548 Pt.2.

MT 65/124   United Nations shipping statistics: analyses and returns for US Administration. 1942. 1947 STATS 366 Pts I and II.

MT 65/127   United Nations tonnage: estimates of availability. 1942–5. STATS 371.

MT 65/150   United Nations oil and tanker requirements. 1943–5. STATS 430.

MT 9/3739   United States of America (Code 145): Offer by the Fur Trades in the United States of America to provide 50,000 fur vests for distribution to United Nations Seamen. 1942–7. M.13176/42.

POWE 33/1411   United Nations refinery operations: throughput and production. 1944–6. PE/571/1 Pt.1.

POWE 33/645   Tanker tonnage: United Nations shipping statistics. 1942–4. PE/12/56/3 Pt.1.

POWE 34/17   United Nations oil stocks. 1944.

PREM 4/17/7   United Nations Reconstruction and Development Bank. January 1944.

PREM 4/28/10   United Nations Conference on Food and Agriculture. March to June 1943.

PREM 4/29/4   PM's directive on United Nations Relief and Rehabilitation Administration. June to September 1944.

PREM 4/30/4   Proposed United Nations declaration on national independence. March to October 1943.

PREM 4/32/13   United Nations Day celebrations. May 1942 to May 1944.

T 220/19   United Nations Commission on war crimes. 1942–8. IF 46/05.

T 220/83   Location of United Nations Organisations. 1945–9. IF 364/01.

WO 106/2609A   ABDA area: comments by General Sir A. Wavell, Supreme Commander United Nations Forces. Assessment of Malayan campaign. February to October 1942.

WO 106/4968   General Forces: United Nations policy for the cessation of hostilities. June 1943 to February 1945.

WO 106/4972   General Forces: Assistance to the United Nations war effort. September 1943 to July 1945.

WO 106/4973   General Forces: United Nations Commission for the investigation of war crimes. September 1943 to November 1945.

WO 202/540   United Nations: policy on relief and rehabilitation. June to September 1944.

WO 202/551   United Nations relief and rehabilitation administration: personnel recruitment. February to July 1945.

WO 202/604   United Nations relief and rehabilitation: flying squads for work in connection with displaced persons. August 1944 to May 1945.

WO 204/2394   Italy: control of United Nations propaganda in Rome. October 1944. 091.412-8.

WO 204/6331   Algiers: United Nations radio operation schedule. August 1944.

WO 229/1/12   War Crimes: United Nations liaison and searching out teams. 1 January to 31 December 1945. 000.5-5.

WO 229/31/15   Roster of United Nations. 1 January 1945 to 31 December 1945. 092-2.

WO 311/1331   United Nations War Crimes Commission history and research office documents.

WO 32/15298   CIVIL AFFAIRS: General (Code 93(A)): Russian and other United Nations participation in Allied Control Commission for Italy. 1943–5. 033/4828.

WO 32/15298   OVERSEAS: Italy (Code 0/M): Russian and other United Nations participation in Allied Control Commission for Italy. 1943–5. 033/4828.

WORK 21/196   United Nations. 1942–59. AE 9107/12 Pt 1.

Selected general bibliography

Acheson, Dean, *Present at the Creation* (London: Hamish Hamilton, 1970).

Ambrose, Stephen E., *Citizen Soldiers: The US Army from the Normandy Beaches to the Bulge to the Surrender of Germany, June 7, 1944 – May 7, 1945* (New York: Simon & Schuster Trade, 1998).

Armstrong-Reid, Susan and Murray, David, *Armies of Peace* (University of Toronto Press, 2008).

Arne, Sigrid, *United Nations Primer* (New York: Farrar & Rinehart, 1945).

Badoglio, Pietro, *The War in Abyssinia* (London: Methuen, 1937).

Banac, Ivo (ed.), *The Diary of Georgi Dimitrov, 1933–1949* (New Haven: Yale University Press, 2003).

Bathurst, M. E., *The United Nations War Crimes Commission* (American Society of International Law, 1945).

Beevor, Antony, *Stalingrad* (London: Penguin, 1998).

Beevor, Antony and Vinogradova, Luba (eds.), *A Writer at War: Vasily Grossman with the Red Army 1941–1945* (London: Pimlico, 2006).

Beisner, Robert L., *Dean Acheson: A Life in the Cold War* (Oxford University Press, 2006).

Blayney, Michael S., 'Herbert C. Pell, War Crimes and the Jews', *American Jewish Historical Quarterly* 65 (June 1976).

Bloxham, Donald, *Genocide on Trial: War Crimes Trials and the Formation of Holocaust History and Memory* (Oxford: Oxford University Press, 2001).

Blumenthal, David A. and McCormack, L. H. (eds.), *The Legacy of Nuremburg: Civilising Influence or Institutionalised Vengeance?* (Leiden: Martinus Nijhoff, 2008).

Borgwardt, Elizabeth, *A New Deal for the World* (Cambridge, MA: Harvard University Press, 2005).

Bose, Mahir, 'The Two Faces of Empire', *History Today* 58/10 (October 2009).

Brocaw, Tom, *The Greatest Generation* (New York: Random House, 1998).

Bullock, Alan, *Hitler: A Study in Tyranny* (London: Odhams, 1964).

Butler, Susan (ed.), *My Dear Mr. Stalin: The Complete Correspondence of Franklin D. Roosevelt and Joseph V. Stalin* (New Haven, CT: Yale University Press, 2006).

Canadian Army, Report No. 146, Historical Section, Canadian Military Headquarters, Operations Of First Canadian Army in North-West Europe, 31 Jul–1 Oct 44 (Preliminary Report).

Churchill, Winston, *History of the Second World War* (London: Pimlico, 2002).

————, 'Sinews of Peace' (Iron Curtain Speech), at Westminster College in Fulton, Missouri on 5 March 1946, available at http://www.historyguide.org/europe/churchill.html.

Conn, Stetson and Fairchild, Byron, *Framework of Hemisphere Defense* (Washington: Office of the Chief of Military History, 1960).

Conn, Stetson, Rose C. Engelman, and Fairchild, Byron, *'Guarding the United States and Its Outposts'*, volume in *United States Army in World War II: The Western Hemisphere* (Washington: Department of the Army, 1964).

Danchev, Alex, *Oliver Franks: Founding Father* (Oxford: Clarendon Press, 1993).

Danchev, A. and Todman, D. (eds.), *Field Marshal Lord Alan Brooke, War Diaries 1939-1945* (London: Weidenfeld and Nicolson, 2001).

Diebold, Wiliam, 'From ITO to GATT and Back?', in Orin Kirshner (ed.), *The Bretton Woods System: Retrospect and Prospect After Fifty Years* (New York: Sharpe, 1995), pp. 152–70.

Dilks, David (ed.), *The Diaries of Sir Alexander Cadogan, 1938–1945* (London: Cassell, 1971).

Dimitrov, Vesselin, *Soviet Foreign Policy, Democracy and Communism in Bulgaria 1941-1948* (London: Palgrave Macmillan, 2007).

Divine, Robert Alexander, *Second Chance: The Triumph of Internationalism in America during World War II* (New York: Athenaeum, 1967).

Dobson, Alan P., *US Wartime Aid to Britain 1940–1946* (London: Croom Helm, 1986).

Doenecke, Justus D., *Storm on the Horizon: The challenge to American Intervention, 1939–1941* (New York: Rowman & Littlefield, 2000).

Eade, Charles (ed.), *The War Speeches of Winston Churchill* (London: Cassell, 1952).

Eden, Anthony, 'The "Four Power" Plan', Cab 66/30/46 WP (42) 516, 8 November 1942.

Ethiopia, Ministry of Justice, Ethiopia, Documents on Italian War Crimes submitted to the United Nations War Crimes Commission by the Imperial Ethiopian Government, 2 vol. Addis Ababa, 1949, Vol II.

Fenby, Jonathan, *Alliance* (New York: Simon and Schuster, 2006).

Flynn, John T., *The Roosevelt Myth* (San Francisco, CA: Fox & Wilkes; 50th anniversary edition, 1998).

Foreign Relations of the United States, Vol. 1: General, British Commonwealth, The Far East (1942).

Friedlander, Henry and Milton, Sybil, *Archives of the Holocaust: An International Collection of Selected Documents*, Vol. 16, United Nations Archives New York, United Nations War Crimes Commissions (New York: Garland, 1990).

Gallup, George H., *The Gallup Poll: Public Opinion, 1935–1971* (New York: Random House, 1972).

Gaskin, M. J., *Blitz: The Story of 29th December 1940* (London: Faber and Faber, 2005).

General Eisenhower, Order of the Day, 6 June 1944, SHAPE.

Ginsburgs, George and Kudriavtsev, V. N. (eds.), *The Nuremberg Trial and International Law* (Dordrecht, Netherlands: Martinus Nijhoff Publishers, 1990).

Glantz, David M., *The Soviet Strategic Offensive in Manchuria, 1945: 'August Storm'* (Portland, OR: Frank Cass, 2003).

Glantz, David M., *Colossus Reborn: The Red Army at war 1941–1943* (Kansas City: University Press of Kansas, 2005).

Glantz, Mary E., *FDR and the Soviet Union* (Kansas City: University Press of Kansas, 2005).

Goodrich, Leland M. and Hambro, Edvard, *Charter of the United Nations Commentary and Documents* (Boston: World Peace Foundation, 1946).

Goodwin, Doris Kearns, *No Ordinary Time, Franklin and Eleanor Roosevelt: The Home Front in World War II* (New York: Simon and Schuster, 1994).

Hall, H. Duncan, *North American Supply, History of the Second World War* (London: HMSO, 1955).

Hannay, David, speech at SOAS-CISD, GCSP conference 2008, available at http://www.cisd.soas.ac.uk/Editor/assets/hannay_lunchkeynote_geneve.pdf.

Harriman, W. A. and Able, E. *Special Envoy to Churchill and Stalin, 1941–1946* (New York: Random House, 1975).

Hart, Michael (ed.), *Also present at the Creation: Dana Wilgress and the UNCTE at Havana* (Ottawa: Centre for Trade Policy and Law, 1995).

Herring, George C. Jr, *Aid to Russia, 1941–1946: Strategy, Diplomacy, the Origins of the Cold War* (New York: Columbia University Press, 1973).

Hexner, Ervin, 'The Soviet Union and the International Monetary Fund', *American Journal of International Law* 40/3 (July 1946).

Hirschmann, Ira, *The Embers Still Burn: An Eye-Witness View of the Postwar Ferment in Europe and the Middle East and our Disastrous Get-Soft-with-Germany Policy* (New York: Simon and Schuster, 1949).

History of Chief of Staff to Supreme Allied Commander (US Army Center of Military History Historical Manuscripts Collection (HMC), file number 8-3.6A CA).

HMSO 'Co-ordination of the Allied War Effort, Agreements between the Prime Minister and the President of the United States of America' (Great Britain), Parliamentary Papers, Cmd. 6332 (1942).

HMSO 'The Organisation for Joint Planning' (Great Britain), Parliamentary Papers 1941–2, Cmd. 6351 (1942).

HMSO Protocol Of The Proceedings Of The Crimea Conference, Yalta, 11th February, 1945 (London: Foreign Office, HMSO, 1945).

HMSO, Cmd. 6315, Misc. No. 3: Inter-Allied Meeting Held in London at St. James's Palace of September 24, 1941, Report of Proceedings (1941).

HMSO, German Atrocities (HMSO for, the Soviet Embassy, London, 7 November and 6 January 1942).

HMSO, *Punishment for War Crimes* (London: HMSO, 1942).

Hoopes, Townsend and Brinkley, Douglas, *FDR and the Creation of the UN* (New Haven and London: Yale University Press, 1997).

Howard, Sir Michael, 'The United Nations: from Warfighting to Peace Planning', in Ernest R. May and Angeliki E. Laiou (eds.), *The Dumbarton Oaks Conversations and the United Nations, 1944–1994* (Cambridge, MA: Harvard University Press, 1998).

Hull, Cordell, statement for *Foreign Trade Week*, May 1942, in *America's Economic Policy for the War and the Peace* (London: Hutchinson & Co., 1942).

Hull, Cordell, *The Memoirs of Cordell Hull* (London: Hodder and Stoughton, 1948).

Jenkins, Roy, *Churchill* (London: Pan, 2003).

Johnstone, Andrew, *Dilemmas of Internationalism: The American Association for the United Nations and US Foreign Policy 1941–1948* (Aldershot: Ashgate, 2009).

Jolly, Richard, Emmerij, Louis, and Weiss, Thomas G., *UN Ideas that Changed the World* (Bloomington IA, 2009).

Jones, Priscillia Dale, 'British Policy towards German Crimes against the Jews, 1939–1945', *Leo Baeck Institute Yearbook* 36 (1991).

Kagan, Robert, *Of Paradise and Power: America and Europe in the New World Order* (New York: Alfred A. Knopf, 2003).

Kaldor, Mary, *Human Security* (Cambridge, MA: Polity, 2007).

Keynes, John Maynard, *The Economic Consequences of the Peace* (London: Macmillan, 1919).

Kimball, Warren, *The Most Unsordid Act: Lend-Lease 1939–1941* (Baltimore, MD: Johns Hopkins Press, 1969).

Kimball, Warren, Reynolds, David, and Chubarian, A. O. (eds.), *Allies at War* (London: Macmillan, 1994).

Kirshner, Orin (ed.), *The Bretton Woods System: Retrospect and Prospect After Fifty Years* (New York: Sharpe, 1995).

Kochavi, Arieh J., *Prelude to Nuremberg, Allied War Crimes Policy and the Question of Punishment* (Chapel Hill, NC: University of North Carolina Press, 1998).

Kregel, Jan, 'The Discrete Charm of the Washington Consensus', Working Paper No. 533 (Levy Economics Institute of Bard College, Center for Full Employment and Price Stability, Kansas City, and Tallinn University of Technology, April 2008).

Krout, John A. (ed.), *Proceedings of the Academy of Political Science, May 1942* (New York: Columbia University Press, 1942).

Langford Paul (ed.), *The Writings and Speeches of Edmund Burke*, Vols V and VI (Oxford: Clarendon Press, 1991).

Lankevich, George J. (ed.), in Friedlander, Henry and Milton, Sybil, *Archives of the Holocaust: An International Collection of Selected Documents* (New York: Garland, 1990).

Lebedev, Igor, *Aviation Lend-Lease to Russia: Historical Observations* (Hauppauge, NY: Nova Science Publishers, 1997).

Leighton, R. M., *Global logistics and strategy 1941–1943* (Washington, DC: US Army in World War II, US GPO, 1955).

Levering, Ralph B., *American Opinion and the Russian Alliance, 1939–1945* (Chapel Hill, NC: University of North Carolina Press, 1976).

Liberal Jewish Synagogue (London, 19 August 1945).

London School of Hygiene and Tropical Medicine, Finance and General Purposes Committee Minutes, 12 May 1943.

Lorwin, Lewis, *Postwar Plans of the United Nations* (New York: The Twentieth Century Fund, 1943).

Lyttleton, Oliver, 'My American Visit: Some Random Notes' (UK National Archives WP (42) 591, 16 December 1942).

MacMahon, Kevin J., *Reconsidering Roosevelt on Race* (Chicago, IL: University of Chicago Press, 2003).

Mandela, Nelson, *Long Walk to Freedom* (London: Abacus, 1994).

Markwell, Donald, *John Maynard Keynes and International Relations* (Oxford: Oxford University Press, 2005).

Mastny, Vojtech, *Russia's Road to the Cold War: Diplomacy, Warfare and the Politics of Communism, 1941–1945* (New York: Columbia University Press, 1980).

Mastny, Vojtech, 'Stalin and the Prospects of a Separate Peace in World War II', *American Historical Review* 77 (1972).

Matlof, M. and Edwin M. Snell, *Strategic Planning for Coalition Warfare, 1941-42* (Washington, DC: Department of the Army, 1953).

Matthews, W. R., *The Fellowship of Nations* (London: World's Evangelical Alliance, 1944).

Mawdsley, Evan, *Thunder in the East: The Nazi-Soviet War 1941–1945* (London: Hodder, 2005).

Maxwell Fife, David, *War Crimes Trials*, Vol. I, in Cameron John (ed.) (London: Hodge, 1948).

Mazower, Mark, *No Enchanted Palace: The End of Empire and the Ideological Origins of the United Nations* (Princeton, NJ: Princeton University Press, 2009).

McJimsey, George, *Harry Hopkins* (Cambridge, MA: Harvard University Press, 1987).

Mellinger, George, *Soviet Lend-Lease Fighter Aces of World War 2* (Westminster, MD: Osprey Publishing; illustrated edition, 2006).

Miller, James N., 'Origins of the GATT – British Resistance to American Multilateralism' (Working Paper No. 318, Jerome Levy Economics Institute at Bard College, 2000).

Miner, Steven M., *Stalin's Holy War* (Chapel Hill, NC and London: University of North Carolina Press, 2003).

Moran, Lord, *Winston Churchill: The Struggle for Survival, 1940–1965* (London: Constable, 1996).

Morgenthau, Hans J., *A New Foreign Policy for the United States* (New York: Council on Foreign Relations, 1969).

Mortimer, Edward, *The World that FDR Built* (New York: Scribner's and Sons, 1988).

Motter, T. H. Vail, *The Persian Corridor and Aid to Russia, The Middle East Theatre, US Army in World War II* (Washington, DC: Office of the Chief of Military History, Dep. of the Army, 1969).

Neave, Airey, *Nuremburg* (London: Hodder and Stoughton, 1978).

Nevins, Allan, *Herbert H. Lehman and His Era* (New York: Charles Scribner's Sons, 1963).

Nye, Joseph, *Soft Power* (Cambridge, MA: Perseus, 2004).

Office of Lend-Lease Administration (USA), 'All for one, One for all: the Story of Lend-Lease' (US GPO, June 1943).

Orr, Robert C. (ed.), *Winning the Peace: An American Strategy for Post-Conflict Reconstruction* (Washington, DC: Center for Strategic & International Studies, 2004).

Overy, Richard, *Interrogators: The Nazi Elite in Allied Hands, 1945* (London: Allen Lane/The Penguin Press, 2001).

Palumbo, Michael, *The Waldheim Files* (London: Faber and Faber, 1988).

Petrov, G. F., *Red Stars 4: Lend-Lease Aircraft in Russia* (Tampere, Finland: Kustantaja, 2002).

Plesch, Dan, *The Beauty Queen's Guide to World Peace* (London: Politico's, 2004).

Ranshofen-Wertheimer, Egon F., *The International Secretariat: A Great Experiment in International Administration* (Washington, DC: Carnegie Endowment for International Peace, 1945).

Ratner, Sidney, 'An Inquiry into the Nazi War Economy', reviewed work(s): 'Design for Total War: Arms and Economics in the Third Reich' by Bernice A. Carroll, *Comparative Studies in Society and History* 12/4 (October 1970), pp. 466–72.

Reid, Escott, *On Duty: A Canadian at the Making of the United Nations, 1945–1946* (Kent, OH: Kent State University Press, 1983).

Republican Party Platform of 1940 (for the US Presidential Election, 1940), available at: http://www.presidency.ucsb.edu/ws/index.php?pid=29640.

Reynolds, David, *From Cold War to World War* (Oxford: Oxford University Press, 2006).

Reynolds, David, *America, Empire of Liberty* (London: Penguin, 2009).

RIIA, 'War and Peace in the Pacific', a preliminary report of the Eighth Conference of the Institute of Pacific Relations on wartime and post-war co-operation of the United Nations in the Pacific and the Far East, Mont Tremblant, Quebec, 4–14 December 1942 (London: Royal Institute of International Affairs, 1943).

Roberts, Andrew, *The Storm of War: A New History of the Second World War* (London: Allen Lane, 2009).

Roberts, Geoffrey, *Stalin's Wars* (New Haven, NY: Yale University Press, 2006).

Roberts, Sir Adam, 'Britain and the Creation of the United Nations', in William Roger Louis (ed.), *Still More Adventures with Britannia* (London and New York: I.B.Tauris, 2003).

Robins, Dorothy, *Experiment in Democracy: The Story of US Citizens Organisations in Forging the Charter of the United Nations* (New York: Parkside Press, 1971).

Roosevelt, Elliott, *As He Saw It* (New York: Duell, Sloan and Pearce, 1946).

Rotbalt, Sir Joseph, 'Leaving the Bomb Project', *Bulletin of the Atomic Scientists* (Chicago, August 1985).

Ryan, A., 'Klaus Barbie and the United States Government', report to the Attorney General of the United States, submitted by Allan A. Ryan Jnr, Special Assistant to the Assistant Attorney General, Criminal Division, United States Department of Justice (Washington, DC: US Government Printing Office: 20402, 1983).

Samuel, Joseph L., *American Catholics and the Formation of the United Nations* (Lanham, MD: University Press of America, 1993).

Sapir, Jacques, 'The economics of war in the Soviet Union during World War II', in I. Kershaw and M. Lewin (eds.), *Stalinism and Nazism* (Cambridge: Cambridge University Press, 1997).

Schlesinger, Arthur Jr, 'Foreword' to Butler, Susan, *My Dear Mr. Stalin: The Complete Correspondence of Franklin D. Roosevelt and Joseph V. Stalin* (New Haven: Yale University Press, 2005).

Schlesinger, Stephen C., *Act of Creation: The Founding of the United Nations: A Story of Superpowers, Secret Agents, Wartime Allies and Enemies, and Their Quest for a Peaceful World* (Oxford: Westview, 2003).

Sen, Sunil Kumar (ed.), *Burke on Indian Economy* (Socio-Economic Research Institute, Calcutta, Progressive Publishers, 1969).

Seton-Watson, Hugh, *Neither War Nor Peace: The Struggle for Power in Post-War Europe* (London: Methuen, 1960).

Sherwood, Robert, *Roosevelt and Hopkins* (New York: Harper, 1948).

Simma, Bruno, Mosler, Hermann, Paulus, Andreas, Chaitidou, Eleni and Giuliano, Maurizio (eds.), *The Charter of the United Nations: A Commentary* (Oxford: Oxford University Press, 1994).

Simpson, Christopher, *Money, Law, and Genocide in the Twentieth Century* (Monroe, ME: Common Courage Press, 1995).

Skidelsky, Robert, *John Maynard Keynes: Fighting for Freedom 1937–1946* (New York: Viking, 2000).

Smith, Bradley F., *The Road to Nuremberg* (New York: Basic Books, 1981).

Smith, Gaddis, *American Diplomacy During the Second World War, 1941–1945* (New York: John Wiley and Sons, 1965).

Sorensen, Reginald, MP, *India and the Atlantic Charter* (London: The India League, 1942).

Stalin's correspondence with Churchill, Attlee, Roosevelt and Truman 1941–5 (London: Lawrence & Wishart, 1958).

Stettinius, Edward R., *Lend-Lease* (London: Macmillan, 1944).

Stimson, Henry L. and McGeorge, Bundy, *On Active Service for Peace* (New York: Harper, 1947).

Taylor, Paul, 'The United Nations and International Order', in J. Baylis and S. Smith (eds.), *The Globalization of World Politics* (Oxford: Oxford University Press, 2001).

Tucker, Roy S., *Tractors and Chopsticks: My Work with the UNRRA Project in China, 1946 to 1947* (iUniverse.com, 2005).

UK House of Commons, Official Report, 18 January 1945.

UK House of Commons, Official Report, London, 17 December 1942.

UK House of Lords, Official Report, 23 March 1943.

UK National Archives Draft United Nations Declaration On National Independence, PREM 4/30/4 Hush-Most Secret From: Quadrant 15.9.43.

UK National Archives, ADM/15758.

UK National Archives, COS (42) 335, 6 July 1942.

UK National Archives, Eden, Anthony, Cab/66/24/42 W.P. (42) 212, 20 May 1942.

UK National Archives, Foreign Office, War, General, Confidential (16209) L 2136/2136/405, 1 June 1942.

UK National Archives, Halifax to Foreign Office No 1283, 17 March 1943.

UK National Archives, Ministry of Fuel and Power POWE 33/1411.

UK National Archives, PREM 4/32/13: Brendan Bracken to the PM 3 June 42, submitting draft, 1943, PREM 4/32/13 Hodge of MoI to Peck parades London Cardiff and Edinburgh, some concern at war cabinet over stretch of resources on Whit Monday and getting into an annual event. Coordinated with the United Nations Office in London, UK National Archives Halifax to FO No 2341, 19 May 1943; UK National Archives PREM 4/32/13 AS Hodge of the Ministry of Information to JH Peck at Downing St.

UK National Archives, PREM 4/29/4 Prime Minister's Personal Minute Serial No. M(R)8/4.

UK National Archives, Viscount Halifax to Foreign Office 5 June 1943, PREM 4.28/10.

UK National Archives, Viscount Halifax to Foreign Office, No 2413 24, April 1942, repeated 6 May 1942.

UK National Archives, War Cabinet, JP (42) 1017 (S), 17 December 1942.

United Nations Documents 1941–5 (London: Royal Institute for International Affairs, 1946).

United Nations General Assembly, (A/RES/60/1, para. 138 and 139), 2006.

UNHCR, 'Figures at a Glance', 2009, available at http://www.unhcr.org/pages/49c3646c11.html.

UNHCR, 'Global Trends 2008: Refugees, Asylum-seekers, Returnees, Internally Displaced and Stateless Persons', available at http://www.unhcr.org/4a375c426.html, p. 2.

UNRRA, Agriculture and Food in Greece, Operational Analysis Paper No. 19 (UNRRA European Regional Office, Portland Place, London W2, 1947).

UNWCC, Law Reports of Trials of War Criminals: Four Genocide Trials (UN War Crimes Commission; reprinted by Fertig, New York, 1992).

US, Department of State Bulletin, 17 September 1944, Vol. XI No. 273 (Washington, DC: US GPO, 1944).

US, Department of State Bulletin, 29 October 1944, Vol. XI No. 279 (Washington, DC: US Government Printing Office, 1944).

US, FDR statement to Congress on the 2nd Anniversary of Lend-Lease, 11 March 1943 (US GPO, 1943).

US, 'Letter from President Roosevelt', Report to Congress on Lend-Lease Operations (Washington, DC, US GPO, June 1942).

US, The Work of the FAO (Washington, DC: United Nations Interim Commission on Food and Agriculture, August 1945).

US, Treaties and Other International Agreements of the United States of America 1776–1949, Vol. 3, Multilateral 1931–1945, Department of State Publication 8484 (Washington, DC: US GPO, 1969).

Van Tuyll, Herbert P., *Feeding the Bear: American Aid to the Soviet Union, 1941–1945* (New York: Greenwood Press, 1989).

Vorsin, V. F., 'Motor Vehicle Transport Deliveries through "Lend Lease"', *Journal of Slavic Military Studies* 10/2 (1997).

Ward, Geoffrey C. (ed.), *Closest Companion* (Boston and New York: Houghton Mifflin, 1995).

Watson, Mark S., *Chief of Staff: Prewar Plans and Preparations* (Washington DC: US Army, 1950).

Weiss, Thomas G., 'What Happened to the Idea of World Government', *International Studies Quarterly* 53/2 (2009), pp. 253–71.

————, *What's Wrong with the United Nations and How to Fix It* (Cambridge: Polity Press, 2009).

Widney Brown, A. and Laura Grenfell, 'The International Crime of Gender-Based Persecution and the Taliban', *Melbourne Journal of International Law* VI/4 (2003).

Wilcox, Clair, *A Charter for World Trade* (New York: Macmillan, 1949).

Wilcox, Robert, *Target Patton* (New York: Regnery Publishing, 2008).

Wild, Payson S. Jnr, 'Machinery of Collaboration between the United Nations', Foreign Policy Association, Foreign Policy Reports, Vol XVIII No. 8, July 1942.

Willkie, Wendell, *One World* (New York: Macmillan, Simon and Schuster, 1943).

Wilson, Francesca M., *Aftermath* (London: Penguin, 1947).

Wilson, Harold, *Memoirs: The Making of a Prime Minister 1916–1964* (London: Weidenfeld and Nicholson; and Michael Joseph, 1986).

Wood, F. L. W., *Welfare and Peace in Political and External Affairs, The Official History of New Zealand in the Second World War 1939–1945* (Wellington: Historical Publications Branch, 1958).

Woodbridge, George, *The History of the United Nations Relief and Rehabilitation Administration*, in three volumes (New York: Columbia University Press, 1950).

Woolner, David B., Kimball, Warren F. and Reynolds, David (eds.), *FDR's World* (New York: Palgrave Macmillan, 2008).

Woytak, Richard, 'The Promethean Movement in Interwar Poland', *East European Quarterly* XVIII/3 (September 1984).

Wright, Lord and Alderson, Robert, *History of the United Nations War Crimes Commission and the Development of the Laws of War* (London: HMSO, 1948).

Index